Policy-Making in France

Policy-Making in France
From de Gaulle to Mitterrand

Edited by Paul Godt

Pinter Publishers
London and New York

First published in Great Britain in 1989 by
Belhaven Press (a division of Pinter Publishers),
25 Floral Street, London WC2E 9DS

British Library Cataloguing in Publication Data
A CIP catalogue record for this book is available from the British Library

ISBN 0 86187 706 3

Library of Congress Cataloging-in-Publication Data
Policymaking in France.
    Bibliography: p.
    Includes index.
    1. France--Politics and government--1958-
2. France--Economic policy--1945-   . 3. France--
Social policy. 4. France--Foreign relations--1945-
I. Godt, Paul.
    JN2594.2.P63 1989   944.083   89-8630
ISBN 0-86187-706-3

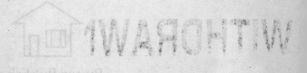

Typeset by Saxon Printing Ltd
Printed and bound in Great Britain by Biddles Ltd of Guildford and Kings Lyn.

Contents

Preface

When the Fifth Republic came to life thirty years ago, few expected it would outlast its founder, General Charles de Gaulle, recalled from retirement to rescue France from the explosive Algerian question. Not only did the regime survive that colonial war, but also the disruptive 'Events' of May 1968, de Gaulle's sudden resignation the following year, the economic and social transformations and crises of the 1970s, and the alternation in power of conservatives and Socialists in the 1980s. The Fifth Republic seems solidly anchored today.

But the world has changed, and certainly the settings in which France functions are no longer the same: her former colonial empire is now at best a zone of influence; Europe has matured, expanded in size and scope, and is preparing for even greater challenges; the bipolarization of the 'Cold War' has yielded to a more complex and uncertain multipolar world; and the 'superpowers' have proven to be vulnerable to both economic and military setbacks. Can the Fifth Republic have remained unaffected? How have institutions and policy-making processes designed to meet de Gaulle's critique of the Fourth Republic responded to the demands of the 1970s and 1980s?

For those of us for whom examining French politics and society is a life-long passion, it is important every now and then to gather together, as friends and colleagues, to take stock of France's evolution. In 1978, William G. Andrews and Stanley Hoffmann organized such a meeting in Brockport, NY; the papers presented there brought many insights to a generation of social scientists. Hoping to perpetuate a tradition, the editor of this volume planned a similar academic conference, under the auspices of The American University of Paris, an institution uniquely situated at the crossroads of French and English-speaking scholars of contemporary France. In June 1988, in the wake of momentous presidential and legislative elections, some 160 participants — from all over Europe and the United States — came to review and discuss the Fifth Republic's accomplishments.

The conference was facilitated by a generous grant from the Mona Bismarck Foundation of Paris, and the encouragement and support afforded by University President Daniel Socolow and Academic Vice-President Charlotte Lacaze. As conference organizer, I owe a special debt to Vincent Wright, Jean-Luc Parodi, and Dominique Moïsi, who, at critical junctures, provided wise counsel and crucial assistance. The conference was of course made by the scholars who presented their research. And it was also greatly enriched by the keynote and concluding speeches of Stanley Hoffmann and René Rémond and by the perceptive contributions from the panel chairs, discussants and other participants, whom I want to thank here: Nicholas Wahl, Howard Machin, Bruno Genevois, Yves Mény, Georges Lavau, Jean-Luc Parodi, Philip Cerny, Kay Lawson, Mark Kesselman, Jean-Marcel Jeanneney, Peter Hall, George Ross, John Goodman, Bruno Jobert, Dominique Schnapper, Catherine Wihtol de Wenden, Martin Schain, Michel Jobert, Jean-François Daguzan, Jérôme Paolini and François Godement.

This volume was designed to make available to a wider public these informed studies of the Fifth Republic's institutions, political forces, and principal policy areas, offering readers a broad overview of politics and policy-making in contemporary France. The set of topics covered is inevitably incomplete: examination of the bureaucracy or the judicial system, for example, would have given additional perspectives on institutional evolution. Space constraints have also obliged us to neglect interesting policy sectors. Cultural policy could have demonstrated the distinctive role played by the French state over the past thirty years. Agriculture, education, Franco-American relations and defence policy, as well, would surely have echoed some of the themes developed herein. In the last analysis, however, a volume such as this must strike a balance between those subjects scholars currently find most exciting and those which are relatively accessible elsewhere in the professional literature.

One of the frequent pitfalls of collected works is overall coherence, as most scholars specialize in one field and are usually less expert in others. We have tried to overcome that by providing a policy-making focus to the chapters, to give the reader illustrative examples of the dynamic interaction between the political process and the public agenda: that is, how the evolution of public policy issues during the Fifth Republic has transformed institutional patterns, and how, conversely, innovations in policy-making have shaped the policy outcomes. The Fifth Republic has proven its capacity to survive, and if this book contributes to a better understanding of French politics, we shall have fulfilled our mission.

Paris, March 1989
Paul Godt

List of contributors

PAUL GODT is Associate Professor of Political Science at The American University of Paris, where he has taught since 1972; he has also been Visiting Professor at the Universities of Grenoble and Nice. His articles on French local government reforms and health politics in France and West Europe have appeared in *The Tocqueville Review, Pouvoirs, The Journal of Health Politics, Policy, and Law* and Public Administration.

OLIVIER DUHAMEL is Professor of Public Law at the University of Paris I, and Co-Editor of *Pouvoirs*. He is author of *Chili ou la Tentative* (Paris: Gallimard, 1974); *La Gauche et la Ve République* (Paris: Presses Universitaires de France, 1980); *Histoire des Idées Politiques* (Paris: PUF, 1982), with François Châtelet and Evelyne Pisier; *Le Nouveau Président* (Paris: Seuil, 1987), with Jérôme Jaffré. In addition, he has edited *Changer le PC?* (Paris: PUF, 1979), with Henri Weber; *La Constitution de la Ve République* (2nd edn., Paris: Presses de la FNSP, 1988), with Jean-Luc Parodi; *Dictionnaire des Oeuvres politiques* (Paris: PUF, 1986), with François Châtelet and Evelyne Pisier; *SOFRES Opinion Publique* (Paris: Gallimard, 1984, 1985, 1986); and SOFRES *L'Etat de l'opinion* (Paris: Seuil, 1987, 1988, 1989).

DIDIER MAUS is Maître de Conférences at the Institut d'Etudes Politiques de Paris and Associate Professor at University of Paris I (Sorbonne). A graduate of the National School of Administration (ENA), he is also Vice-President of the French Association of Constitutionalists. He recently served as Chief of Staff to the Minister for Parliamentary Relations.

ALEC STONE is a graduate student now completing his dissertation on the Constitutional Council at the University of Washington, Seattle. His articles have appeared in professional journals such as *West European Politics* and *Pouvoirs*, and in collective works.

SONIA MAZEY is a Senior Lecturer in Politics at the Polytechnic of North London. She is co-editor of *Mitterrand's France* (London: Croom Helm, 1987) and co-author of *The European Community: Theory and Practice* (London: McGraw Hill, forthcoming 1990). She has also published several articles on French politics and public policy-making in Western Europe.

FRANK L. WILSON is Professor of Political Science at Purdue University, and author of *The French Democratic Left: 1963–1969* (Stanford, Calif: Stanford U.P., 1971), *Political Parties under the Fifth Republic* (New York: Praeger, 1982), *Interest-Group Politics in France* (Cambridge: Cambridge U.P., 1987), as well as numerous articles on French and European political parties and interest groups.

MARTIN A. SCHAIN is the author of *French Communism and Local Power* (London: Frances Pinter, 1985), co-editor and author (with Philip G. Cerny) of *French Politics and Public Policy* (London: Frances Pinter, 1980) and *Socialism, the State and Public Policy in France* (London: Pinter, 1985). He has also written numerous articles on the French Communist Party, the National Front, and problems of immigration in France. He is Professor of Politics, and is associated with the Institute of French Studies, at New York University.

YVES MENY is Professor of Political Science at the Institut d'Études Politiques de Paris, and author of *Politique Comparée* (Paris, 1987) and *Les Politiques Publiques* (forthcoming, 1989), with Jean-Claude Thoenig. He is also co-editor, with Vincent Wright, of *Centre–Periphery Relations in Western Europe* (London: George Allen & Unwin, 1985), and of *The Politics of Steel: Western Europe and the Steel Industry in the Crisis Years (1978–1984)* (Berlin: De Gruyter, 1986). He has written numerous articles on French public administration and center-periphery relations.

CHRISTIAN STOFFAËS is currently Associate Director of Economic and Strategic Studies at the EDF (Electricité de France). He has long worked at various high-level posts in the Ministry of Industry. He is author of *La Grande Menace Industrielle* (Paris: Calmann-Lévy, 1978), and co-editor of *French Industrial Policy* (Washington: The Brookings Institution, 1984), with James Adams.

HOWARD MACHIN is Professor of Politics at the London School of Economics and Political Science. He is the author of *The Prefect in French Public Administration* (London: Croom Helm, 1977); editor of *National Communism in West Europe: A Third Way to Socialism?* (London: Methuen, 1983); Co-editor, with E. Lisle, of *Traversing the Crisis: Social Science Research in Britain and France* (London: ESRC, 1984); with Michael Hebbert, *Regional Government and Economic Policy in France, Italy and Spain* (London: ICERD, 1984); with Vincent Wright, *Economic Policy and Policy-making in Mitterrand's France* (London: Frances Pinter, 1985); with Peter

Hall and Jack Hayward, *Developments in French Politics* (London: Macmillan, 1989, forthcoming). He has also contributed many articles to *West European Politics* and *Government and Opposition*.

PHILIP G. CERNY is Senior Lecturer in Politics at the University of York (England), and has been Visiting Professor at New York University, Harvard University, and Dartmouth College. He is the author of *Une Politique de Grandeur: Aspects idéologiques de la politique étrangére de De Gaulle* (Paris: Flammarion, 1986); editor of *Social Movements and Protest in France* (London: Pinter, 1982), and co-editor of *Elites in France* (London: Pinter, 1981). He is currently preparing *The Financial Revolution and the State* and *The Architecture of Politics: A Theory of Political Structuration*. He has also published articles in a number of journals, including the *British Journal of Political Science*, the *European Journal of Political Research*, the *International Political Science Review*, and *West European Politics*.

MARK KESSELMAN is Professor of Political Science at Columbia University, and author of *The Ambiguous Consensus: A Study of Local Government in France* (New York: Knopf, 1967), editor of *The French Workers' Movement* (New York: Allen and Unwin, 1984), co-editor and author of *European Politics in Transition* (Lexington, MA: D.C. Heath, 1987) and *The Fading Rose* (Cambridge: The Polity Press, 1988). He has written extensively on local government reform, the Communist Party, and labour issues in France.

WILLIAM SAFRAN is Professor of Political Science at the University of Colorado, Boulder, where he has been teaching since 1965. He has contributed numerous articles to professional journals and chapters in nine books, and has also written five books on comparative politics, including *Veto-Group Politics* (San Francisco: Chandler, 1967), *Ideology and Politics: The Socialist Party of France* (Boulder, Colorado: Westview Press, 1979), with William Codding; and *The French Polity* (New York: Longman, 3rd edn. forthcoming 1989).

DOMINIQUE MOÏSI is Associate Director of the Institut Français de Relations Internationales (IFRI) and Editor of *Politique Etrangère*. He is a frequent contributor to professional journals such as *Foreign Affairs*, *International Security, Atlantic Quarterly, Politique Etrangère*, and commentator on international affairs for several periodicals, including the *International Herald Tribune* and the *Los Angeles Times*.. His books include: *L'Historien entre l'ethnologue et le futurologue; Crises et guerres au XXe siècle: analogies et différences; and Le système communiste: un monde en expansion*.

PHILIPPE MOREAU DEFARGES is consultant at the Foreign Affairs Ministry, Professor at the Institut d'Etudes Politiques de Paris, and Assistant to the Director of the IFRI. He has written *Les Relations Internationales dans le Monde d'Aujourd'hui* (3rd ed., Paris: Editions S.T.H., 1986); *L'Europe et son Identité dans le Monde* (Paris: Editions S.T.H., 1983);

Quel Avenir pour quelle Communauté? (Paris: IFRI, 1986); and articles in professional journals such as *Commentaire, Politique Etrangère,* and others.

MARIE-CLAUDE SMOUTS is Research Director in the CNRS, associated with the Centre d'Etudes et de Recherches Internationales (CERI), and Professor at the Institut d'Etudes Politiques de Paris ; she is co-author of *La France dans le nouveau désordre Nord-Sud* (Paris: Editions Karthala, 1989); co-editor of *La Politique Etrangère de Valéry Giscard d'Estaing* (Paris: Presses de la FNSP, 1985); and author of *La France à l'ONU* (Paris: Presses de la FNSP, 1979). She contributes regularly to professional journals such as *Politique Etrangère, La Revue Française de Science Politique,* and others.

VINCENT WRIGHT is Fellow at Nuffield College, Oxford, and Joint-Editor of West European Politics. In addition to the works cited above, he was also co-editor of *Local Government in Britain and France* (London: George Allen & Unwin, 1979), with Jacques Lagroye; and *The Politics of Privatization in Western Europe* (London: Cass, 1988), with John Vickers. He edited *Continuity and Change in France* (London: George Allen & Unwin, 1984), and has written several books, including *The Government and Politics of France* (3rd edn, New York: Holmes & Meier, 1989) and numerous articles on French and European politics for professional journals and collected works.

List of Acronyms

ACP	African, Carribbean and Pacific Countries
ANVAR	Agence Nationale de Valorisation de la Recherche (National Agency for the Promotion of Innovation)
CAC	Chambre Syndicale des Agents de Change (Stock Brokers' Association)
CAPES	Certificat d'Aptitude de Pédagogie de l'Enseignement Secondaire (Secondary School Teaching Certificate)
CCC	Commission constitutionnelle consultative (Constitutional Consultative Committee)
CEA	Commissariat à l'Energie Atomique (Atomic Energy Commission)
CEPII	Centre d'Etudes Prospectives et d'Informations Internationales (Centre for Forecasting and International Information)
CEPREMAP	Centre d'Etudes Prospectives d'Economie Mathématique Appliquées la Planification (Center for Mathematical Economic Forecasting Applied to Planning)
CERC	Centre d'Etudes des Revenus et des Coûts (Centre for the Study of Incomes and Cost-of-Living)
CFDT	Confédération Française et Démocratique du Travail (Democratic French Labour Confederation)
CGT	Confédération Générale du Travail (General Labour Confederation)
CIASI	Comité Interministériel pour l'Aménagement des Structures Industrielles (Inter-ministerial Committee for the Adjustment of Industrial Structures)
CII	Compagnie Internationale pour l'Informatique (International Data-Processing Company)

CNAMTS	Caisse Nationale d'Assurance Maladie des Travailleurs Salariés (National Health Insurance Fund for Salaried Workers)
CNES	Centre National d'Etudes Spatiales (National Centre for Space Studies),
CNEXO	Centre National pour l'Exploitation des Océans (National Centre for Ocean Development)
CNIP	Centre National des Indépendants et des Paysans (National Centre of Independents and Peasants)
CNJA	Centre National des Jeunes Agriculteurs (Young Farmers' Union)
CNPF	Conseil National du Patronat Français (National Council of French Employers)
CNRS	Centre National de Recherches Scientifiques (National Centre for Scientific Research)
CODER	Commission de Développement Economique Régional (Regional Economic Development Commission)
CODIS	Comité de Développement des Industries Stratégiques (Strategic Industries Development Committee)
CORDES	Comité de Recherches sur le Développement Economique et Sociale (Research Committee on Economic and Social Development)
CREDOC	Centre de Recherches pour l'Etude et l'Observation des Conditions de Vie (Research Centre for the Study and Observation of Living Conditions)
CSMF	Confédération des Syndicats Médicaux Français (Confederation of French Medical Unions)
DATAR	Délégation à l'Aménagement du Territoire et à l'Action Régionale (Territorial Development Agency)
DGRST	Délégation Générale de la Recherche Scientifique et Technique (Agency for Scientific and Technical Research)
ECSC	European Coal and Steel Community
EDC	European Defence Community
EDF	Electricité de France (Electricity of France)
FGDS	Fédération de la Gauche Démocratique et Socialiste (Federation of the Democratic and Socialist Left)
FMF	Fédération des Médecins de France (French Doctors' Federation)
FN	Front National (National Front)
FNSEA	Fédération Nationale des Syndicats d'Exploitants Agricoles (National Federation of Farmers' Unions)
FO	Force Ouvrière (Labour Force)
GATT	General Agreement on Tariffs and Trade
IDI	Institut pour le Développement Industriel (Institute for Industrial Development)

IFOP	Institut Français de l'Opinion Publique (French Public Opinion Institute)
IMF	International Monetary Fund
INSEE	Institut Nationale des Statistiques et des Etudes Economiques (National Institute for Statistics and Economic Studies)
MATIF	Marché à Terme des Instruments Financiers (Financial Futures Market)
MEP	Member of the European Parliament
OECD	Organisation for Economic Co-operation and Development
ORTF	Office de la Radiodiffusion et Télévision Française (Office of French Radio and Television)
PAP	Programme d'Action Prioritaire (Priority Action Programme)
PAPIR	Programme d'Action Prioritaire d'Initiative Régionale (Regional Priority Action Program)
PCF	Parti Communiste Français (French Communist Party)
PFN	Parti des Forces Nouvelles (New Forces Party)
PS	Parti Socialiste (Socialist Party)
PSU	Parti Socialiste Unifié (United Socialist Party)
RPR	Rassemblement pour la République (Rally for the Republic)
SICAV	Société d'Investissement à Capital Variable (mutual fund or unit trust)
SNCF	Société Nationale des Chemins de Fer Français (National Railway Company)
SOFRES	Société Française des Etudes par Sondage (French Opinion Research Company)
STABEX	Stabilization of Exports
UDC	Union du Centre (Union of the Centre)
UDF	Union pour la Démocratie Française (Union for French Democracy)
UDR	Union pour la Défense de la République (Union for the Defence of the Republic)
UNCTAD	United Nations Conference on Trade and Development
UNR	Union pour la Nouvelle République (Union for the New Republic)

Part I: Institutions of the Fifth Republic

1. President and Prime Minister*

Olivier Duhamel

For those yet unaware, the experience of the two years preceding the thirtieth anniversary of the Fifth Republic demonstrated conclusively that the French constitutional system has a very particular form of dualism at the head of the power structure. Of course, a double-headed executive is common to other European parliamentary regimes, and no one questions that governmental authority is exercised by the Prime Minister, whatever the role incumbent upon the head of state. Such is not the case in France, where a number of factors combine to suggest the possibility of a real dyarchy.

First, the inherited tradition of the parliamentary regime, confirmed in 1958, distinguishes between the head of state and the head of Government. And yet, the principal innovation of the 1958 Constitution was the considerable and unprecedented extension of presidential prerogatives. Moreover, the Constitution is ambivalent concerning the roles attributed to these two authorities: on the one hand, the President 'shall ensure, by his arbitration, the regular functioning of the governmental authorities, as well as the continuity of the state'; on the other hand, the Prime Minister 'directs the operation of the Government'.

In addition, the presidential and Prime Ministerial powers are inextricably intertwined. The Prime Minister must countersign the President's ordinary acts, and those few that are specifically exempted never concern, except for Art. 16's emergency powers, matters of public policy decisions. Consequently, Michel Debré was correct to assert, when he presented the text of the Constitution to the Council of State in 1958, that 'the President of the Republic has no power of his own; he may only appeal to another authority'.[1]

The two leaders coexist in the media, are the subjects of journalists' special attention, their relative popularities regularly compared in

* Translated by the editor.

opinion polls measuring the public's confidence in them. Even the nation-wide elections have assumed a duality, linking the two heads of the executive branch to the people, the President directly, as in the USA, and the Prime Minister indirectly, as is common in parliamentary systems, by means of legislative elections.

These basic characteristics of the French bicephalous executive do not make it easy to define simply stable relations between President and Prime Minister. But in the light of thirty years of varied institutional practice, the four presidencies and the eleven Prime Ministerships, and the different variants of political alternation witnessed since 1981, it is possible to sketch out a certain number of more or less irreversible features. Although these do not clear up all the uncertainties, nor settle the disagreements concerning the sharing of executive power, we can attempt to disentangle the distribution of power by analysing the conditions for exercising it.

Choosing President and Prime Minister

No other fundamental aspect of the Fifth Republic was more contested than the popular election of the head of state, when it was proposed in 1962. No other aspect is better accepted after thirty years of a Constitution whose spiritual father never dared imagine a measure so radically opposed to French republican tradition. The direct election of the President today no longer raises any public objections of principle, at least among political actors, with the exception of the French Communist Party, which still remains resolutely hostile. As it can no longer even propose turning back, the PCF focuses its challenge instead on the election rule — the decisive one — which restricts the run-off round to the top two candidates. In this way, the Communists show their refusal to accept the constraints of electoral bipolarization. They know their limited proposal has no chance of success; dropping their demand for the elimination of the direct election is therefore not a sign of realism on their part, but of the awareness of the distance between their conceptions and their voters' preferences, a tribute to the depth of the consensus.

Other questions about the election method relate to considerations of electoral strategy. Thus it was for the 1988 reform which extended to regional council members the right to sponsor presidential candidates. Some found it inconceivable that a political force representing 10 per cent of the electorate, like the National Front, be denied a place in the first-round campaign, where the mini-groups of the extreme Left can express their subtle nuances. Most Frenchmen, however, were more anti-Le Pen than they were democratic, and massively preferred his absence from the election. By deciding not to follow their view, the Minister of the Interior — Charles Pasqua, Jacques Chirac's campaign manager — acted less out of commitment to pluralism than because electoral analyses showed that Le Pen's absence would help Raymond Barre's chances more than those of Chirac.[2] As a result of these calculations, Le Pen was an official candidate, obtaining barely 114 signatures more than the 500 required (thanks to the regional councillors), and Barre did not make it into the run-off.

For the future, thought must be given to the major political forces, especially the neo-Gaullist RPR and the centrist UDF, which will need to devise, if not a single party, then at least common rules for selecting a single candidate. A presidential election can be lost, bringing Communists and Socialists to power, because of divisions among their adversaries. Even a second can be lost in the same way, returning to office a Socialist President two years after the defeat of his party in legislative elections. But an obsession with defeat has its limits. The selection of a single conservative candidate to oppose the Socialist candidate would certainly have positive effects on the coherence of a presidential coalition, on the management of the moderate Right's internal divisions, on the density of presidential leadership; such unity is not, however, considered primarily in that perspective, but rather more trivially as a means of winning the presidential battle. This conclusion, still debatable in 1981, appears inescapable in 1988, when Barre and Chirac separately scored a total of 36 per cent in the presidential election, whereas the joint slates for the legislative elections won 40 per cent.[3]

The selection of the President raises only questions of party strategies; the choice of Prime Minister cannot be so readily settled, even if the first twenty-eight years of the Fifth Republic seemed to support the pre-eminence of the President's role. The head of state has in fact been able to have his own way, naming to Matignon a leader of his supporters' party (e.g., Michel Debré, Jacques Chaban-Delmas, or Pierre Mauroy), a high civil servant he himself brought into politics (Georges Pompidou, Maurice Couve de Murville, Raymond Barre, or Laurent Fabius), or an intermediary figure, with a parliamentary identity more or less distinct from the head of state but presumed to serve him faithfully (e.g., Pierre Messmer, or Jacques Chirac in 1974). In none of these nine cases was the appointed Prime Minister imposed in any way on the President.[4] Even in 1974, Valéry Giscard d'Estaing could have chosen a different Gaullist, or even someone outside the Gaullist party, as he in fact did when Chirac resigned in August 1976. Nearly forgotten was the government's responsibility before the National Assembly: the alternative between the appointment of someone acceptable to a majority of MPs — or, more exactly, one not totally unacceptable to a majority — and the dissolution of the Assembly.

The change of parliamentary majority in March 1986 served to remind those who may have overlooked this reality that, if the government no longer emanated from the Parliament, it could still be toppled by it. When the Assembly's majority is opposed to the head of state — that is, when a new coalition is victorious over the one which had earlier elected the President — legitimate doubt is cast on presidential freedom of choice. Nothing prevents him from toying with a minority Prime Minister, as long as he recognizes that such a course is only a holding operation until a dissolution or the emergence of a restructured legislative majority. The latter hypothesis is conceivable in the case of a pure cohabitation (i.e., when proximate elections grant the presidency to one camp and a legislative majority to the other, as nearly took place in May–June 1988). In that circumstance, the President must make his choice from among his adversaries in the new parliamentary majority. His freedom of man-oeuvre is inversely proportional to the degree of cohesiveness of the majority, to the degree of its leader's authority. The limits went untested in 1986, as François Mitterrand immediately chose the RPR's leader, who had already convinced his troops to refuse any other appointment. Mitterrand's choice was not for constitutional reasons — naming the leader of the leading party in the legislative majority — but rather for tactical reasons: to revive the competition within the Right by provoking challenger Raymond Barre. In any case, the precedent now exists, and will be used, if political conditions allow.

In short, a consensus exists around the choice of Prime Minister by the President , but in relation to the legislative majority, which, according to the circumstances, leaves him either very wide discretion — or nearly none at all.

Terminating the executive functions

A similar consensus does not exist, however, on ending the terms of office of President and Prime Minister. Concerning the President, there are three sources of disagreement. First, there is nothing sacred in the seven-year term: a majority of Frenchmen favour reducing it to five years,[5] a majority of the political elite has at one time or another expressed support for such a change, and the current President indicated during the 1988 campaign that he would welcome it. The seven-year term is not finished, though, because public opinion matters little in this instance, and the views of political leaders vary according to their most immediate interests, which happen to conflict on this question.

The second subject of disagreement is the use of the referendum, and particularly the degree to which presidential responsibility is involved in such a procedure. The Gaullist thesis — that the referendum is inevitably a question of confidence before the people — may appear to have been condemned by de Gaulle's defeat of 1969, or by the poor turn-out for Pompidou's referendum of 1972, or even by Mitterrand's aborted effort in 1984. None the less, and despite these three contrary examples, one cannot exclude definitively the use of the referendum as a plebiscite:

Raymond Barre has supported this position, the procedure offers opportunities to coalesce the most disparate opposition groups, and the public seems to feel that in a referendum, it is saying 'yes' or 'no' to the person asking the question.

The third source of eventual discord concerns the consequences of legislative elections on presidential authority. Here again, uncertainty reigns. On the one hand, one could argue that an electoral defeat of the Right under Mitterrand in 1988 supports Barre's idea of a presidential commitment during legislative elections. On the other hand, one cannot forget that the division of the candidates of the Right made Mitterrand's victory possible; a future President facing a situation like that of Mitterrand in 1986 will be tempted to follow his precedent. Moreover, the relative first-ballot success of the parties of the Right in the 1988 legislative elections obliged them to call for a 'renewed cohabitation'. As a consequence, the view common in other countries that a President remains in office for the duration of his elected term — a novel idea for France — is taking root.

It is less easy to resolve the question of ending the Prime Minister's term in office. The Constitution is of no help, as it provides only for his resignation, either voluntary or mandatory following the Government's overthrow by the Assembly. The experience of the Fifth Republic is interesting in that it at once has filled in a constitutional gap and has come closer to the original intentions of 1958, after deviating from them initially.

It now appears certain that the Prime Minister must offer his resignation following a presidential election. All have followed this practice, either when a new President was elected (the resignations of Couve de Murville, Messmer, and Barre), or when an incumbent was reelected (the resignations of Pompidou, reappointed; and of Chirac, replaced by Rocard). As a result of this custom, the presidential election has a consequence for the cabinet not explicitly provided for in the Constitution of 1958. It can be seen most clearly when a President is elected with a political base different from that of the sitting parliamentary majority.

Let us consider for a moment the situation if the Prime Minister in place could, or even must, remain in office. The newly elected President would have to admit that the cabinet and its head were responsible only to the Assembly, reducing the President's choices to accepting the situation or dissolving the Assembly: On the contrary, by immediately accepting the presidential election's effect on the cabinet, political forces have sanctified not only the Gaullist doctrine that the cabinet proceeds from the President, but also a majoritarian conception of the Fifth Republic, in which alternation in power is favoured over cohabitation. During the presidential campaign of 1988, Valéry Giscard d'Estaing put forth the opposite point of view, asserting that it was advisable to arrange for the coexistence of France's two halves, that is, both the presidential and the parliamentary majorities. He did not go so far as to defend keeping Jacques Chirac at the head of the Government, but explained that the new Prime Minister had to be acceptable to the RPR–UDF parliamentary majority. However, no one followed the former President along this ultra-cohabitationist line; the Fifth Republic thus fell back on its natural presidentialism.

This presidentialism has also been reinforced by the regular practice of Government resignation following legislative elections, whatever the outcome. It matters not that the Prime Minister directs the electoral campaign, nor even that he occasionally wins it; it is the President who alone interprets the popular will, which allows him to change Prime Minister. François Mitterrand was thus faithful to the Gaullist heritage when he commented on Michel Rocard's fate following the 1988 legislative elections: 'A priori, there is no reason for me to replace him'.

There remains the question of changing the Prime Minister between elections, at the President's initiative — or to put it clearly, when the President fires his Prime Minister. We know that the Constitution does not provide for it, that General de Gaulle excluded the possibility when the document was being written, and that both he and his successor, Georges Pompidou, resorted to it. It would appear that, on this point, the Fifth Republic has undergone a clarification. No Prime Minister has been fired against his will since July 1972. In August 1976, Jacques Chirac left on his own initiative. In July 1984, Pierre Mauroy's departure was by mutual agreement, in so far as he wished to be replaced. In a period of cohabitation, no one challenges the view that the President cannot remove the Prime Minister; he is, to use Giscard d'Estaing's expression, *'indé-boulonnable'*. As for the future, François Mitterrand allowed for no distinction between circumstances of cohabitation or compatible major-ities when he asserted: 'The Prime Minister, who implements the policies of the parliamentary majority, can be removed only by that majority'.[6]

One should evidently not overestimate the consequences of this evolution, since a President has always had to have the acquiescence of a Prime Minister from his own political family before replacing him. Still, the disappearance of the theory of the Prime Minister's removability at will is significant. It indicates a new state of mind more aware of the need to share power. It requires that the President who wishes to replace his lieutenant must respect certain procedures and await — or create — the appropriate circumstances. It also guarantees prime ministers a certain lease in office. Incidentally, they have generally averaged three years at Matignon; those who did not last that long were victims not of presidential rejection, but of a change of President or of parliamentary majority. The assurance, albeit relative, of a certain time in office strengthens the Prime Minister in the difficult exercise of sharing power.

Decision-making authority

The respective influence of President and Prime Minister in political decision-making is above all a function of the conditions under which power was conferred, and most especially those which determined the choice of Prime Minister. At bottom, the significant distinction is between periods of presidential domination — whether tempered or not — when presidential and parliamentary majorities are congruent, and periods of cabinet domination, under incompatible majorities.[7]

In the first case, the President may always exercise his powers to the fullest extent in his 'reserved domain': constitutionally, that includes foreign affairs, defence, the institutional functioning; and, by tradition, it includes France's European policies, relations with the overseas territories, and major cultural projects. Here, the Prime Minister's subordination is without question. In other areas, the power-sharing is contingent. It will depend on whether or not the President has made commitments during the election campaign; whether or not he wishes to implement them; whether or not the Prime Minister and the responsible ministers know how to carry out a policy without challenging the presidential establishment or any interest group sufficiently powerful to appeal to it; and finally, whether or not these ministers are willing to rely directly on the President or his staff to circumvent the Prime Minister.

But whatever the variations, the head of government's power is always limited by the fact that, in the final analysis, he must yield to a presidential order, regardless of the area, no matter how insignificant (unless he is willing to offer his resignation, an exceptional gesture by definition). The President's power will always be limited by the fact that he does not control the administrative machinery and must go through the Prime Minister's office and/or the ministries in order to carry out his will, keeping in mind all the different interpretations that implementation may entail.

In the second case, when the President has lost legislative elections during his term of office, the Prime Minister gains real decision-making power for all public policy issues outside the President's constitutional reserved domain. The head of state no longer has a power of command. He participates in the appointment process, in the numerous cases where his signature is required, and thus retains a capacity to negotiate. In return, for strictly political decisions, his resources are limited to delay (especially if the Prime Minister offers him the opportunity by resorting to the ordinance procedure) or to public criticism. In the reserved domain, the head of state no longer can decide in full sovereignty, but contends with the Prime Minister to arrive at a consensual decision. At the end of this process, 'France speaks with a single voice', even in situations in which the double-headed executive is the least unequal.

The Fifth Republic has thus known a number of variations in the distribution of power between its two heads. Many intermediary patterns could be found between the two extreme hypotheses raised above. Among them, for example, is that of the new legislature opening in June 1988, an unprecedented situation of an Assembly without a majority: the legislative elections gave to no governmental coalition an absolute majority, despite the majority polling system, and despite the fact that the Socialist Party repeated its 1981 score, and despite the fact that the Left scored 50.3 per cent of the votes on the decisive round — because the Union of the Left no longer exists. With an additional 1 per cent of the votes either way, the Socialists or the RPR–UDF coalition would have obtained an absolute majority, thus restoring an ordinary Fifth Republic situation. The voters, however, managed miraculously to get their way by granting the Socialists only a relative majority.

In this unprecedented configuration, the President's power was increased in one specific area: he is to decide the meaning of the vote. By making compromises in one direction or another, François Mitterrand could have tried to constitute a new majority with the centrists, or to create a broad coalition in light of the Europe 1992 horizon, or even to revive a new Union of the Left. He preferred bolstering the pre-eminence of the presidential election by appointing a minority Socialist cabinet, reserving the possibility of a progressive evolution toward a new alliance with the Centre.[8]

Once this initial choice had been made, the Prime Minister can be expected to acquire additional decision-making power, in so far as it is he who must build issue-based majorities, alternating among each of the options rejected for the long term (centrist support, consensus, or Communist support). But this Prime Minister of the third type, neither executive assistant to an all-powerful President, nor leader of a majority opposed to the President, can play the role of grand negotiator only as long as the head of state does not seek to transform the political circumstances. His task of managing the activities of government and Parliament has a limited time framework which he does not control. The constraints of a relative majority thus bestow on him an importance as decisive as it is precarious.

These variations in power-sharing at the top of the state are without parallel in other Western democracies. It is ironic to note in conclusion that, if this situation derives from the different articulations of two phenomena completely unforeseen in 1958 — presidential and parliamentary majorities — it nevertheless brings the regime full circle back to the compromises and incertitude of its origins.[9]

Notes

1. Michel Debré, 'Discours devant le Conseil d'Etat, 27 août 1958', in Didier Maus (ed.), *Les Grands Textes de la pratique institutionnelle de la Ve République* (4th edn., Paris: La Documentation Française, 1988), p. 6.

2. See Olivier Duhamel and Jérôme Jaffré, *Le Nouveau Président* (Paris: Seuil, 1987), p. 196.

3. The complete results can be found in two special publications of *Le Monde*, devoted to the presidential and legislative elections.

4. See Olivier Duhamel, 'The Fifth Republic under François Mitterrand', in George Ross, Stanley Hoffmann and Sylvia Malzacher (eds.), *The Mitterrand Experiment* (Cambridge: Polity Press, 1987), p. 144.

5. SOFRES, *L'Etat de l'opinion: clés pour 1987* (Paris: Seuil, 1987), p. 216.

6. François Mitterrand, in an interview with the author, 'Sur les institutions', in *Pouvoirs*, no. 45, April 1988.

7. See Olivier Duhamel and Jean-Luc Parodi (eds.), *La Constitution de la Cinquième République* (2nd edn., Paris: Presses de la FNSP, 1988), p. 542.

8. SOFRES, *L'Etat de l'opinion: clés pour 1989* (Paris: Seuil, 1989).

9. See *Documents pour servir à l'histoire de l'élaboration de la Constitution du 4 octobre 1958*, Volume I, *Des origines de la loi constitutionnelle du 3 juin 1958 à l'avant projet du 29 juillet 1958* (Paris: La Documentation Française, 1987); and Volume II, *Le Comité Consultatif Constitutionnel, de l'avant projet du 21 août 1958* (Paris: La Documentation Française, 1988).

2. Parliament in the Fifth Republic 1958–1988*

Didier Maus

In order to appraise the evolution of the French Parliament under the Fifth Republic since 1958, one must first determine the model of reference. Should one compare the situation to that experienced prior to 1958, under the Fourth Republic, that is, to the period of parliamentary sovereignty and its excesses, or should one attempt to evaluate Parliament's role in the light of the expectations of the founding fathers of the 1958 Constitution? Depending on the alternative chosen, the answer is likely to be quite different. The role of French parliamentary assemblies today is without doubt less than it was in preceding republics. Nevertheless, Parliament continues to be perceived through the image of ancient recollections.

On assuming his Speaker's chair in July 1981, Louis Mermaz (Socialist) declared: 'Today we must restore to Parliament its rights and its dignity'.[1] Looking back over Parliament's performance during the seven years of the Mitterrand presidency, one of the best observers of parliamentary practice concluded that the 'redistribution of powers between the legislative and the executive did not take place; ... over seven years, the weight of the institutions has proven to be greater than both the will of men and the pressure of events'.[2]

Throughout the Fifth Republic, various men and political parties have expressed dissatisfaction with Parliament's place in the workings of the Republic. In 1971, several Gaullist dignitaries in the National Assembly complained about the lack of autonomy, even lack of freedom, of the nation's representatives.[3] The manifesto of the FGDS in 1965–7,[4] the Common Programme of the Left in 1972,[5] candidate Mitterrand's 110 proposals in 1981,[6] clearly reflect this same reaction. It goes without saying that such an attitude has been less common among orthodox Gaullists: the respect due to the text of 1958 outweighs other considerations in their view. Among the opposition centrists, the theme of

*Translated by the editor.

enhancing Parliament's authority was quite evident, at least until they clearly joined the majority in 1974. Although the Communist Party's interest in institutional problems is bewildering, one cannot overlook its consistent rhetoric on the muzzling of Parliament's most basic rights; from the beginning, the Fifth Republic's Constitution has never been in their good graces.[7] At the other end of the political spectrum, the National Front's MPs have very often since 1986 used the theme of 'Parliament, the defender of Democracy', occasionally rather violently, to stress the 'rights of the people's representatives'.

These several elements justify an analysis from a double perspective: first, by recalling the intentions of the Constitution's authors and their vision of 'rationalized parliamentary government'; and then, by analysing the ground covered and attempting to compare it to the 'model of 1958'.

Parliament in 1958: the end of a disequilibrium?

The Fourth Republic, like the Third Republic between the two wars, suffered from the weakness of the executive and, as a consequence, from the excessive power of Parliament. *La République des députés* was one of the causes, but not the only one, of France's political instability. It was to remedy this situation that the authors of the 1958 Constitution sought to create a new equilibrium between the two principal institutions of the Republic.

Drafting the text of the Constitution

The drawing up of the articles concerning Parliament[8] was not at the heart of the difficulties of the summer of 1958. The constitutional act of 3 June 1958 already provided some useful indications. Its very first paragraph made the legislative and the executive branches equal before universal suffrage. Consequently, the legislature would no longer enjoy an absolute superiority and would have to deal with an executive vested with a legitimacy — and thus a power — equal to its own.

The second paragraph reinforces this analysis by pointing out that the two authorities must 'be effectively separated'. One can thus no longer be subordinated to the other. In order to be clear, the article affirms that each of the two authorities 'assumes, under its own responsibility, the full measure of its powers'. There can be no doubt: the instructions given by Parliament itself to the authors of the future Constitution considerably modified the customary constitutional practice as it had existed before. The fact that the third paragraph asserts that the government is responsible to Parliament in no way modifies this view; it only confirms the parliamentary, not presidential, nature of the new French regime.

Michel Debré's speech before the Council of State, in August 1958, constitutes the best account of the motives behind the new Constitution, and certainly the only one which is complete, coherent and unquestionably faithful to the thinking of the text's authors. In a somewhat surprising manner, in light of the subsequent polemic, the Minister of Justice indicated clearly that the object of the new charter was not to eliminate Parliament's role: 'The government has sought to renovate the parliamentary regime. I am even tempted to say that it wanted to establish it ... The proposed Constitution, as it is submitted to you, aspires to create a parliamentary regime'.[9]

The available documents and other information seem to emphasize that Parliament's status was not in general among those arrangements most debated between June and September 1958. In any case, the basic outlines took shape rapidly.

De Gaulle asserted on 6 June 1958, according to François Luchaire, that 'there must be an absolute distinction between the functions of member of Parliament and those of minister'.[10] The incompatibility rule of Articles 23 and 25 was already in evidence. He likewise indicated that 'the government must in no case emanate from Parliament'. On the other hand, it is quite curious to note that de Gaulle was considering a Senate composed of three sections: the first political, the second economic, and the third for the overseas territories. This idea came up again 13 June, during the first meeting on the constitution with the Ministers of State at the Hotel Matignon, where, under pressure from Guy Mollet, Pierre Pflimlin and Michel Debré, it was dropped.[11] None the less, it was revived in 1969, and was one of the reasons for the defeat of the 27 April referendum, and thus for de Gaulle's resignation.

During the second meeting on the constitution, 23 June, de Gaulle insisted on the necessity for the President of the Republic to be able to dissolve the Assembly or replace the government, if one or the other exceeded its authority.[12] Many of the elements of 'rationalized parliamentary government' appear in the documents of the 1 July meeting of the working group set up around Michel Debré: the verification of the election of MPs by an *ad hoc* judge, the limits on parliamentary sessions, the election of the Assembly's Speaker for the full five-year legislative term, the individual nature of MPs' votes, the idea of a distinction between the Parliament's law-making authority and the government's rule-making authority.[13]

The draft of the sections dealing with the relations between the government and the Parliament was examined during the 2 July meeting, during which the rules concerning the government's responsibility to the Assembly were spelled out quite specifically, and it was proposed to grant priority to the government's agenda. The idea of a joint committee to facilitate conflict resolution between the two chambers was also introduced. The next days' meetings confirmed that an overall vision, very close to that of the final text, was taking shape. Title IV, on the relations between Parliament and government, of the first complete draft (the 'Celle St. Cloud' text) is nearly the same as Title V of the final version; only the mechanism of Article 49, paragraph 3, was missing. The linkage of the government's responsibility to the Assembly and the vote on a bill appeared with the meetings of the working group on 16 July and the interministerial council 16–18 July.[14] The wording would hardly be altered during the later drafting stages.

The roles of the Constitutional Consultative Committee and the Council of State were in general, we know, rather modest. The text's overall architecture was not noticeably modified, at least as far as the institutions of the Republic are concerned. On the Parliament, the debate dealt essentially with the incompatibility between a seat in Parliament and a post in government, and the distinction between the law-making and rule-making powers. The members of the CCC, mainly MPs, considered rather accurately that the incompatibility rule the government was so set on was not realistic.[15] It was mainly the Council of State which drafted the future Article 34 on the distinction between Parliament's and government's areas of activity. This transformation, in many ways very symbolic, was not opposed by the CCC.[16] There were, on the other hand, some very real difficulties in drafting: how to define clearly what came under the law-making power and what did not. Failing to come up with a satisfactory solution, the government sent the Council of State two drafts, its own of 29 July and that put forth by the CCC. Faced with this indecision, the Council of State drew up a new text for Article 34, with the government's approval, adding headings under the law-making power, creating a somewhat artificial distinction between 'rules' and 'principles', and perfecting the mechanisms of Article 37.[17]

The agreement

The absence of any real political difficulties in the drafting of a new status for Parliament, and especially the favourable treatment for the government in the rules concerning the relations between the executive and the legislature, require some explanation. Such a broad agreement is indeed surprising, in so far as the goal was to constrain the power of the national representative body. In reality, all the responsible politicians recognized the defects of the Fourth Republic's procedures; they knew, as did the experts, that a new definition of the respective responsibilities of the government and the Parliament was an absolute necessity. The failures of the reforms attempted in Parliament by Paul Coste-Floret in 1957[18] or those of the Gaillard government in 1958[19] had demonstrated at one and the same time the agreement on a certain number of changes and the impossibility of achieving them from the inside. This blocked situation was excellently described by Guy Mollet, one of the key men of the period,[20] before the National Assembly's Committee on universal suffrage, on 1 June 1958: 'The government is perfectly convinced that the Assembly will not succeed in proposing constitutional revision. This has been attempted for a long time. It is not an absence of good will. It is a near impossibility, for everyone sticks to his position'.[21]

Detailed analysis of the principal measures concerning Parliament leads to the conclusion that, to a considerable extent, the framers of the 1958 Constitution drew the lessons from the failures of the 1946 Constitution and from their own meditation on the reform of the parliamentary system. Men like Guy Mollet, Pierre Pflimlin, or Michel Debré, among the politicians, or like Jérôme Solal-Céligny, André Chandernagor, or François Luchaire among the specialists, had all taken part in previous reform efforts. They retained the ideas and proposals that they had been unable to implement earlier. One should not go too far in asserting that the whole Constitution of 1958 consists of the failed proposals of the end of the Fourth Republic; yet there are entire sections which strongly resemble the assortment of unachieved recommendations of the 1956–8 period.[22]

Parliament in 1988: a new equilibrium?

Given the foregoing observations, it appears more logical to compare Parliament's role in 1988 to that of 1958, rather than before. Any evaluation must take into account real practice which, during the past thirty years, has been both rich and controversial, in both institutional and political dimensions.

A favourable institutional evolution

In a somewhat paradoxical manner, Parliament in 1988 has at its disposal more significant and more diversified means of action than it did in 1958. This does not mean, however, that the 1958 objective of 'rationalized parliamentary government' was a failure. While not challenging the initial framework, the legislative assemblies were able to perfect parliamentary techniques, by knowing how to exploit all available opportunities. In addition, the evolution of the Constitutional Council transformed the institutional landscape.

LEGISLATIVE PROCEDURE

The constitutional articles dealing with legislative procedure very clearly confined the law-writing process. Through the sections granting government priority on the legislative calendar and dealing with out-of-order motions, the government acquired the means of permanent intervention, more than means of pressure. The assertion that legislative procedure has evolved in favour of the Parliament is thus surprising; as is often the case, it is a question of looking at the appropriate factors.

Legislative amendments — both the number proposed and the number adopted — have undergone an extraordinary expansion over the past twenty years, and especially during the last ten.[23] Even if a large number of the amendments proposed since 1980 were intended as delaying tactics, the phenomenon is none the less a real one. During the everyday elaboration of a law, the government is more and more open to suggestions from deputies and senators, especially if the competent legislative committee makes the amendments theirs. The amendment process has taken on considerable importance due to three main causes: the government has virtually abandoned its rights under Art. 41 to declare motions out of order for intruding upon its rule-making authority;[24] pressure groups are more familiar with the opportunities to intervene through members of Parliament;[25] and the government itself is anxious to appear very open to co-operation with the legislative assemblies.

The procedures provided in Art. 45 concerning the shuttle between the two chambers has in general functioned in a satisfactory manner, respecting a very effective, if not complete, bicameralism. Recourse to the Assembly's 'final word' became a significant phenomenon only between 1962 and 1969, when the Senate was in the opposition,[26] and between 1981 and 1986, due to the total political opposition between the majorities in the Senate and the National Assembly.[27] Quite evidently, recourse to the emergency procedure, which allows the government to convoke a joint committee after only one reading in each chamber, has been overused, but its real effects have been limited. In the name of bicameralism, the government has increasingly introduced its bills first in the Senate, or given the Senate the first reading after a joint committee.

Only modest use has been made — and with only sporadic political significance — of the procedures under Art. 38 for temporarily conferring Parliament's legislative authority upon government, a legacy of the 'special powers' laws of old.[28] In so far as the Constitutional Council, by a series of decisions,[29] has considerably restrained the succinctness of such laws, the authority-delegating mechanism which allowed the government to pass ordinances in the place of laws has not been as widely used as some feared in 1958.

The most widely criticized procedure has undoubtedly been that of Art. 49, paragraph 3, which in certain cases allows a law to be considered adopted without having been submitted to any positive vote in either of the chambers. It is indisputable that the mechanism which allows the government to place the deputies — and them alone — before a clear and simple choice ('either overthrow me or accept the law') has a certain coercive character, but can one condemn a procedure intended to have this effect for functioning correctly? Moreover, the procedure has not been used as much as is often supposed: the government has invoked it on only twenty-three bills over the course of thirty years.[30] An analysis of the various real instances suggests that it has been used much more as a weapon again the temperamentalism of the majority than to prevent the opposition from expressing its views, except when the latter practices a paralysing obstructionism, as was often the case between 1981 and 1986.

PARLIAMENTARY CONTROL

The founding fathers of the Constitution of 1958 sought a profound transformation of the mechanisms of parliamentary control. By attempting to accustom France to the 'difficult'[31] procedure of the motion of no confidence, and by eliminating, directly or indirectly, the other means of challenging the government's responsibility, they gave birth to an entirely new procedure. It was necessary that the government have time before it and that its existence no longer be put in question at any moment. In somewhat curious fashion, the actual development of parliamentary control techniques has not given public opinion the sentiment that this aspect of parliamentary function has been carried out in good conditions.

The question procedures foreseen in 1958 have functioned poorly. On the other hand, the 'Questions to the government', introduced empirically, have worked out satisfactorily. By obliging the authors of a motion of censure to obtain the signatures of at least one-tenth of the Assembly membership, the Constitution sought to end the practice of interpellation, a challenge by a lone deputy. To compensate for abrogating this right, Art. 48 provided that at least one session a week had to be set aside for question procedures. Introduced as oral questions with or without debate, such mechanisms have only rarely led to a real control over government activity: in the National Assembly, oral questions with debate have to all intents and purposes disappeared since 1977, although Michel Debré saw in them the true substitute for interpellation; oral questions without debate, set for Friday mornings, take place before a generally empty chamber and concern mainly local problems (which are not negligible);[32] in the Senate, both procedures have been maintained due to the tenacity of the Senators, but their repercussions are more than difficult to identify.[33]

The 'Questions to the government' procedure, origins of which go back to an initiative of President Pompidou in 1969, has been modified a number of times, but has on the whole been considered a success. With the help of television, Wednesday afternoon has become the week's regular political event. Before a properly full chamber, party groups share speaking time more or less equitably, which allows them to prod government to the limits on the most current issues. This mechanism was so successful that the Senate adopted it on a monthly basis, as of 1982. Beyond the media-show aspect, this procedure has made it impossible, during an ordinary legislative session, for the government to circumvent occasionally very rough questioning.

Written questions, whose role has remained very technical, have had an extraordinary growth. From barely 4,000 a year in 1959, the number has risen spectacularly to well over 20,000 a year in the 1980s.[34]

The legal status of committees of inquiry or audit was evidently very constrained in 1958. The Law of 19 July 1977, adopted on a parliamentary initiative, relaxed the operating conditions of these committees somewhat, but did not really alter the situation.[35] The parliamentary majority continues to make its weight felt in these committees. Although the Senate attempted to use these procedures as weapons against the government between 1981 and 1986, its success was only moderate.[36] In order to avoid the fetters of these committees, both chambers — especially the Senate[37] — have gone beyond the formal framework to establish *ad hoc* committees (*missions*) set up by each chamber as it wishes, the role of which is to gather information on a temporary or permanent basis. On the whole, those committees which were created have fulfilled their tasks properly.

Experience has also witnessed the extension of the procedure of parliamentary missions (*délégations*). Initiated with the 1972 Law on the ORTF (the Public Radio and Television Corporation), the goal of these missions is either to associate members of Parliament in the study of a broad theme (such as European affairs or the Plan) or to grant them additional means of information (e.g., the Parliamentary Office on Technological Choices). While not very spectacular, these missions have carried out high-quality work whose influence can, in the long run, be quite perceptible.[38]

In equally praetorian fashion, the Senate has put in place a mechanism for following up the execution of laws which allows it, twice annually, a full review of the delays or the progression of the administrative decrees needed to implement the laws.[39]

The very real flourishing of these different means of information and control has none the less encountered a certain scepticism in the opinion of the average as well the informed public. How can parliamentary control be functioning properly when, on the one hand, the government is never overthrown (nor even put in difficulty) and when, on the other hand, matters considered 'sensitive' never arouse any curiosity among the representatives of the national sovereignty? It is probable that one of the conditions for improving the functioning of the committees of inquiry or audit would be to allow them to be created outside the constraints of the parliamentary majority, for example, by a significant number of deputies or senators, as was done for referral to the Constitutional Council.

THE ROLE OF THE CONSTITUTIONAL COUNCIL

The Constitutional Council's now recognized place among French
institutions is the result of a veritable 'adventure'.[40] No one in 1958 had
either imagined or hoped that an organ of this type would become an
authentic constitutional court. Here is not the place to review the
evolution of the Constitutional Council, but simply to draw attention to its
influence on parliamentary behaviour.[41]

The first consequence of the creation of the Constitutional Council was
the control — some would say the tutelle — that it exercised over the
setting up of the institutions: the decisions of June 1959[42] on the by-laws
of the National Assembly and the Senate were poorly received and
obliged the chambers to integrate all the more rapidly the new logic of
power distribution. The loss of each chamber's right to accredit its own
members was not greatly regretted, because of the bad memories of the
non-accreditations of 1956. During the first decade, the perception of the
Council was frankly negative: the decision of 6 November 1962[43]
rejecting the appeal of the Speaker of the Senate on the law concerning
the election of the President of the Republic by direct universal suffrage,
adopted by referendum, was perceived to be out of weakness toward de
Gaulle, regardless of its quite serious judicial reasoning. In the same light,
the decision of 30 January 1968[44] concerning the modified conditions for
financing public television was deemed poor, in so far as the Council could
not answer a question which was not explicitly posed.

It was not until the very famous decision of 16 July 1971[45] (nine months
after the death of the Fifth Republic's spiritual father) that the image of
the Council was altered and that the idea began to emerge that an
effective judicial review of constitutionality might reinforce Parliament's
position and not impair the sacrosanct sovereignty of both Parliament and
the Law. The constitutional amendment of 29 October 1974 — granting a
right of referral to the Council to any sixty deputies or sixty senators —
translated this new perception. Since then, and whatever the government
in power, the Constitutional Council has settled in as the great regulatory
agency of constitutional life.[46] It is well known that it takes great care,
quite regularly, to point out that it does not have a 'power of value
judgment and decision-making equivalent to that of Parliament',[47] but
this has not prevented every great political conflict over the past fifteen
years (if embodied in law) from finding its way to the Council's nine
members.

The Council's influence has been felt along two main axes. First, the
Constitutional Council judges the regularity of legislative procedure.
Through a variety of decisions, it has had occasion to spell out, for
example, the extent of the right of amendment, the notion of resolution,
various aspects of the procedures for joint committees, and the right to
vote. Concerning finance laws, numerous decisions (every annual finance

law since 1973 has been referred to the Council) have allowed it to clarify such issues as budgetary 'riders', the separate voting on the first part of the law (concerning revenues and the overall balance) and on the whole text, the special status of revised budget laws, and the import of the time limits for considering the budget spelled out in Art. 47 of the Constitution and in the Ordinance of 2 January 1959. Through these decisions, the most classical parliamentary law, as it was described by Eugène Pierre in 1893,[48] has lost its autonomy — or at least jurisprudence has become a source of law equivalent to the written rule.[49] In certain respects, it is even superior, since the decisions of the Constitutional Council are binding on all authorities, and thus especially on the parliamentary chambers.

Second, judicial review of the substance of the law, that is, its constitutionality, is now well known, even making the news headlines in some cases. Here it is important simply to note the transformation resulting from this review: constitutionality has become an element of political debate. The controversies and the decisions of the Council concerning the 1982 nationalizations or the 1986 privatizations demonstrate that it is no longer possible to overlook eventual intervention by the Constitutional Council.[50] Without going so far as to conclude, on the basis of statistics of Council decisions, that any new majority's normative freedom of manoeuvre has been reduced,[51] one has to admit that the threat — indeed the certainty — of a referral to the Constitutional Council modifies the parameters of governmental and parliamentary decision-making. In the final analysis, the essence of the Council's reasoning is not to say, in case of unconstitutionality, 'You have no right to make such a rule', but rather to assert: 'You must use another procedure, such as a constitutional amendment, for example'. In this perspective, the Council becomes a pointsman who, after a parliamentary deliberation, verifies if the means chosen correspond to the deepest intentions of the bill's authors. To date, it has never seemed either desirable or possible to supersede a decision of the Constitutional Council and to initiate a constitutional amendment in order to enact the reform declared unconstitutional.

The rise of the parliamentary majority

The collective memory of the French political system in 1958 had but very distant recollections of the existence and the functioning of a parliamentary majority. Since the First World War, France was better known for the chronic absence of majorities, and when they did appear, for their rapid disaggregation. The immediate example of the Fourth Republic confirmed this vision. Michel Debré seemed to express a unanimous opinion when he exclaimed in August 1958, before the Council of State, 'Oh, if we only had the possibility of calling forth tomorrow a clear and constant majority ... '[52] One of the great surprises of the past thirty years is precisely the appearance and the durability in the National Assembly of a 'clear and constant' parliamentary majority.

Contrary to widely held opinion, however, the phenomenon was not born with the Fifth Republic in 1958: the National Assembly elected by majority ballot in November 1958 had no majority, at least in the sense we understand it today.[53] To use the apt expression of Pierre Avril, this was a 'transitional election'.[54] Even if the Gaullist dynamic was clearly in evidence, the Union for the New Republic party group had only 206 members, out of a total of 579 seats. The 'Algerian' legislature, which concluded in 1962 with the fall of the Pompidou government and the dissolution of 9 October, was characterized by fluctuating majorities and the government's difficulty at times in finding real support. Thus it was that the law creating the strategic nuclear force (the *force de frappe*) could be adopted only by making it a question of confidence (Art. 49, paragraph 3).

The Autumn 1962 crisis, an authentic parliamentary crisis, finally brought a majority into existence.[55] The hostility of the 'Cartel des Non ' to any constitutional amendment and the adoption by its members of an anti-de Gaulle stance led the UNR and its Independent Republican allies to campaign alone. The result was noteworthy: 268 seats out of 482. A parliamentary majority was born; it soon became a habit.

The legislative elections of 1967 and 1968 present quite different aspects: in the first case, the majority was just barely obtained; in the second, it was enormous, since the UDR (the new name for the Gaullist party) won an absolute majority on its own. The difficulties of the brief legislature of 1967–8 can be explained by the narrowness of the parliamentary majority, but one is obliged to acknowledge that, without the 'events' of May 1968, it would not have come to an end so rapidly.

The general elections of 1973 and 1978 confirmed the incumbent majority, or its successive versions after the opposition centrists were invited to join in 1969 and 1974.[56] Beginning in 1972, the competition became clearly bipolar: the signatories to the Common Program of the Left on one side, and every one else on the other. In both camps, there was a certain amount of theatrics around this bipolarization, leading to the birth of the quadri-party system which remained more or less in place until 1986 ('the Gang of Four', to use the expression coined by Jean-Jacques Servan-Schreiber in 1979).

The alternation of 1981 did not alter the particulars of the problem: one stable, united, coherent and disciplined majority replaced another. On this occasion, France came to know a change of majority very much like that of other Western democracies. The break-up of the governmental coalition upon the withdrawal of the Communists in 1984 had no parliamentary consequences, since the Socialist Party alone had an absolute majority of the seats, like the UDR in 1968.

The revised electoral law introducing proportional representation did not prevent the formation of a new majority in 1986. Even if it was, like that of 1967, very narrow, it did not suffer any defections during the two years of its life prior to the May 1988 dissolution.

This brief overview of the political history of the Fifth Republic demonstrates that the existence of a parliamentary majority has become a commonplace circumstance. Moreover, the French seem to have adopted it as well.

The workings of the majority

The development and the durability of a parliamentary majority have evidently influenced the functioning of Parliament, first the National Assembly and then, by way of reaction, the Senate in certain cases.[57] The majority contract has become the source for the policies pursued by successive governments. No one could communicate this constraint better than President Mitterrand in his message to the the newly-elected Parliament in July 1981: 'I have stated on numerous occasions that my electoral commitments constitute the charter of governmental action. I would add, since universal suffrage has spoken a second time, that they have become the charter of your legislative action'.[58] Things are thus clear: there exists a solidarity among all those elected on the same programme. Since in addition the contract was drawn up before the country, and prior to the elections, it can only be undone in the same conditions, that is, with new elections. This majority contract mechanism certainly played a role between 1978 and 1981, when the RPR supported the Barre government only tepidly (to say the least), but dared not overthrow it.

The majority phenomenon brought with it two other consequences, both important for the functioning and the image of Parliament. First, it became necessary to organize the internal workings of the majority by setting up among the coalition parties a variety of consultative and decision-making instruments, depending on the moment and the majority in question. These have included the minister responsible for relations with Parliament, periodic meetings of the majority parties' whips, breakfasts at the Elysée, lunches at Matignon, etc., some more successful than others. They were useful in so far as they assured co-ordination between the government and its majority.

Second, the displacement of the debate among the parties of the majority deprived it of its often spectacular and particularly public nature. Since 1962, no majority party leaders have ever had to worry about the outcome of an important vote. Regardless of the tone — even violent — of its speakers, the opposition remained a minority. In such a context, the real political negotiations took place not between a government and parliamentary parties, but within the majority by means of the procedures indicated above. The British or German situations are hardly different from this description. In the end, the government is only formally responsible to Parliament: it is in reality responsible to the majority. And the majority has but one simple question to answer: 'Will the government I support allow me to win the next elections?' The question is more easily raised than answered.

Conclusion

It is only logical now to return to the question posed at the beginning of this essay: what is the model of reference, the pre-1958 Parliament, the 1958 Parliament, or other Western parliaments?

Since 1958, the Fifth Republic's Parliament has been caught in a vice between the Constitution and the majority. Both of these parameters are external to Parliament: the former is considered the basic law, and the latter is the combined result of the party system and the voters' choice. Within this framework, the chambers have done their utmost to expand their democratic functions of making the law and protecting democracy. These ideals are perpetually under construction.

The authors of the Declaration of the Rights of Man in 1789 had hoped that 'the acts of the legislative power and those of the executive power might be forever compared to the goal of all political institutions'. This wish has been incorporated into positive law thanks to the Constitutional Council. The commemoration of the bicentennial of 1789, after that of 1787, is the demonstration that Parliament has remained the best symbol of democracy.

The 'crisis of Parliament' is one of the more permanent themes of political and constitutional discourse. Pragmatic reflection based on observable facts and not memories leads one to more optimism. In a country like France under the Fifth Republic, Parliament has managed to use fully all the opportunities available to it. It seems probable that future political circumstances will give rise to other practices or the discovery of other possibilities. In the end, the institutional framework is but the 'armature' of a political situation. It is this situation which shapes parliamentary behaviour and gives to the institution its true role. Since 1958, France has without doubt adopted a new parliamentary model. It gave up Parliament's absolute sovereignty in exchange for a system in which the political unity between the government and its Assembly majority is assumed to exist, at least as long as the contrary is not demonstrated.

From a political point of view, one is obliged to admit that the notion of 'governmental crisis' has disappeared from the vocabulary, and that France has been governed without interruption since the beginning of the new Constitution: thirty years of constitutional stability have not been common in the country's history. There is no doubt that Parliament can play an even more important role, but it is certain that it has fulfilled the role foreseen by the 'founding fathers' in 1958.

Notes

1. *Journal officiel*, Assemblée Nationale, 2 July 1981.
2. Thierry Bréhier, 'Bilan du Septennat, 1981-1988', *Le Monde*, p. 49.
3. Manifeste du 12 juillet 1971, Le Monde, 14 July 1971.
4. The Program of 14 July 1966, in *Les Cahiers de la Convention des institutions républicaines*, No. 4, supplement to *Combat républicain*, no. 19, September 1966.
5. *Programme commun de gouvernement du Parti communiste et du Parti socialiste* (Paris: Editions Ouvrières, 1972).
6. In Claude Manceron and Bernard Pingaud, *François Mitterrand: l'homme, les idées, le programme* (Paris: Flammarion, 1981).
7. See for example the proceedings of the 25th Congress of the PCF (6–10 February 1985).
8. See the proceedings of the Aix-en-Provence colloquium, published as *L'Écriture de la Constitution* (Paris: Economica, 1989).
9. The text of the speech may be found in Didier Maus (ed.), *Les Grands Textes de la pratique institutionnelle de la Ve République* (4th ed., Paris: La Documentation Française, 1988) (hereafter referred to as *Les Grands Textes*) document 00-100.
10. In *Documents pour servir à l'histoire de l'élaboration de la Constitution du 4 octobre 1958* (Paris: La Documentation Française, 1987 [I], 1988 [II], (hereafter referred to as *Documents pour servir...*), p. 235.
11. Ibid., p. 246.
12. Ibid., p. 277.
13. Ibid., p. 319.
14. Ibid., p. 457.
15. Letter from Paul Reynaud to Gen. de Gaulle, in *Documents pour servir...*, Vol. II, p. 557.
16. Ibid.
17. *Documents pour servir...*, Volume III (1989).
18. *Journal Officiel: Documents parlementaires, Assemblée Nationale*, 1956-1957, no. 4663.
19. *Journal Officiel: Documents parlementaires, Assemblée Nationale*, 1957-1958, no. 6327.
20. See Didier Maus, 'Guy Mollet et l'élaboration de la Constitution de 1958', in *Guy Mollet: Un camarade en République* (Lille: Presses Universitaires de Lille, 1987), p. 349.
21. In *Documents pour servir ...*, Volume I, p. 155.
22. See Didier Maus, 'De la IVème à Vème République', in *Des Républiques françaises* (Paris: Economica, 1988).
23. See Didier Maus, 'L'article 44' in F.Luchaire et G.Conac (eds.), *La Constitution de la République française*, (Paris: Economica, 1987), p. 859, and sources cited therein.
24. *Les Grands Textes...* document 41–100.
25. Thierry Bréhier, 'Les groupes de pression à l'Assemblée', *Pouvoirs* 34 (1985) p. 107.

26. 'Dans l'adversité' was the expression used by Prof. Georges Vedel.
27. *Les Grands Textes...*, documents 45–100 and 200.
28. Ibid., document 38–100.
29. Bruno Genevois, *La jurisprudence du Conseil constitutionnel* (Paris: Editions STH, 1988), p. 117ff.
30. See *Les Grands Textes...*, documents 49–300 and 399.
31. According to the expression of Michel Debré in his speech before the Council of State (see note 9 above).
32. Yves Michel, 'Les questions du vendredi à l'Assemblée nationale', paper presented at the Colloquium 'L'Assemblée nationale aujourd'hui', sponsored by the AFSP (French Association of Political Science), 1985.
33. For statistics on the use of the question procedures, see *Les Grands Textes...*, documents 48–301, 302, 303, 304.
34. See *Les grands textes...*, document 48–300; also Jean-Francois Tribondeau, 'A propos des questions écrites', paper presented at the 1985 AFSP Colloquium.
35. Jacques Desandre, 'Les commissions d'enquête ou de contrôle', *Pouvoirs* 34 (1985), p.51.
36. See *Les Grands Textes...*, document 43–210.
37. Pierre Avril, 'Les innovations sénatoriales', Pouvoirs no. 34 (1985), p.114.
38. Jacques Desandre, 'Les délégations parlementaires', *Revue de droit public*, (1984), p. 77.
39. Avril, 'Innovations', p. 113.
40. Jean Rivero, 'Fin d'un absolutisme', *Pouvoirs* no. 13 (1980), p.p. 5ff.
41. On the Constitutional Council, see: Louis Favoreu and Loïc Philip (eds), *Le Conseil constitutionnel* (3rd ed.,Paris: Que Sais Je-Presses Universitaires de France, 1985); Favoreu and Philip (eds), *Les Grandes Décisions du Conseil constitutionnel*, (4th ed., Paris: Sirey, 1986); Francois Luchaire, *Le Conseil constitutionnel* (Paris: Economica, 1980); D. Turpin, *Contentieux constitutionnel* (Paris: Presses Universitaires de France, 1986); Bruno Genevois, *La Jurisprudence du Conseil constitutionnel*, as well as the chapter by Alec Stone in the present volume, and the sources cited therein.
42. Favoreu and Philip, *Les Grandes Décisions...*, p. 36.
43. Ibid., p. 172.
44. *Recueil des décisions du Conseil constitutionnel* (Paris: Imprimerie nationale, 1968 volume), p. 23.
45. Favoreu and Philip, *Les Grandes Décisions...*,p. 239.
46. See Louis Favoreu, 'Le Conseil constitutionnel et l'alternance', in Olivier Duhamel and Jean-Luc Parodi (eds), *La Constitution de la Ve République* (Paris:Presses de la FNSP 1985), p. 422, et *La Politique saisie par le droit* (Paris: Economica, 1988).
47. Conseil constitutionnel, 14–15 January 1975, in Favoreu and Philip, *Les grandes Décisions...*, p. 291.
48. Eugène Pierre, *Traité de droit politique, électoral et parlementaire* (1st ed, Paris: Librairies-Imprimeries réunies, 1893).
49. In 1957, Prof. Marcel Prélot was still correct in observing: 'The place of jurisprudence in parliamentary law is of little importance' (Paris: IEP Cours du droit, 1958), p. 32.
50. See 'Le Conseil constitutionnel et les partis politiques', a 1987 colloquium of the French Association of Constitutionalists (AFC), (Paris: Economica, 1988).

51. Favoreu, *La Politique saisie par le droit*, p. 127.
52. *Les Grands Textes...*, document 00–100.
53. Ibid., document 24–401.
54. Pierre Avril, *Histoire politique et institutionnelle de la Ve République* (Paris: PUF, 1987), p. 24.
55. For the political history of the Fifth Republic, see Pierre Avril, ibid., and Jacques Chapsal, *La Vie politique en France sous la Ve République* (3rd ed., Paris: PUF, 1987), 2 volumes.
56. Since 1973, *Le Monde* has published substantial brochures following every national election.
57. A thorough discussion of the evolution of the Senate is not possible in this space. It is important none the less to point out that a co-ordination among the Senate's majority parties got under way during the 1981–6 legislature, and has been maintained since.
58. *Les Grands Textes...*, document 18–110.

3. Legal constraints to policy-making: the Constitutional Council and the Council of State

Alec Stone

'If we allow the Constitutional Council's jurisprudence to develop as it has recently', asserted the Minister of Justice in October 1986, 'we will find ourselves in a situation where the governments of tomorrow ... will no longer have anything to do'. Albin Chalandon's voice was only one in a chorus of protests orchestrated by the majority during the 1986 legislative sessions and directed at the French constitutional court. The view, which has been expressed in a variety of forms by majorities on both the Right and the Left in the 1980s, holds that policy-makers are in danger of losing their power to legislate, caught in a constantly narrowing spiral of constitutional constraints, jurisprudential precedent, and legal debate.[1]

The accuracy of this (probably exaggerated) assessment is questionable. What is undeniable, however, is the increasingly important place which judicial, that is, constitutional, considerations have come to occupy in the policy-making process. Indeed, the process can no longer be adequately understood without taking into account the direct and indirect influence of the Constitutional Council on legislative outcomes, and by extension, the influence of the Council of State as the government's official legal adviser.

In 1958, no one would have predicted that we would be discussing such influence today. As the Fifth Republic begins its fourth decade, it may be useful to cast our sights backward to the Constitutional Council's creation and the subsequent development of constitutional review (Section I). This is followed (Section II) by a general discussion of the impact this development has had on the policy-making process.

Section III briefly examines the direct effects the Constitutional Council may have on legislative outcomes, illustrated by its decisions on two important and controversial reform sectors of the 1980s: nationalization and communications (print and audiovisual media).

I

That the practice of judicial review has long been anathema to the French legal system is well known. As David has written: 'A fundamental principle of French law denies judges the power to declare a statute unconstitutional or the right to refuse to apply it on the basis of its violation of the Constitution. No one questions this principle. It is so well established that successive French constitutions have seen no need to state it'.[2]

The framers of the 1958 Constitution followed this tradition, but added an important wrinkle. They created the Constitutional Council, a nine-member body appointed by the President and the Presidents of the Senate and the National Assembly which, once petitioned by the proper authorities according to the procedures of Art. 61.2 of the Constitution, possesses the power to invalidate, in whole or in part, any bill adopted by Parliament on the grounds that it is unconstitutional.[3] A bill referred to the Council can only be promulgated after the Council has ruled on its constitutionality. The Council's decisions are not subject to appeal; and a bill once promulgated, even if the Council had not been asked for a ruling, is immune to judicial review.

This new institution was thought essential to the proper functioning of the parliamentary regime established by the 1958 Constitution. As discussed elsewhere, the Constitution redistributed public powers away from Parliament and toward the executive by, among other things, limiting the domain of *loi* (what the Parliament is empowered to do) and expanding the domain of *règlement* (what the government is empowered to do). The Council was the mechanism expressly created to police the boundaries between these two domains, and to ensure that Parliament would not trespass on executive prerogatives. This it did effectively, contributing to the success of the 'rationalized' Parliament, or, for critics, the 'servile' legislature.

From 1958 to 1971, the Council rendered seven decisions on the basis of Art. 61.2, six times at the request of the Prime Minister and once at the request of the President of the Senate (until 1974 only these two authorities and the President of the Republic and of the National Assembly could convene the Council). In each case it decided in favour of the executive. Moreover, it demonstrated consistent constraint when presented with opportunities to expand its interpretative powers. While one might argue that the Council 'ratified' policy-making procedures chosen by executive authorities, legislative outcomes during this period were not in any meaningful sense altered or formed by the existence of a constitutional review mechanism.

This is not surprising. In all countries where constitutional review of legislation by non-elected bodies exists, confrontation between governments and courts may flare periodically; in France, where hostility to judge-made law is fiercely dogmatic, problems of democratic theory are especially acute. French public authorities in this period were simply not accustomed to thinking of their constitutions — relatively malleable and transient documents — as providing substantive constraints on policy-making. In legislative circles, the traditional doctrine of parliamentary sovereignty and the related conception that law — the parliamentary act — embodied the concrete expression of the 'general will' largely precluded such notions. On the executive side, the dominant political figure of the early period, General de Gaulle, had little patience for legal niceties, once stating:

Three things count in constitutional matters. First, the higher interest of the country ... and of that I alone am judge. Second, far behind, are the political circumstances, arrangements, tactics ... Third, much further behind, there is legalism. ... I have accomplished nothing in my life except by putting the welfare of the country first and by refusing to be entrapped by legalisms.

And later the General asked of a biographer: 'Do you really believe I am bound by the Constitution?'[4]

On only one instance during this period was the Council asked to rule against the executive, when the President of the Senate, Gaston Monnerville, asked the Council in 1962 to invalidate de Gaulle's attempt to amend the Constitution by referendum — a procedure not provided for by the Constitution. The proposal, to require the direct election of the President, brought immediate protest from politicians, the media, and constitutional scholars, largely to the effect that it was unconstitutional and would lead to authoritarian, 'presidential' rule. The government had consulted with both the Council of State and the Constitutional Council, and both had advised that the procedure was unconstitutional. De Gaulle ignored these opinions and, in effect, challenged the constitutional system to stop him. In November 1962, after the referendum had passed, the Council ruled on Monnerville's petition and declared themselves without jurisdiction to control a law directly voted by the people. 'The Constitutional Council just committed suicide', the Senator said afterwards, and asked: 'If the Council does not have the competence to judge a violation so patent and so grave of the Constitution, who does in our country?'[5]

A related, more general question was left largely unanswered: would the Council, in exercising its powers — formidable on paper — ever thwart aspects of major policy initiatives?

The 1971–81 period yielded two major events. The first occurred in July 1971 when the Council, for the first time, annulled a government bill. As important, the Council's decision settled long-running arguments about the constitutional status of phrases contained in the Preamble of the Constitution, which, among other things, mentions the French people's 'attachment' to the Declaration of the Rights of Man in 1789, 'reaffirmed and complemented' by the Preamble of the 1946 Constitution. The government's bill, which would have allowed administrative authorities to restrict the rights of certain groups to legal personality, was struck down on the basis that it violated one of the 'fundamental principles recognized by the laws of the Republic' (in this case a law guaranteeing free association adopted in 1901) — principles proclaimed by the above-mentioned Preamble of the 1946 Constitution. The decision thus effectively incorporated an unexplored but expansive bill of rights which, the Council was asserting, could be used as a source of future Council jurisprudence and annulments. Lastly, as a matter of partisan politics, it produced the somewhat ironic spectacle — mundane today — of opposition groups in Parliament celebrating limitations on what Parliament could do.

A second event led to the development of a major role for the Council in the day-to-day politics of the Fifth Republic. In October 1974, Art. 61.2 of the Constitution was amended, empowering any sixty members of either the National Assembly or the Senate to petition the Council for a ruling on any bill adopted by Parliament. The impact of this amendment on the Council's activities is remarkable: the number of decisions which the Council was required to make jumped dramatically — almost doubling from 45 between 1974 and 1981 to 89 between 1981 and 1988; annulments became commonplace — more than 25 per cent of the laws referred to the Council between 1975 and 1981 were judged to be in whole or in part unconstitutional as adopted, a figure which jumps to 50 per cent after 1981; and the number of petitions emanating from other enabled authorities dropped and is today virtually nil (the primary source of the early petitions, the Prime Minister, has not used his petitioning powers in the 1980s).

To cut a long story short, parliamentary life was gradually 'juridicized', and revitalized, as constitutional debate and Council petitions came to be viewed as effective — at times the most effective — means of opposition available to parliamentary minorities. During the Giscard presidency, this juridicization was weak and uneven, the executive being, in a general sense, unwilling to compromise policy-making objectives in the name of constitutionality. Stated differently, before 1981, governments were not greatly preoccupied with the threat of Council censure, even when these threats were made explicit by the opposition or by its own advisers. This preoccupation became commonplace after 1981 as elections brought, in rapid succession, two radically different reform-minded governments to power.

II

Policy-making can be described as 'juridicized' to the extent that Council decisions, the pedagogical authority of past Council jurisprudence, and the threat of future Council censure alter legislative outcomes.[6] When the Council annuls legislative provisions, this influence is direct, and, as will be shown (III below), is not always negative. But the Council can also have an indirect influence to the extent that policy-makers sacrifice policy preferences in order to avoid constitutional censure. This indirect influence also constitutes the Council's policy-making behaviour.

Juridicization can potentially be examined at each stage of the legislative process today. The first crucial juridicizing role is played by the Council of State. Article 39 of the Constitution requires that all government bills must be referred to the Council of State for an *avis* — a non-binding, formally secret advisory opinion — before they are discussed in cabinet or communicated to Parliament. Discussions of constitutionality are today central to this opinion. As early as 1982, the body's annual report declared that:

When the Council of State examines government bills... its first concern is to verify their conformity to the Constitution. It proceeds in this examination in order to assure the government a maximum of judicial security, not unaware of the fact that this security is all the more necessary since the expansion of the petitioning procedure to the Constitutional Council has multiplied the risks that a new law will be referred to the latter.[7]

The government thus begins its own deliberations and later moves on to Parliament, apprised of the constitutional issues which may come into play and, in the Council of State's words, 'of the risks it takes of its bills being censured by the Council'.[8]

In addition, the Council of State performs other important policy-making roles. It works to harmonize government initiatives with existing legal regimes, that is, to verify that a new bill will not conflict with existing statutes or lead to incoherence in its application. It also may identify and study judicial and administrative aspects of social problems on its own, and make policy recommendations to governments based upon these studies.[9]

That said, the Council of State cannot impose its policy choices on politicians. While the increased efficacy of constitutional review has added more weight to its *avis*, the government is free to disregard it. Furthermore, it is important to remember that the Council of State only considers the initial version of a bill, and is thus not consulted on amendments made in Parliament.

Like its legal adviser, government must assume that important bills will be referred to the Constitutional Council. Indeed, Council intervention can be said to be systematic: all budgets since 1974 have been reviewed by the Council, as have most major reform initiatives since the first *alternance* in 1981. In consequence, governments try to cut potential losses by compromising where initial policy-making objectives seem to conflict with constitutional obligations. This is done, and often. But the task is not a simple one, since the Council of State, its own constitutional experts, and the parliamentary opposition may have differing conceptions of these obligations, and predict different Constitutional Council rulings. More important, governments usually set limits on how far they are willing to compromise, and these are largely determined by partisan and not legal considerations.

In Parliament, a bill, and especially an important one, may become the focus of systematic, unrelenting obstruction by opposition groups. Procedural manoeuvres are employed, and hundreds, sometimes thousands, of opposition amendments are discussed and debated, clogging up the process and disrupting the parliamentary calendar. Constitutional considerations are part and parcel of this obstruction. When opposition parliamentarians raise what are called motions of *irrecevabilité* — a demand for a vote on a law's constitutionality before its discussion on the floor or in committee — often sophisticated arguments are made citing past Council decisions, rumors or leaks concerning the Council of State's opinion, and the work of respected law professors. These motions are, of course, routinely voted down by the majority (since their passage would kill further discussion), but not before its own legal specialists or spokesmen have responded to the charges levelled against the bill. Once the amendment process begins, the arguments begin all over again, often in minute detail, as the opposition works — at times, with surprising success — to force the majority to compromise by invoking the spectre of Council censure and proposing changes which will allegedly insulate beleaguered provisions from negative rulings.

The development and reinvigoration of parliamentary techniques of obstruction are linked to the juridicization of the policy-making process. Between 1959 and 1974, for example, only four exceptions of *irrecevabilité* were voted on the floor of the National Assembly, compared with forty-two between 1981 and 1985, and fifty-one in 1986–7 (more than 100 more were raised but not voted in 1986–7!). Moreover, it is precisely those bills which raise the greatest constitutional controversy that elicit the greatest numbers of amendments: during the first reading of the 1982 nationalization bill, for example, more than 1,400 amendments were considered, then a record; 2,491 amendments were tabled during the first reading of the 1984 bill on press pluralism — more than the total registered during some entire legislative years in the 1960s.

The opposition understands that the government and its majority, for all of its mastery of the legislative process, cannot prevent Constitutional Council scrutiny of its policies. It engages in constitutional debate and petitions the Council in order to have its policy choices ratified or the government's choices watered down or vetoed. Constitutional debate and the petition to the Council are thus patently partisan activities: in France, judicial politics is legislative politics by another name.

III

All courts which exercise constitutional review of legislation have the power to make public policy. The Constitutional Council's policy-making role is a relatively visible and direct one because of its structural mandate and the inclination of politicians to use its offices as a means of opposition.

As a matter of form, each Council decision necessarily constitutes the final, substantive stage of the policy-making process, and is itself an integral part of a referred bill's legislative history. A referral automatically suspends a bill duly adopted by Parliament; the subsequent decision may have one of several effects on this suspension. These can be summarized as follows: if a bill is judged not to be unconstitutional, the suspension is lifted and the bill is promulgated; if judged to be unconstitutional, the bill remains in permanent suspension, vetoed; a bill judged to be in part unconstitutional (a partial annulment) may be promulgated, but 'amputated' of the offending provisions (which remain in permanent suspension); or a bill may be judged to be only in part unconstitutional but non-promulgable nevertheless, that is, the Council may rule that the offending provisions are so important to the whole bill that the bill can have no separate integrity as law without them. In the latter two cases, the government may elect to go through the whole legislative process again in order to 'correct' and 'revise' the bill by incorporating the Council's prescriptions into new legislation.

The legislative histories of the 1982 nationalizations and the 1984 and 1986 reforms of the press and audiovisual regimes provide good examples of how and why the more complicated of these effects can be produced. While space does not allow for thorough treatments, these cases are generally illustrative of juridicized policy-making processes and of the complexity of the constitutional obligations the Council is asked to force policy-makers to observe.

For each of these laws, the parliamentary stage of the legislative process was dominated by the kind of juridicized debate discussed above. *Exceptions d'irrecevabilité* were raised and rejected, long, often violent sessions ensued, and the opposition threatened publicly to petition the Council. As important, and especially for the bills on media policy, the bills were substantially rewritten in Parliament because of fears of Council censure. During the debates on the 1986 reforms of the press and audiovisual regimes, the Socialist opposition was even joined by parts of groups within the majority (Barristes, UDF, and others) to force the government to compromise in the name of constitutionality. But it is the more direct effects of Council of State and Constitutional Council intervention which are of interest here.

From the beginning, the Mauroy government recognized that nationalizations[10] would raise constitutional controversy, and a judicial committee composed of cabinet officials and members of the Council of State was established to study and report on the legal problems involved. The stickiest of these problems concerned how to compensate expropriated shareholders, and how to justify why some companies were and others were not to be nationalized. Both of these problems have bedeviled courts and legal scholars of nationalization around the world, and little consensus concerning the concrete application of very general principles has emerged. The government proposed to the Council of State a compensation formula based largely on the average public trading values of companies to be nationalized during a three-year period (1978–80), and decided on nationalizing only those banks which had more than 1 billion francs in deposits, excepting foreign and certain co-operative and mutual institutions.

The Council of State, after two long days of debate, accepted the compensation formula as constitutional, but suggested to the government that it could enhance its judicial security if the profits and assets of the companies to be nationalized were also taken into account. The Council of State also criticized as a potential violation of the principle of equality before the law the criteria for deciding which banks would and would not be nationalized, arguing, among other things, that foreign banks should not be excluded. The government accepted the former criticism, adopting the Council of State's compensation formula, but rejected the latter criticism, arguing that the exclusionary criteria could be defended.

As is often the case, the Constitutional Council was asked to decide both general and specific issues of policy. In its petition, the opposition argued that nationalization itself was unconstitutional since, among other things, a socialist republic was incompatible with the Constitution, and that property was, according to the 1789 Declaration, an 'inviolable, sacred right' which, in the absence of 'public necessity' could not be infringed. It also argued that even if the Council were to find that the nationalizations were constitutional in principle, specific aspects of the legislation should be struck down, in particular the compensation provisions and the exclusionary criteria for banks. On the other side, the majority argued that the general power to nationalize was explicitly recognized by Art. 34 of the Constitution, which states that Parliament is to 'fix the rules concerning nationalizations', and that such rules would necessarily include the determination of what is a 'fair and prompt' compensation formula required by the Declaration. It also pointed out that the Preamble to the 1946 Constitution seemed to require nationalization in certain cases.

The Council decided, agreeing with the Council of State's initial finding on this point, that it was for Parliament to decide if public necessity required nationalizations or not. This part of the decision was largely expected. The Council did not, however, accept that Parliament was therefore free to fix the details of nationalization without reference to other constitutional principles. The Council then annulled the Council of

State's compensation formula as inadequate, and the exception allowing co-operative and mutual banks to escape being nationalized was judged to be contrary to the principle of equality before the law. Moreover, since a law nationalizing industries could not logically be applicable without providing for their purchase, the legislation could not be promulgated at all.

After again consulting the Council of State, the government revised the law by, in its words, 'mechanically' accepting the consequences of the decision, and resubmitted it to Parliament. The new bill raised the number of nationalized banks to thirty-nine from thirty-six, in spite of the fact that the government judged this to be contrary to the 'general interest' (these three banks would be denationalized later after the government had developed arguments, in line with Council jurisprudence, as to why the difference in treatment before the law could be justified by differences in kind, or 'situation'). As for compensation, the government followed what it called the 'outline of a solution' made by the Council in its criticisms: share-prices were determined by the highest monthly average achieved during the period from October 1980 to March 1981, dividends added, and the total raised 14 per cent to take into account monetary depreciation.[11] The opposition referred this new bill to the Council, largely on the basis that compensation was still inadequate, but the Council did not accept these arguments and the bill became law.

This decision shows clearly how blurred are the lines between judicial and legislative decision-making in the French system. Council decisions can never be separated from legislative outcomes. Michel Rocard's criticism of the decision (one of the most moderate heard from the majority) is revealing: 'instead of stating the law, [the Council] is stating the price'.[12] Of course, in this instance, a statement of law is a statement of price. We must always consider how legislative outcomes would have differed in the absence of constitutional review. In this case, among other things, the whole economy of the bill was altered by the direct and indirect effects of review: by accepting the changes in the compensation formula suggested by the Council of State, for example, the cost of nationalizations was raised more than 20 per cent; by incorporating the Constitutional Council's prescriptions into the bill, the cost was raised by nearly 30 per cent — an increase of nearly 50 per cent in all.

The search for coherent, stable, and pluralistic press and audiovisual regimes has been a controversial one this past decade. It has occupied vast amounts of the time and resources of governments, parliamentarians and bureaucrats, has led to the creation of numerous regulatory commissions, and has opened up new areas of law and administration. The impact of constitutional review on these regimes has been profound and enormously complex, and cannot be adequately traced here. Focus on the more manageable problem of media pluralism, however, will illustrate how reform can be structured, even produced, by the legislative effects of constitutional decision-making.[13]

In October 1984, the Constitutional Council was asked to rule on the Socialists' bill to ensure the financial accountability and the pluralism of the press. The bill's most controversial provisions established anti-trust rules according to which no person or group could control more than 15 per cent of the total market for national dailies or 15 per cent of all regional dailies. The path through Parliament had been a brutal one, breaking all records for hours of public debate and amendments proposed, and leading to several censures of deputies. The Council rejected nearly all of the opposition's arguments, and upheld the fixed market ceilings, vigorously opposed by the Right, but amputated the bill of one very important provision — its retroactivity.

The Socialists had designed the legislation, among other things, to dismantle the Hersant press group, which then controlled three national dailies, including the rightist *Figaro,* and fifteen regional dailies, numerous weeklies, specialized publications, and periodicals (the group's head, Robert Hersant, was also a National Assembly deputy on the Right). The Council ruled that not only was the Parliament free to work to protect press pluralism but that this pluralism was itself an 'objective of constitutional value' without which Art. 11 of the 1789 Declaration — which enshrines the free expression of thoughts and opinions — could not be effectively exercised. However, it ruled that restrictions on the right to press ownership, also being a public liberty, could not apply to 'existing situations' in normal circumstances. The main impulse and thrust of the bill was thus thwarted, the Hersant group having escaped the reach of the legislation.

Even before the Right won the 1986 elections, the opposition in the Senate wrote and voted a bill to abrogate the 1984 press law, which among other things, would have rescinded the market ceilings. During the debates on this bill, the Right argued that anti-trust provisions were not essential to the protection of pluralism, and that concentration had actually strengthened it, since otherwise weak dailies would have gone out of business had they not been absorbed by stronger groups. But the new majority, fearing Council censure, finally wrote into the bill a new fixed ceiling for market shares — set at 30 per cent — but as the opposition complained, the provision would only apply to new acquisitions and would not forbid groups from buying up titles and then liquidating them. In July 1986, the Council agreed with this argument and amputated the provision.

A similar fate befell the government's audiovisual reform, which was being discussed in Parliament when the press decision was rendered. Its anti-trust mechanism was almost entirely revised to take the decision into account, but the opposition still warned that the measures — which restricted control to 25 per cent per person or group over each private television station — would be judged unconstitutional since nothing in them forbade ownership of 25 per cent of all stations, and a related criticism was made with respect to provisions regulating the acquisition of frequencies. In September, the Council agreed with the opposition and a number of other articles were also declared non-promulgable due to their 'inseparable' relationship to the censured anti-trust rules.

Although both the press and audiovisual bills were promulgated, the Council's rulings all but required the government to legislate again. In the case of the press law, the Council's amputations had left the press regime governed by a number of statutes inspired by conflicting legislative philosophies (the 1984 anti-trust provisions still stood, for example, because of the 1986 amputations). For the audiovisual regime, the Council's extensive rulings of inseparability left dormant certain crucial articles which could only be revived by new legislation taking into account the Council's criticisms. The mess was cleaned up in one single bill — 'unwished for' legislation, the government protested — 'a required text' which was 'dictated ... by the Council'.[14]

The bill became law without being referred to the Council, not surprisingly, since the law is a simple synthesis of the Council's rulings and the amputated legislation. The government had simply copied into the law — word-for-word at times — sections of the Council's rulings into the vetoed articles.

Two general points should be made. First, lines of jurisprudence (and this is true wherever constitutional review exists) can result in ongoing restrictions of legislative discretion, at least until jurisprudential authority is reversed. In the French case, this phenomenon is evident in many legislative areas — penal law, electoral law, and so on. It can lead to curious outcomes. The constitutionalization of anti-trust mechanisms for the protection of media pluralism, for example, had little to do with the initial policy objectives of the legislation in question. The Socialists were not successful in dismantling the Hersant group; and the Right was not subsequently successful in eradicating from the legal regime fixed ownership ceilings of a sort designed by the Left. The anti-trust formulas now prevalent in this area, certainly not the only ones imaginable, seem to have acquired a kind of indirect constitutional value of their own.

Second, complex rulings of inseparability, as in the nationalization, audiovisual, and other cases, lead to Council-written legislation. That is, governments would rather secure constitutionality by mechanically copying the terms of Council decisions into new, revised bills than search for more imaginative solutions (both risky and time-consuming). The Council does not, therefore, only possess a power of veto, but can create new law. In an interesting, colourful and apt phrase, the majority characterized the forced revision of the audiovisual law as a 'taking of constitutional hostages', since the effect of the decision was to 'suspend the application of the law until the legislator had agreed to vote new provisions which have in fact been dictated by the Council itself'.[15]

IV

Students of French policy-making can no longer ignore the impact of constitutional review on the legislative process.

First, the development of constitutional review has transformed the customs, habits and conduct of politicians and policy-makers. Striking confirmation of this point was recently provided by Michel Rocard in his prime ministerial circular stating a general code of conduct for his new government (May 1988). In stark contrast to the traditional French model of parliamentary sovereignty and to a general aversion to 'legalism', evident in the early years of the republic, Rocard called 'respect for the state of law' his government's first priority, and ordered his ministers do 'everything' possible to 'eliminate the risks of unconstitutionality', even for bills not expected to be referred to the Council. He also requested them to communicate all potential problems of constitutionality raised during preparatory work to the Council of State before it renders its *avis*, and to leave enough time for that body to deliberate effectively (the Council of State has long complained of inordinate governmental pressure to hurry its opinions, thus reducing their efficacy). Lastly, he urged that constitutional vigilance be maintained as the bills make their way through parliamentary committees and on to the parliamentary floor.[16] The juridicization of the policy-making process is now official.

Even with the best intentions of governments, however, judicial security can never be complete, since the opinion of the final authority can only be known when it is too late to change anything. In 1982, addressing criticisms of its role in the nationalizations case, the Council of State put it this way:

It is inevitable that distinct authorities may judge differently the same legal question. While this risk is small when interpreting a text whose [legal nature] is precise, it is greater in the case of applying a principle whose character is more general; the judgement necessarily becomes more subjective.[17]

This risk, of course, is inherent in the very nature of constitutional review. However, if the era of reform mania is truly over in France, less strain will be placed on the review system and on these judgements generally, and the decisions of the Constitutional Council will likely give rise to fewer polemics about the discretionary powers inherent in constitutional review.

In terms of its direct influence on the legislative process, students of policy-making can profitably conceptualize the Constitutional Council, if not the Council of State, as an associate — in partnership or rivalry — to 'legislative' authorities traditionally conceived.[18] Political scientists can and should view the Council as a kind of third legislative chamber: the Council operates entirely within parliamentary space, and its decisions effectively constitute a final 'reading' of referred legislation, the effects of which are wholly legislative. These effects can be negative — a simple veto authority — or positive, that is, decisions may shape and even produce policy outputs.

Notes

1. *Lettre de la nation* (notes bleues), 7 October 1986. For a very different perspective on these constraints by an eminent public law specialist, see Louis Favoreu, *La Politique saisie par le droit* (Economica: Paris, 1988), pp. 17–41 and pp. 78–122.

2. René David, *French Law: Its Structure, Sources, and Methodology* (Louisiana State University Press: Baton Rouge, 1972), p. 124.

3. While the Constitutional Council does have other important duties, some of which are relevant to policy-making (such as its mandatory jurisdiction over organic laws), only the review powers flowing from article 61.2 of the 1958 constitution are treated here.

4. Quoted in James E. Beardsley, 'Constitutional Review in France', The Supreme Court Review (1976), pp. 212–13.

5. *Le Monde,* 8 November 1962. The indispensable reference for the most important Council decisions is Louis Favoreu and Loïc Philip, *Les Grandes Décisions du Conseil constitutionnel* (PUF: Paris, 1986), not least because it includes invaluable bibliographies and commentary on the most important of the Council's rulings.

6. For a more complete treatment of the juridicization phenomenon, see Alec Stone, 'In the Shadow of the Constitutional Council: The "Juridicization" of the Legislative Process in France', *West European Politics* (September 1988).

7. *Rapport annuel 1981–1982* (Council of State, 1982), p. 15.

8. *Rapport annuel 1987* (Council of State, 1987), p. 54.

9. See generally G. Braibant, 'Les nouvelles fonctions du Conseil d'Etat', *Revue administrative,* no. 239 (1987), pp. 415–21.

10. For an overview, see André G. Delion, Michel Durupty, *Les Nationalisations 1982* (Economica: Paris, 1982).

11. *Rapport* of the Commission Spéciale, Assemblée nationale, no. 700, 22 January 1982; Rapport of the Commission des finances, Assemblée nationale, no. 779, 1982.

12. For reactions to this decision, see *Le Monde,* 19–20 January 1982.

13. Discussion on the 1984 Press law is largely based on John T. S. Keeler and Alec Stone, 'Judicial-Political Confrontation in Mitterrand's France', in Stanley Hoffmann, Sylvia Malzacher and George Ross, eds., *The Mitterrand Experiment.* On the 1986 media reforms, see Stone, 'In the Shadow of the Constitutional Council'.

14. *Rapport* of the Commission des Affaires Culturelles, Sénat no. 19, 21 October 1986, p. 3, p. 7.

15. Ibid, p.22, and *Rapport* of the Commission des Affaires Culturelles, Assemblée nationale no. 371, 7 October 1986, p. 19.

16. Text printed in *Le Monde*, 27 May 1988.
17. *Rapport annuel 1981–1982* (Council of State, 1982), pp. 15–16.
18. A perspective developed in Alec Stone, 'Towards a Political Science of Constitutional Council Behavior: Reflections on *La Politique saisie par le droit* by Louis Favoreu', forthcoming in *Revue du droit public* (1989).

4. Centre–periphery relations in the Fifth Republic: the legitimization of local politics

*Sonia Mazey**

Introduction

The centralized 'one and indivisible' Republic, established initially by the Jacobins and consolidated by Napoleon I, was left untouched by the Constitution of the Fifth Republic. Since 1958, however, local government reform has rarely been absent from the political agenda as successive governments have sought to rationalize and reform the complex structure of centre–periphery relations. Territorial reform has nevertheless been a slow and piecemeal process; each initiative has modified only slightly the existing arrangement. The cumulative impact of these marginal adjustments, however, has been a significant restructuring of centre–periphery relations. Three parallel developments have contributed to this change: the piecemeal establishment of regional government; the progressive extension of the financial and political autonomy of municipal and departmental councils; and the concomitant *déconcentration* of administrative responsibilities. Although the precise nature of centre–periphery relations, in practice, varies from place to place, in formal terms at least, the French state is now in several respects less centralized than in 1958. This chapter outlines these developments and highlights those factors which have determined the incremental nature of the policy-making process in this sector.

While economic and administrative considerations have consistently persuaded governments of the need to reform local government structures, the precise nature of the changes proposed has varied in accordance with the ideological beliefs and political ambitions of those in power. External factors, including financial pressures, the national political configuration and public opinion, have further helped to determine the pace and nature of territorial reform. In particular, all governments have

*The author wishes to acknowledge research relief granted by the Humanities Faculty of the Polytechnic of North London in relation to this work.

had to accommodate the effective opposition of local administrative and political elites to any change which might undermine their traditional power base — the department and commune. The vertical and horizontal integration of these elites into the national politico-administrative system and decision-making structures (through *cumul des mandats* and informal alliances between administrative officials and politicians) has enabled these groups to maintain their privileged position within the framework of any local government reform. Entrenched in the local-administrative system, these groups have also been able to control the subsequent implementation of local government reform.[1]

The Gaullist Republic: functional regionalism

Gaullist governments of the 1960s and early 1970s, while unambiguously opposed to political decentralization, were none the less painfully aware of the need to rationalize French local administration. The system had been designed for a rural nation and was patently unable to meet the administrative and economic planning needs of a modern industrialized economy. The ninety-six departments were simply too small to be viable units for the purposes of economic planning, while demographic change had rendered the communal structure obsolete: by 1968, 95 per cent of the 37,708 communes had fewer than 5,000 inhabitants; 10 per cent contained fewer than 100 people and some had no population at all. Most communes lacked the financial resources to build or maintain even the most rudimentary amenities and were, in consequence, totally dependent upon state financial and technical aid.[2]

Despite their constitutional and parliamentary strength these governments nevertheless found local government reform a difficult and delicate task. Given the national political influence of the — generally conservative — 'apolitical' and centrist local notables, intent on maintaining their power base, comprehensive modernization of the system was out of the question. Equally, the *étatiste* nature of Gaullist ideology and the growing strength of left-wing opposition parties at local government level during the 1960s and 1970s precluded substantive political decentralization. Gaullist governments, therefore, pursued two pragmatic strategies; inter-communal co-operation and functional regionalism.

Attempts by successive Gaullist governments to rationalize the vast mosaic of ineffectual communes met with only limited success. Few mayors welcomed the new opportunities provided for voluntary inter-communal co-operation in the provision of services and urban planning provided by the Multi-Purpose Inter-Communal Syndicates (SIVOM) and Districts created by decree in 1959 and the Urban Communities established by law in 1966. By 1976 there were only 148 districts including 1,259 communes and just over 4 million people; by the same year 1,703

SIVOMs were established affecting some 19 million people and 17,000 communes. The 1966 law created four Urban Communities based upon the cities of Bordeaux, Lille, Lyon and Strasbourg. Despite plans to extend the scheme throughout France, only five other Urban Communities were subsequently established. Meanwhile, government plans for compulsory mergers of small and impoverished communes were abandoned after the events of May 1968 and the replacement of the Gaullist Minister of Interior, Christian Fouchet, by Raymond Marcellin, local notable *par excellence* and leader of the Republican Party. The 1971 Marcellin law on the subject was much less draconian; mergers were to be voluntary. The proposal was greeted unenthusiastically by local *élus* ; by 1975 only 1,957 communes had merged and the total number of communes had been reduced by a mere 800.[3]

Government objectives of administrative rationalization and state-led economic growth together with the need to bypass the politically unsympathetic local political elites led naturally to the consideration of the region as a functional unit of administrative and economic organization. Rudimentary regional administrative structures which had been established during the Fourth Republic were therefore developed in a series of regional reforms in the 1960s. The purpose of these reforms was twofold: to establish a regional administrative framework for the purposes of economic planning; and to incorporate politically sympathetic, dynamic socio-economic elites into the policy-making process.

In 1960–1 twenty-one planning regions were established and a collegiate Interdepartmental Conference established within each region comprising the the heads of the ministerial field services and departmental prefects of the region. The reforms also introduced official, consultative bodies in the form of Regional Economic Expansion Committees comprising the so-called *forces vives* within the region — representatives from banking, agriculture, commerce and industry who were invited to comment on state investment in the region. These initiatives were further developed by the 1964 regional reforms. The prefect of the principal department in the region became the official regional prefect with authority over other departmental prefects in the region and responsibility for the co-ordination of all planning and public investment activities within the region. The Interdepartmental Conference was replaced with an advisory Regional Administrative Conference which brought together under the chairmanship of the regional prefect the departmental prefects and heads of the regional field services. Two new institutions were also created: the Regional Missions and the Commissions for Regional Economic Development (CODER). The former comprised a small group of senior administrative and technical officials appointed by the Prime Minister and intended to act as the 'independent' personal 'brains trust' of the regional prefect. The CODER extended the degree of regional representation previously afforded by the Regional

Economic Expansion committees. Designed to unite 'experts' with local politicians and representatives of various socio-economic groups within the region, the CODER were consulted on regional aspects of the national economic plan and state investment. Politically, the CODER represented an attempt to bypass traditional local elites.[4]

The 1960s regional reforms were, in fact, a compromise as earlier proposals for regional structures divorced from traditional local political and administrative elites put forward by the Planning Commission and DATAR (the Territorial Planning Agency) were modified in the light of opposition from groups affected by them. The prefectoral corps, supported by the Minister of the Interior, would agree only to a regional reform which was to its advantage; plans to establish an independent regional planning administration directly accountable to the Prime Minister were thus abandoned. (Of this scheme, only the Regional Mission survived.) Supervision of the ministerial field services by the regional prefect was challenged by government ministers who, as compensation for this loss of autonomy, demanded representation within the Regional Administrative Conferences. And local political notables, anxious to protect their local power base, insisted upon representation within the CODER. These conflicts of interest inevitably affected the subsequent functioning of the new regional institutions: prefects continued to defend the interests of their own department in regional negotiations; the Regional Missions were marginalized; and the CODER were effectively colonized by traditional local political notables who used them as an additional forum for the defence of local interests. While these factors obviously limited the effectiveness of the new regional institutions, the reforms were were important in so far as they laid the foundations for the future institutional and political development of the region.[5]

Despite their essentially administrative nature, the above reforms also added momentum to a wider political debate towards the end of the 1960s on centre–periphery relations which was accompanied by growing support for further decentralization. Although President de Gaulle's proposals for regional (and Senate) reform were rejected by French voters in the 1969 referendum, public support for further decentralization continued to grow. The issue was no longer simply one of administrative efficiency; the events of May 1968 had given fresh impetus to disparate regionalist movements and prompted widespread support for increased citizen 'participation'.[6]

Elected in the wake of the 1969 referendum, President Pompidou had no desire to revive the regional issue, but was unable to ignore the disparate demands for further regional reform coming from within the government, the administration, political parties, regional associations and the general public. Pompidou's personal antipathy towards the region was reinforced by his policy of *ouverture* towards the centre parties at the national level. The weight of these parties within municipal and general councils effectively ruled out the possibility of a regional reform involving a reduction in the status of the department and commune. The prefectoral corps was equally determined to preserve its position within the departmental and regional structures. Pompidou's desire to appease reformist elements within his ruling coalition sympathetic to political decentralization was also constrained by the growing electoral popularity of left-wing parties at local levels.

The effects of these conflicting pressures upon the policy-making process were reflected in the provisions of the 1972 regional reform. The Frey Act granted the twenty-two planning regions the legal status of territorial public establishments with responsibility for regional economic and social development. The CODER was replaced by two new representative assemblies: a regional council comprising all national politicians within the region — who were *ex officio* members — together with an equal number of local elected politicians; and a consultative Economic and Social Committee comprising representatives from socio-economic and professional associations, who were appointed by the prefect. The regional executive remained the regional prefect, assisted by the Regional Mission. Government suspicion of the region and the influence of local *notables* were evident in the pivotal role accorded to the regional prefect and the composition of the regional council. Similar considerations were reflected in the limited powers and meagre financial resources granted to the new authorities. In addition to being consulted over the formulation of the regional section of the plan, regions were responsible for raising and spending their own budget, the size of which was strictly limited by law and which was derisory when compared to those of traditional local authorities. It was essentially an investment budget since the regions were prohibited from establishing independent technical and administrative services. They could contribute financially to projects of direct regional interest which none the less had to be authorized and implemented by either the state and/or the constituent local authorities. The regional institutions thus remained federations of communal and departmental interests. However, the legal, institutional and financial status of the regions had been further strengthened.[7]

The Giscardian Presidency: rationalizing resources and responsibilities

Elected President in 1974, the reformist Valéry Giscard d'Estaing — at that time an advocate of further regional decentralization — declared local government reform to be an urgent priority. Yet, despite two major government reports on the subject and extensive parliamentary debate, no major structural reforms took place between 1974 and 1981. In practice, the political obstacles to any far-reaching reform proved insurmountable. Elected with an extremely narrow majority, Giscard d'Estaing's government was heavily dependent upon the support of Gaullist deputies and centrist local *notables*, who were for the most part hostile to further regional reform. The local electoral success of the Socialists and Communists during the 1970s further inhibited the introduction of substantive regional decentralization. None the less, Giscard d'Estaing's own reservations about centralized planning, the persistence of the regional debate and the need to counter growing public support for left-wing opposition proposals for decentralization and *autogestion* (see below) convinced the President of the need to address the issue. The result was a series of piecemeal changes which transferred powers and resources from the state to local authorities.

In 1975 Giscard d'Estaing publicly announced that there would be no further regional reform. The President's abrupt change of attitude towards the region was followed by the publication in 1976 of the Guichard Commission's report (*Vivre Ensemble*) on the subject of local government reform. The report recommended a clarification of the functions of local and central government, increased responsibilities and financial powers for communes, relaxation of the *tutelle*, more powerful departmental councils, and the creation of a local administration and communal federations. The region was hardly mentioned. The Guichard proposals met with immediate opposition from the Senate, the prefectoral corps and the many local *élus* from small communes. Anxious to conciliate the centrist *notables* within the presidential coalition, the government promptly sought the views of all French mayors on the subject in a questionnaire. The responses provided the basis of — less radical — government legislation on communal reform presented to the Senate in 1978. These proposals represented a victory for the mayors as their principal demands — preservation of the existing communal structure, less central government control and increased financial resources in the form of a block grant — were met.

Only two reforms were actually passed before the 1981 presidential elections. In January 1979 the numerous government subsidies granted to communes by individual ministries for specific projects (which at that time accounted for more than 34 per cent of municipal and department resources) were replaced by a single block grant (Dotation Globale de Fonctionnement), to be freely disposed of by local authorities. Then, in January 1980, a package of local financial reforms was adopted: local business taxes were slightly increased; the principle of progression was introduced into local taxation; the government agreed to reimburse local authorities for VAT costs; and loans were made easier for small communes to obtain.

Although Giscard d'Estaing abandoned in 1975 his earlier promise to introduce directly elected regional assemblies he did extend the budgetary and policy-making powers of the regions after 1976. The government devolved to the region deliberative power over the allocation of departmental state subsidies and allowed the regional budgets to grow. Regions were also increasingly encouraged after 1976 to intervene in the economy by guaranteeing loans to private industry, giving subsidies to firms locating in the region, contributing to the funds of regional development societies and establishing regional employment schemes. Regions also began to play a larger role in the formulation and implementation of the national economic plan with the result that regional investment was increasingly channelled into government priority programmes in the form of Regional Priority Action Programmes financed jointly by the State and the region (together with other local authorities and public establishments) for the duration of the Seventh Plan.[8]

These developments were facilitated by economic recession. Beset by financial problems, the government was happy to 'offload' new financial responsibilities on to the regions and communes. Moreover, the introduction of more flexible planning mechanisms was perfectly consistent with Giscard d'Estaing and Raymond Barre's antipathy towards uniform, centralized planning. The strategy was also politically acceptable; while the above initiatives did little to meet regionalists' demands, they went some way towards accommodating the wishes of both reformists and local *notables* within the presidential coalition. By the time the Socialists came to power in 1981, important changes in centre–periphery relations had already been initiated: regional administrative and representative assemblies had been established; local and regional authorities had already begun to assume a more interventionist role; rationalization of local government finance was under way; support for further decentralization was widespread (even among local *élus*); and local government reform was already on the political agenda.

The Mitterrand *Septennat* : political decentralization

Shortly after his election in May 1981 President Mitterrand declared that political and administrative decentralization would be *la grande affaire du septennat*. The announcement came as no surprise. Since 1972 the Socialists and Communists had repeatedly promised that a future left-wing government would implement a comprehensive programme of decentralization. In 1945 left-wing parties had been united in their support for the centralized administrative state which they regarded as the primary guarantee of democratic equality and essential for socialist economic planning. During the 1960s, however, several left-wing intellectuals, many of whom were later to join the new Socialist Party became vocal supporters of regional decentralization — notably Michel Rocard, author of the provocative *Décoloniser la Province*. Meanwhile, the Communist Party, stirred into action by these developments, publicly declared in 1971 its commitment to decentralized economic planning and greater democratic participation in local and regional government.

The ideological shift towards decentralization on the part of the Left was prompted partly by the need to respond to — and present a democratic alternative to — earlier reforms undertaken by right-wing administrations. It was also a response to widespread disillusionment with centralized planning. Growing economic disparities between regions — notably between Paris and the provinces — which were exacerbated by the economic recession of the 1970s, convinced many on the Left of the need for decentralized economic planning. The 1960s were also characterized by the revival of regionalist movements which tended to equate regionalism with socialism. Meanwhile, economic and industrial disputes began to assume the character of regional protests against a capitalist, centralized state. Inevitably, party political considerations were also involved. Although the Left had been out of power at the national level since 1958, local electoral agreements between the Socialists and Communists had produced impressive results: after the 1977 municipal elections left-wing parties controlled 153 of the 221 largest towns and many left-wing councillors — particularly younger ones — were eager for more local autonomy. As a broad coalition movement the rejuvenated and modernized Socialist Party attracted support from regionalists, environmentalists and *autogestionnaires* in favour of increased local democracy, technocrats committed to decentralized planning, and local *notables* eager for more power.

The law on the Rights and Liberties for Communes, Departments and Regions was adopted in March 1982. Over the next four years a further twenty-two laws and 170 government decrees completed the decentralization programme.[9] Yet, while the Socialist measures were undoubtedly more extensive than previous initiatives, they did not constitute a radical break with the past. Essentially, they confirmed existing practices and trends. Executive power at the departmental and regional levels was transferred from the prefects to the elected presidents. The state administrative services and local officials were placed at the disposal of the local and regional presidents who were also free to appoint additional political, administrative and technical advisers. The prefects became *Commissaires de la République* (this title was officially changed back to prefect in 1987) who are now the official representatives of the Prime Minister. While they lack the local executive powers of their predecessors the *commissaires* enjoy new powers in relation to economic planning and greater control over ministerial field services. All forms of *a priori tutelle* over local authority decisions were abolished; local government activity is now subject only to the *a posteriori* legal and financial control exercised by the administrative tribunals and newly-created regional Cours des Comptes which audit local authority budgets. The twenty-one metropolitan regional public establishments and the four overseas territories became fully-fledged local authorities with directly elected regional councils and full revenue-raising powers. The major concession made to the regionalists and autonomists was the Special Statute granted to Corsica in March 1982 which set the territory apart legally from other regions and granted the island additional state subsidies and greater autonomy over educational, cultural and social policies.

The reforms attempted to clarify the responsibilities of the various tiers of local government. The *raison d'être* of the region remained economic planning and socio-economic development. Regions were accorded a key role in the formulation and implementation of the decentralized Ninth Plan. Departments were given special responsibility for *solidarité* — socio-medical and social security provision (amounting to 75 per cent of all such expenditure). The primary task of communes was defined as town planning and urban development. *Plans d'occupation du sol,* drawn up by one or more communes and approved by the Commissaire, leave mayors free to grant planning permission for specific projects without further recourse to the central government. The reforms continued the process of financial rationalization initiated during the 1970s. Devolved responsibilities were accompanied by fiscal transfers and a new index-linked block grant the *Dotation Générale de Décentralisation.* Individual capital investment grants previously allocated to local authorities for specific projects by various ministries were similarly replaced by a further block grant, the *Dotation Globale d'Equipement* (which accompanies the *Dotation Globale de Fonctionnement* introduced in 1979).

Several factors facilitated the above reforms. First, the changed national political configuration made further decentralization possible. Unlike previous regimes, the Socialists came to power with a large parliamentary majority and a commitment to decentralization. In contrast to previous right-wing administrations, the Mitterrand government could also rely upon the support of politically sympathetic local councillors. Second, Interior Minister Gaston Defferre was careful to avoid antagonizing key groups. The principal beneficiaries of the reforms were the *grands notables* who had for many years demanded more autonomy. No attempt was made to reduce the number of communes, no choice was made between the department and the region and only minor limitations to the practice of *cumul des mandats* were imposed (from 1992 an individual may hold only two 'significant' elective offices — deputy, senator, MEP, mayor of a commune with more than 20,000 inhabitants). Comprehensive reform of local government finance was evaded and concessions made to ministers who refused to relinquish control over their budgets. Third and more generally, the Defferre reforms were facilitated by the existence of a widespread consensus in favour of further decentralization and the extent to which the proposals simply accelerated existing trends.

Conclusion

Important changes in centre–periphery relations have taken place during the Fifth Republic. All governments have been forced to respond to the pressures for administrative and political decentralization — economic planning, industrial modernization, administrative rationalization and growing public demand for greater local democracy. However, as highlighted in this chapter, the pace and nature of these changes have — throughout the period under discussion — been determined as much by pragmatism as by principles as successive governments have had to trim their objectives to fit the options open to them. Political ideology, the national political configuration, financial constraints, public opinion and the policy-making influence of traditional local and administrative elites have to varying degrees shaped both the formulation and implementation of territorial reform.

Nevertheless, piecemeal reforms introduced by successive administrations have consistently — albeit gradually — increased the economic and political importance of local and regional authorities. In practice, the impact of these developments has been extremely diverse, depending on local politics, personalities, financial circumstances and relations between local administrative and political personnel. But, in formal terms at least, the cumulative effect of successive territorial reforms has been a potentially important shift in the balance of power between Paris and the provinces: resources and responsibilities have been devolved to local and regional levels of government; local politicians, who have traditionally sheltered behind the prefect, are now directly accountable for their actions; and regionally elected governments have been established which, in theory at least, might provide a platform for assertive campaigns against the national government. Centre–periphery relations have thus been modernized and local politics legitimized. Yet, while important changes have occurred within the politico-administrative system, the system itself has not been transformed. As the 1986 regional elections revealed, the traditional politico-administrative elites continue to dominate French politics at all levels.

Notes

1. For details of traditional French local government structures, see Howard Machin, 'Traditional patterns of French local government' in Jacques Lagroye and Vincent Wright (eds), *Local Government in Britain and France* (London: George Allen & Unwin, 1979).

2. On the subject of informal relationships within the French politico-administrative system, see Jean-Pierre Worms, 'Le préfet et ses notables', *Sociologie du Travail*, vol. 8, 1966, pp. 249–75; Pierre Grémion, *Le Pouvoir Périphérique* (Paris: Editions du Seuil, 1976); Jean-Claude Thoenig, 'La Relation entre le centre et la périphérie', *Bulletin de l'Institut International d'Administration Publique*, no. 36 (1975), pp.77–123; François Dupuy, 'The politico-administrative system of the *département* in France', in Yves Mény and Vincent Wright (eds), *Centre–Periphery Relations in Western Europe* (London: George Allen & Unwin, 1985).

3. See Douglas Ashford, *British Dogmatism and French Pragmatism: Central–Local Policy-Making in the Welfare State* (London: George Allen & Unwin, 1982).

4. For details of regional reforms undertaken during the 1960s, see Jean-Louis Quermonne, 'Vers un régionalisme "fonctionnel"?' in *Revue Française de Science Politique*, vol. 13 (1963), p. 851; Catherine Grémion, *Profession Décideurs: Pouvoir des Hauts Fonctionnaires et Réforme de l'Etat* (Paris: Gauthier-Villars, 1979); Pierre Grémion and Jean-Pierre Worms, 'The French regional planning experiments', in Jack Hayward and Michael Watson (eds), *Planning Politics and Public Policy* (London, 1975); Howard Machin, 'Local government change in France: the case of the 1964 regional reforms', *Policy and Politics,* vol.2 (1974), pp. 249–65.

5. See Howard Machin, *The Prefect in French Public Administration* (London: Croom Helm, 1977); Pierre Grémion, 'Résistance au changement de l'administration territoriale: le cas des institutions régionales', *Sociologie du Travail*, vol. 8 (1966), pp. 276–95.

6. On the subject of the 1969 referendum on regional reform, see Jean-Luc Bodiguel (ed.), *La Réforme Régionale et le Référendum du 27 avril 1969* (Grenoble: Presses de l'Institut d'Etudes Politiques, 1970).

7. For details of the 1972 regional reform, see P. Ferrari and C .Vier, 'La réforme régionale: loi du 5 juillet portant création et organisation des régions', *Actualités Juridiques — Droit Administratif,* October 1972, pp.491–510; Vincent Wright and Howard Machin, 'The French regional reforms of 1972: a case of disguised centralisation', *Policy and Politics,* vol. 3, 1975, pp.3–28; Vincent Wright, 'Regionalisation under the French Fifth Republic: the triumph of the functional approach', in L.J. Sharpe (ed.), *Decentralist Trends in Western Democracies* (London: Sage, 979).

8. For details of local government reform and the development of the region during the Giscard presidency, see Yves Mény, 'Central control and local resistance', in Vincent Wright (ed.) *Continuity and Change in France* (London: George Allen & Unwin, 1984); Pierre Sadran, 'La régionalisation française en pratique: esquisse d'un bilan', in Yves Mény (ed.), *Dix Ans de Régionalisation en Europe 1970-1980* (Paris: Editions Cujas, 1982).

9. There is an extensive literature on the Defferre decentralization reforms. See M. Keating and P. Hainsworth, *Decentralisation and Change in Contemporary France* (London: Gower, 1986); Sonia Mazey, 'Decentralisation: la grande affaire du septennat?', in Sonia Mazey and M. Newman (eds), *Mitterrand's France* (London: Croom Helm, 1987); Yves Mény, 'The Socialist decentralization', in George Ross, Stanley Hoffmann and Sylvia Malzacher (eds), *The Mitterrand Experiment* (Oxford: Polity Press, 1987); Paul J. Godt, 'Decentralization in Socialist France: A Strategy for Change', in *The Tocqueville Review*, vol. 5, no. 1 (1983); and Paul J. Godt, 'Decentralization in France: Plus ça

change ...?', *The Tocqueville Review*, vol. 7 (1986). On the 1986 regional elections see Sonia Mazey, 'The French regional elections of 16th March 1986', *Electoral Studies*, vol. 5 (1986), pp. 297–312.

Part II: Political Forces

5. Evolution of the French party system

Frank L. Wilson

In the fifteen years between 1962 and 1977, the French political parties underwent profound transformations resulting in a substantially new party system.[1] This new party system was characterized by the emergence of a dominant majority coalition composed of the Gaullists and their allies; the formation of a durable Socialist–Communist alliance based on a renewed and radicalized Socialist Party and a more moderate Communist Party; a trend towards a dualist party system with two stable multiparty coalitions and the marginalization of centrist or extremist parties that remained outside these two alliances; a movement toward the well-demarcated government/opposition dialogue characteristic of 'party government'; the nationalization and personalization of parties and election campaigns; and strengthened party organization and discipline under hierarchical control in and out of Parliament.

As these trends in party transformation became evident in the 1970s, the one question that remained in assessing the reality and significance of these changes was whether or not they would survive the transfer of political power from the Right to the Left. The victory of the Left in 1981 provided the test of the permanence of these new characteristics in the French party system. And they did prove durable through 1986.[2] Some adjustments in party alignments and styles occurred but the basic features of well-organized, competitive, bipolar blocs of parties continued with the Socialists in power just as they had emerged during a conservative era.

However, the era of cohabitation from 1986 to 1988 introduced new elements that have raised questions about the viability of the party system that emerged in the earlier years of the Fifth Republic. Many of the features enumerated above as important changes are now evolving in new directions.

The end of Gaullist hegemony

The successful development of a broad-based, well-organized Gaullist party under the leadership of Georges Pompidou permitted the survival of a party with origins in de Gaulle's personal charisma.[3] The party gradually abandoned some of de Gaulle's views as Pompidou steered clear of adventurous reforms and moved toward more traditional conservative principles. The Gaullist party remained a convenient political vehicle for the diverse leaders and voters who had rallied to de Gaulle. In 1974, Pompidou died without leaving a clear successor as party leader, thus opening a period of uncertainty for his party. Eventually, Jacques Chirac assumed leadership of the party and moved it toward positions on economic liberalism more like those of traditional French conservatives than the economic views of de Gaulle.[4]

By the end of the 1970s, the Gaullist party, renamed the Rally for the Republic (RPR), had renewed its organization under the leadership of Jacques Chirac.[5] It had fended off efforts by Valéry Giscard d'Estaing to translate his presidential victory into a rebalanced conservative coalition based on his own Republican Party. The Gaullist party remained the best-organized party on the Right in terms of structure and networks of grass roots support. While its voting strength was reduced and it now shared the right and centre votes that it had once consolidated alone, the RPR remained the right-wing party capable of winning the most votes in national and local elections. But it lost the breadth of electoral support that the Gaullist party under de Gaulle had been capable of attracting.

The RPR lost even more of its Gaullist character as its leadership was renewed. The passing of the Resistance leaders, who had formed the core of the original party, brought the recruitment of new leaders and workers by Chirac at the end of the 1970s.[6] The leadership renewal gained added momentum after 1981 when Chirac took advantage of the time in opposition to eliminate older and ineffective leaders and former Parliament deputies. He brought into positions of influence a new generation of party leaders loyal to himself rather than to the ideas of Gaullism. At the level of the rank and file, the RPR gained new members and strengthened its organization. Many express scepticism about the strength of the Gaullist party organization and the activity of its purported members.[7] But the organizational capability and activity of party members was demonstrated well in 1988 when the RPR organized a rally in Paris of over 80,000 supporters from all over the country to back Chirac's presidential bid.

Chirac dominated the Gaullist party and during the 1980s became the public spokesman for the Right. But his ambition and combative political style made him a controversial and problematic leader for the conservative forces. The personal nature of Chirac's leadership in the party left little room for the development of alternative leaders who might challenge or replace him. His defeat in the 1988 presidential election left his party and his coalition weakened and without a leader at a crucial time in their history. However, Chirac's recuperative powers should not be underestimated in a country where Mitterrand fought an often lonely battle for sixteen years before winning the presidency. Nor should the RPR be counted out. It has already survived a number of challenges that were expected to lead to its demise. It is likely to remain the single most important party on the Right. But it cannot expect to regain the hegemonic position it held for the first fifteen years of the Fifth Republic.

The weakening of the RPR has had important consequences for the party system. It is important to remember that the RPR's successes earlier in the Fifth Republic were among the most important stimuli for reforms in other parties.[8] Now the model of party reform must be found elsewhere as the RPR struggles to adjust to a loss of its hegemony.

There have been three consequences of the RPR's loss of predominance with effects for the party system as a whole. First, the RPR's decline has opened up competition among centre–right parties for leadership of the Right. Prior to 1974, there was diversity in the presence of Giscard's then small Independent Republican Party and several other smaller parties. But the leadership of the Gaullists was unchallenged: the Gaullist party received the vast majority of votes for the conservative coalition with only a small percentage of votes and National Assembly seats controlled by the other rightist and centrist parties. This Gaullist superiority kept competition to a minimum and within the bounds of civility. After 1974, however, the rivalry became intense as the Giscardian party and its centrist allies grew and openly challenged the dominance of the Gaullists. Table 5.1 shows the increased competitiveness of the right-wing parties in elections in the 1970s and 1980s.

Table 5.1: The Gaullist-Giscardian Rivalry: Percentage of votes cast

	National Assembly elections*		Presidential elections		
	1978	1981	1974	1981	1988
Gaullist candidates	22.6	20.8	18.3	21.9	20.0
Giscardian candidates	21.5	19.2	32.6	28.3	16.5

*Not all elections are included since the Gaullists and Giscardians agreed on single candidates for National Assembly elections prior to 1974 and again in 1986 and 1988.

The two groups were involved in a very close battle for pre-eminence. The Gaullists lost two of the three first-ballot presidential contests and saw their once overwhelming edge in the National Assembly dwindle to a margin of a few seats. With the two contenders so close to each other in strength, they focused much of their election campaigns on each other in order to win an advantage on the first ballot of the two-ballot legislative and presidential elections. The policy differences between the RPR and its conservative rivals tended to be minimal and their electorates were virtually indistinguishable in terms of socio-economic or attitudinal differences. The competition thus tended to be over style and personality. Such rivalries proved to be particularly divisive. They resulted in hurt feelings and tensions that were not easily healed in time for the second ballot. Indeed, the Socialist victory in the 1981 presidential election was due less to Mitterrand's appeal than to the failure of Gaullist voters to support Giscard on the second ballot.

Second, one of the key electoral advantages that the Gaullist coalition had during the first twenty years of the Fifth Republic was its unity. At election time, Gaullists would point to the disunity between the Socialists and Communists and raise questions about the ability of the Left to provide stable government. The Left's real and potential divisions would be contrasted with the unity of their own coalition. Marginal voters were swayed by such appeals, overcoming their dislike for the style or policies of the Right in order to vote for effective government. However, once the Gaullists lost their predominant position and the feuding on the Right increased, this advantage was lost. The Left continued to have its own problems with disunity. But no longer could the disunity of the Left be contrasted with the unity of the Right: both sides showed signs of division that nullified the electoral advantage that its earlier cohesion used to give to the Gaullist-dominated coalition.

The third consequence of the new balance of power on the Right was that the competition facilitated the revival of the far Right. A major contribution of the Gaullist party in the early years of the Fifth Republic was its integration of the extreme Right. The breadth of Gaullist appeal to conservative voters reduced the electoral base of radical right-wing groups. Voters on the extreme Right were tempted to vote effectively and support the Gaullists even if they disliked the General's Algerian or decolonization policies. And the Gaullist party did not have to make concessions to the priorities of the far Right to capture these voters. Several efforts to rebuild a far Right party were made but the Gaullist hold over right-wing voters was not to be broken while the Gaullists were as predominant as they were.

Once the Gaullists' dominant position was lost, however, bidding for votes by the two rival conservative groups opened up the possibility of gaining policy concessions in exchange for the votes of the far Right. When this ploy yielded minimal results, the more fragmented situation on the Right (and proportional representation for the 1986 elections) opened up the possibility of amassing votes in a new far Right party that would make it impossible for the main conservative parties to ignore the new issues of immigration and law and order. Thus, the large vote for Jean-Marie Le Pen's National Front in the 1988 elections should not be interpreted as a groundswell of support for the undemocratic positions of Le Pen but rather as a way voters may have tried to force the mainline conservative parties to acknowledge their dissatisfaction with the deterioration of public security and with the presence of so many immigrants.

The breaking of the Gaullist hegemony has thus had far-reaching effects for the entire party system and especially for the political position of the Right. There is little chance that today's neo-Gaullist party can rebuild that dominant position but its continuing strength, even in the aftermath of the 1988 defeat, will prevent another right-wing or centre party from building a new hegemonic single party for that portion of the political spectrum.

The Union of the Left in the Socialist Party

Through the first twenty years of the Fifth Republic, a main feature of party politics was the search for a union of the Left based on co-operation between the Communist Party (PCF) and the Socialist Party (PS). The campaign for a united Left was made possible by changes in the Communist Party as it abandoned its once Stalinist stance to flirt, if only briefly, with Eurocommunism. The PCF moderated many of its doctrinal positions, moved away from close alignment with the Soviet Union on foreign policy matters, and based its hope for coming to power on an alliance with the Socialists. The more moderate stance of the PCF permitted Communists to emerge from the political ghetto of the 1950s and early 1960s. Appearing more and more as a party like other parties, the PCF assumed the role of one of the four main actors in French politics. This opened the way for the Socialists to form an opposition coalition with the PCF and to prepare for governing together. By the mid-1970s, left-wing unity was made formal in an agreement on a common government programme for the Left once it came to power.

In the early years of this alliance, the PCF deferred to Socialist leadership even though the PCF had the larger electoral base. The Communists did so because they recognized that a PCF-led coalition could not attract the majority needed to win the presidency or a parliamentary majority. However, this tactical deference to the Socialists contributed to the growing dominance of the Left by the Socialists. After standing as the candidate of all the Left in the presidential elections of 1965 and 1974, François Mitterrand emerged not only as leader of the Socialists but as *de facto* leader of the Left in the eyes of the public.

By the mid-1970s, it became clear to the Communists that their moderation was not winning them new votes. While PCF vote totals remained stable, the Socialist Party was rapidly gaining votes. The PCF's moderation was gaining votes for the Socialist Party, not for itself. Marginal centrist voters decided that the PCF no longer posed a threat and that they could then vote for the PS in spite of its alliance with the Communists. The result was that the PCF's long dominant position on the

Left was eroded by growing support for the PS while their own voting strength remained stagnant (see Figure 5.1). By 1981, the Socialists had become the largest party on the Left for the first time since the Second World War.

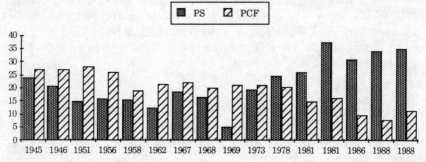

Figure 5.1: Voting strength for the Socialists and Communists, 1945–1988
(*Note:* Results are for the first ballot for legislative elections between 1958 and 1981, and for all presidential elections.)

Communist leaders calculated correctly that the new balance of power on the Left would permit the PS to ignore the PCF's policy agendas once the Left was in power. But by that point, the process of unity had proceeded so far that the Communists could not unilaterally break with the Socialists without serious repercussions. After fifteen years of urging left-wing unity, PCF voters and party members had become attached to the Union of the Left. When the PCF shifted in 1977 to a new aggressive stance toward the Socialists and more hard-line doctrinal positions, the new dogmatism provoked serious division within the party; it destroyed party morale; and it drove voters away from the party to the Socialists. Most Communist voters were unwilling to leave the union of the Left that the party had so long advocated at the moment when victory was at hand.

The result was to leave the Socialists in the hegemonic situation on the Left that the Gaullists had enjoyed on the Right during the 1960s. The Communists were left with only a minor role in the government of the Left between 1981 and 1984. Their voters defected in large numbers so that by the 1988 presidential election the PCF candidate took less than 7 per cent of the vote. That represented a loss of some 2.4 million votes from the already shrunken Communist electorate of the 1981 presidential election and a loss of 3.75 million votes since 1978. Party leaders have been unable to devise a strategy to reverse the party's collapse. Internal divisions over the appropriate countermeasures and loss of *élan* have left the party in a state of near-paralysis. Indeed, there are indications that the PCF's decline is not yet over. The return to the two-ballot electoral system for the National Assembly leaves the PCF in danger of falling short of the number of seats required for a separate parliamentary group. By the end of the 1980s, the PCF is at risk of being confined in a new political ghetto, no longer one of exclusion but rather one of uselessness.

Despite the collapse of the PCF, the union of the Left persists. But the union is now in a single party: the Socialist Party. The consequences of this for the party system as a whole have been important. First, the hegemony of the PS permitted the Left to come to power. With the Socialists dominant on the Left, marginal voters were no longer frightened by the presence of a weakened Communist Party alongside the Socialists. It was not so much that *la grande peur* had disappeared by 1981 as that the PCF had been weakened to the point that it no longer frightened many voters. Indeed, with the decline of left-wing extremism, the new fear is of the radical Right, a fear that works to the benefit of the Socialists as moderate voters worry now about the conservative parties' allying with Le Pen's National Front in local politics and potentially at the national level.

Second, the decline of the PCF left protest voters free to shift to the other political extreme where they voted for Le Pen's National Front. Not all of the strength of the far Right came from the disruptions of the Gaullist hegemony. The PCF had long benefited from the votes of those dissatisfied with the existing system. As the PCF declined and even its negative impact waned, these voters sought more aggressive and fashionable ways to express their discontent and they found it in the anti-immigrant National Front. Many voters in working-class suburbs around Paris and in the large cities in the South of France, where the presence of immigrants has coincided with declining factories and economic distress, appear to have shifted their allegiance from the PCF to the National Front.

Third, the near-disappearance of the PCF permits the Socialists to abandon their once strident, class-based rhetoric and doctrine. Such a hard-line position was necessary as long as the PS was flanked by a powerful Communist Party in order to prevent the defection to the Communists of voters who responded to the old ideologies of the Left. Now, however, that threat is reduced with the PCF attractive to few such individuals. These voters now are content to work within the PS to attain their goals. In the meantime, the Socialist Party can shed the ideological baggage that other European Socialist parties abandoned three decades ago.

The Socialist Party is in fact making this adjustment to a more pragmatic doctrine and style. It entered government in 1981 with a party policy statement correctly described as 'a museum piece, a Marxist delirium in which most of the world's woes were blamed on imperialist exploitation, multinational enterprises, and capitalist contradictions'.[9] The experience in government from 1981 to 1986 served as a school for Socialist leaders. After early efforts to achieve some of its ideological goals proved illusory, the Socialist government concentrated on moderate economic and social policies grounded more in realities than in doctrinal models. By 1984, most of the class rhetoric was also gone. One commentator suggested that a major achievement of the Socialist government may very well have been the freeing of French socialism from its ideology: 'The Left came to power with an ideology and a social base belonging to the past. Today, faced with reality, ... we are witnessing the progressive liquidation of these old dogmas.'[10]

The Socialist retreat from doctrine is still tenuous. There are elements within the PS who are uncomfortable with this retreat from the party's ideological heritage. Its official programme remains unchanged. But the Socialist Party's new-found pragmatism survived the move to opposition after 1986 and back into government again in 1988. The pragmatic PS campaign themes both in 1986 and 1988 suggest the party's less doctrinaire approach. If this continues, the long-established ideological character of French politics may yield to the pragmatism more typical of party politics elsewhere in Europe.

Thus, the Union of the Left continues but in a new form. The union is now essentially achieved within the Socialist Party instead of through an alliance between two equal partners. The PCF has no alternative strategy for coming to power even if it dislikes its subordination. The PS benefits from the PCF's collapse: it has become the dominant party on the Left and it may well establish a new hegemony in the party system as a whole like that of the Gaullists from 1958 to 1974.

An end to party polarization?

The easing of ideological commitments might be expected to assist in solving the excessive polarization of French parties. Party polarization was one feature of the old multiparty system that persisted after the emergence of a new party system in the 1960s and 1970s. Parties from the Left and Right presented entirely different visions of the nature of the actual society and of the desired future society. Under the Fifth Republic, the once moderate PS, excluded from power, rejected social democracy and renewed its commitment to a fundamental, class-warfare brand of socialism.

While ideological commitment finally appears to be waning in France, this does not necessarily portend the ebbing of party polarization. French polarization involves more than ideological conflict. It has important affective and psychological dimensions as well. It is deeply ingrained in the style of French politics. Inter-party rivalries go beyond the normal tensions between rivals for electoral support to the view that one's political opponents are dangerous enemies. In their rhetoric, parties are vitupera-tive in their descriptions of their rivals. At the level of the individuals, the exchanges are often so bitter and irresponsible that slander suits between national politicians are frequent.

Such polarization makes rotation in power difficult and filled with tension. Even the successful experience of the 1981 rotation — the first since 1936 — failed to ease apprehensions on both sides about the willingness of their rival to observe elementary democratic standards in such transitions. While the conservatives ruled in the 1960s and 1970s, the left-wing opposition did more than simply decry the government's policy choices and offer their alternatives. It threatened disorder, subversion and anarchy to discredit the government and block its policies. The victory of the Left in 1981 brought little change in this intense style of political exchange. Then it was the Right which opposed the government as if it were illegal and illegitimate, using the same tactics that the Left used in the past against conservative governments. For its part, the Left government protested against the undemocratic nature of their opponents' tactics in terms not unlike those used by the Right against the Left during the 1960s and 1970s.[11] Cohabitation brought a new form of this polarization with a conservative government handing Mitterrand legislation he was obliged to sign that undid many of the major Socialist changes, notably the nationalizations. At the same time, Mitterrand acted behind the scenes to discredit the government that he presumably headed.

Mistrust and mutual hatred were so intense as to make even ceremonial gestures at co-operation and civility difficult. The spirit of this polarization is well captured by two quotations by prominent political figures from the opposing camps. In 1981, a leading Socialist engendered apprehension when he rashly urged that 'heads fall' shortly after the 1981 Socialist victory. In the country of the Reign of Terror such a comment could only stir opposition extremism. Likewise, a prominent Giscardian fuelled tensions in anticipating a victory by the Right in 1986: 'To François Mitterrand, we say ahead of time: we will cut off your telephone, water, gas, and electricity and we will govern immediately and without sharing power!' The fact that actual behaviour does not correspond with the violent rhetoric in no way reduces the tensions produced by such verbal sparring.

Since the polarization goes beyond ideological commitments, the spread of pragmatism will not eliminate polarization. It is a situation where the political party elites have developed an intense polarization without great ideological, socio-economic, or issue distances between them. To overcome such psychological polarization may well require a wait for the emergence of a new generation of more tolerant political leaders.

Back to multipartyism?

The simplification of the party system that developed in the 1960s and 1970s was not a pure two-party system, but a dualism based on durable and cohesive coalitions on the Left and Right. Four major parties monopolized the overwhelming majority of the vote in national elections and accounted for virtually all the members of the National Assembly. This represented a striking deviation from the traditional multipartyism of previous French democratic regimes. Out of this dualism emerged a dialogue between government and opposition that had not been possible under the loose centrist coalitions that governed nearly always in earlier French multiparty systems. The old centrist parties were eliminated during the 1960s in the polarization between de Gaulle's supporters and the left-wing opposition. There was no political room for a middle course by parties not willing to align themselves with or against the Gaullists. Nor were voters attracted by the centrist options available to them. For the most part, centrist voters and politicians were absorbed by the Gaullist party in the first five years of the Fifth Republic. The remnants of the Centre were integrated into the broadened Gaullist–Giscardian coalition fashioned by Giscard at the time of his election as President in 1974.

In the past few years, the dominant pattern of dualism has seemed to be in danger of giving way to a new multipartyism. The first reason has been the emergence of a new far Right movement. Le Pen's National Front has taken such extreme stances that its integration into the rest of the Right is unlikely.

The second challenge to dualism is the possible re-emergence of centrism. Recent public opinion polls leave little doubt that a sizeable portion of the French electorate professes to prefer government by the Centre to government by either the Right or the Left. Indeed, the initial popularity of cohabitation in 1986 was due in part to the public's desire to enforce a moderation on the two sides by saddling a Socialist President with a conservative National Assembly. A centrist government coalition, tilting sometimes to the Left, sometimes to the Right, is seen by many observers and citizens alike as the natural source of government.

Two related factors also seemed to support this return to centrism. Since 1983, the growing pragmatism of the PS has reduced significantly the policy differences between Right and Left. With the Socialists no longer talking about a rupture with capitalism, centrists can envisage co-operating with them again. National elections no longer appear to the voters as choices between parties supporting alternative views of society; instead, the selection is between alternative sets of leaders whose policies are likely to differ more in nuance than in nature. Second, the development of a broad consensus on political and socio-economic issues in France would seem to obviate the bipolarized party system of the past three decades.

During the 1988 presidential election, Mitterrand appealed to this popular sentiment favourable to centrism by suggesting he would try to govern with the existing majority by attracting centrists to a new coalition with his Socialists. However, the size of his victory margin tempted him to use his new momentum to seek a new Socialist parliamentary majority. After an almost derisory effort to recruit some marginal centrists,

Mitterrand dissolved the National Assembly. In the new election campaign, the Centre-Right closed ranks to offer a clear conservative alternative to the Socialists. Again, the centrist option was absent from the choices offered voters in the ensuing parliamentary elections.

Despite the electoral failure of centrism, the new National Assembly opened an opportunity for a centrist revival. The elections failed to produce a parliamentary majority for the first time since 1962. Sensing a chance to set themselves apart from their conservative allies, a number of centrist politicians elected under the Gaullist–Giscardian label opted to form a new parliamentary group rather than continue their affiliation with the Giscardian Union for French Democracy (UDF). With forty-one deputies, the new Union of the Centre (UDC) hoped to obtain some ministries and policy influence in the new Socialist-led minority government. The Rocard government did include a few centrists but policy control remained solidly in Socialist hands. The UDC remains formally in opposition but it announced it would consider proposed laws on their merits rather than practice the systematic opposition of the RPR and UDF.

The future of this new centrist option is still uncertain. The centrists have been attacked as traitors by their erstwhile friends in the UDF and RPR. they have been scorned by the Socialist Party rank and file, who remain hostile to these 'opportunists' and suspicious of their own leaders' willingness to deal with them. Within the Socialist Party, most activists and leaders would see a renewed centrism as a retreat to the discredited 'third force' strategy of the Fourth Republic. Hence, the PS selected Pierre Mauroy, a more traditional Socialist, as party secretary in 1988 rather than Laurent Fabius, a pragmatist linked with support for a coalition with the Centre. An additional concern for all parties at the present time is the consequence on local elections of such a shift in alliance patterns. With municipal elections due in 1989, few politicians were interested in realigning their local coalitions to conform to a new national strategy that links them with the parties and leaders they have opposed for twenty years at the local level. This concern about the local ramifications of a shift in party alliances is a real one for national political leaders, since nearly all of them also hold local elected offices.

The greatest threat to the new centrism is the electoral obstacle. Whatever the talk about centrist inclinations, few voters are willing to abstain from the choice between the Right and the Left by voting for a centrist movement. Not since 1973 has there been a centrist electoral success. And in that year, the 'Reformers" 13 per cent of the vote was insufficient to prevent their absorption by the Gaullist–Giscardian majority the following year. The two-ballot system has worked to the disadvantage of the centrist parties in the past and is likely to do so in the future. The current centrist deputies are in Parliament because they ran under the RPR and UDF label. Many will find it difficult to win re-election as centrists.

Thus, the dualist pattern is under siege but still prevails. Table 5.2 illustrates the prevalence of electoral dualism even in the 1980s. The National Front and the new centrism pose potential threats to that dualism. But so far, the confrontation between a left-wing coalition now incorporated into the Socialist Party and a moderate conservative coalition has continued to be the dominant political configuration.

Table 5.2: Strength of the Four Largest French Parties

Period:	Number of elections	Percentage of votes cast for candidates endorsed by PCF, PS, UDF, RPR	Percentage of seats in National Assembly won by candidates endorsed by PCF, PS, UDF, RPR
1946-1956	3	76.6	72.9
1958-1978	6	85.3	87.2
1981-1988	3	89.8	96.8

The elusive goal of party government

The revitalization of French parties did not bring with it a strengthened role for parties in the policy process. Under de Gaulle and his successors, parties were kept at a distance from the policy process. Even the crucial issues of cabinet formation and the distribution of portfolios among the majority parties were imposed by the President without consultation with the party leaders. Individually and collectively, Gaullist and Giscardian party figures were able to bring new ideas or point out problems to the executive; but the executive steadfastly resisted bargaining with parties *per se* over programmes or policies or ministerial appointments. Such dealings with parties were scornfully rejected as part of the Fourth Republic legacy that the General had overcome.

There were some signs that this situation might change with the Socialist accession to power in 1981. The PS had long criticized its conservative rivals for their puppet status and had insisted that democratic procedures required greater respect for the ideas of the government parties and their parliamentary groups. In practice, Mitterrand and his prime ministers worked to increase dialogue with their party colleagues. These regular meetings with Socialist Party and parliamentary leaders drew the government's attention to the concerns of the rank-and-file party members and aided the government in deflecting opposition within its parliamentary majority. On occasion, the resulting impact on policy was even important. The most dramatic, and ultimately disastrous, party intervention was the pressure to toughen the proposed restrictions on private schools in 1984.

With the return to conservative rule in 1986, the narrow majority supporting Jacques Chirac's government and the difficult setting of cohabitation might have opened up the possibility of greater dialogue between the executive and party leaders. But in fact there was little evidence of consultation between Chirac and the parties supporting him in the National Assembly. Indeed, he antagonized his supporters in the UDF by his lack of consultation and occasional high-handed executive dominance. The narrow majority only increased Chirac's ability to dominate the process, since dissenting majority deputies knew that their defection would not simply send a distress signal to Chirac, but would topple the government at a difficult time.

The role of parties in forming the cabinet seems to have been slightly expanded in the 1980s in that consultations between the executive and party leaders have taken place during the formation of new governments. In 1981, the entrance of the Communist Party into government was prepared by negotiations between the PCF and PS leaders, although Mitterrand retained the final power to determine which Communist leaders were to be named and which ministries were to be allocated to them. As far as other ministerial appointments were concerned, in 1981, 1984 and 1988, Mitterrand proceeded without consulting the Socialist Party leaders or those of other parties.

When the parliamentary majority shifted in 1986, the leaders of the new conservative majority signalled to Mitterrand that Chirac was the only acceptable choice as Prime Minister. This was unprecedented in the Fifth Republic but it resulted from the peculiar setting of cohabitation that was also unique. Otherwise, the role of parties in cabinet building was similar to the Socialist period with the Prime Minister taking the initiative rather than the selections coming from the Elysée. Conforming to Mitterrand's practice in 1981 and to the realities of a coalition of nearly equal political forces, Chirac consulted with the party leaders of the right-wing coalition as he formed his government in 1986. But he retained final say over the party composition and specific ministerial assignments in his government.

The minority situation of the Rocard government after the 1988 legislative elections required a new sensitivity to the interests of those parties needed to remain in power. The PS had less impact since its deputies knew that total loyalty was essential in such difficult times. But the government had to pay heed to the direct and indirect messages from the centrists and the Communists in order to shape legislation that would attract these parties' support on the floor of the National Assembly.

Both Mitterrand and Chirac in their respective cabinet-building gave greater preference to established party figures than had earlier executives. To some extent, this reversed the earlier tendency toward technocratic and non-partisan government that de Gaulle had introduced. Despite some increased party influence, both conservatives and Socialists have been reluctant to give the impression that they would permit a return to the bad old days of cabinet formation and policymaking through endless negotiations among party notables. The key powers of cabinet- and policy-making are guarded jealously by the executive. The executive remains free from dependency upon the parties to govern France.

Party stagnation or vitality?

The rebuilding of the party system during the 1960s and 1970s made the parties the centre of public attention. Increased internal discipline, strengthened organization, and new vitality made the French parties a sharp contrast with the declining parties of other Western democracies in the 1970s.

Now, as these parties have matured, have they lost the vitality that they had earlier? The answer is not yet clear. Certainly, the Communist Party is in the midst of a crisis that may well determine its ability to survive as anything more than a small, unimportant party on the fringes of French politics. The electoral strength of other parties has deteriorated, notably that of the Gaullists. Heightened factionalism has weakened both the Socialists and the Giscardians.

There are other signs suggesting continued strength. All parties continue to exercise firm discipline and central control. There is no indication of a breakdown in voting cohesion in the National Assembly; local party units remain obedient to central directions on policy and strategy. Party membership claims remain high for most parties. While doubts about the accuracy of these claims are probably well founded, the Socialists and Gaullists remain able to muster very large numbers of activists for electoral work and for periodic rallies. These same two parties have extensive party structures throughout the country with large, permanent staffs at both the national and local levels. Election postmortems often include complaints about organizational weakness, but the principal French parties are better off than their counterparts in many parts of Europe.

It is at the level of public commitment that concern about the vitality of the French parties is the greatest. There are indications that the voters' willingness to identify with specific political parties or even with broad political families has decreased from the comparatively high levels of the 1970s. In addition, there is growing evidence of voter volatility. Part of this is seen in the success of the National Front in breaking into the party system in a way that new parties elsewhere have been unable to do. Further evidence is found in the rather dramatic swings between Right and Left during the 1980s (see Figure 5.2).

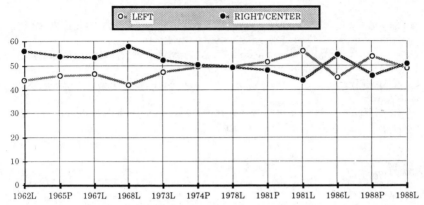

Figure 5.2: Voter Volatility, 1962-1988
Note: Results are for first ballot of legislative elections (L) and second ballot of presidential elections (P). (The 1969 presidential election is omitted since there was no left-wing candidate on the second round.)

Thus, the Right's share of the vote shifted rapidly from 43.1 per cent in the 1981 legislative election to 54.7 per cent of the vote in 1986 to 46 per cent of the second ballot in the presidential elections in 1988 and then to 51 per cent of the first ballot in the legislative elections a few weeks later. Such sharp shifts in voter support in a short period of time suggest instability in voter alignment and in the party system.

It is still too early to determine the long-term meaning of voter volatility and lower levels of party identification. It is clear that the party system of the 1970s is in flux and these shifts have produced citizen uncertainty. It is too early to tell if the party changes will result in an entirely new set of relationships such as a new centrism might bring, or whether they will simply involve the maintenance of the characteristics of the party system of the 1970s with a new hegemonic party on the Right to replace the Gaullist hegemony of the past.

Notes

1. Frank L. Wilson, *French Political Parties Under the Fifth Republic* (New York: Praeger, 1982).
2. Frank L. Wilson, 'Continuity and Change in the French Party System in the 1980s' in Steven B. Wolinetz (ed.), *Parties and Party Change in the 1980s* (London: Routledge and Kegan Paul, 1988).
3. Jean Charlot, *Le Phénomène gaulliste* (Paris: Fayard, 1970).
4. Jean Baudoin, '"Gaullisme" et "chiraquisme": Refléxions autour d'un adultère', *Pouvoirs*, no. 28 (1984).

5. William R. Schonfeld, 'La Stabilité des dirigeants des partis politiques: le personnel des directions nationales du Parti socialiste et du mouvement gaulliste', *Revue Française de Science Politique*, 30 (June 1980).
6. Ibid.
7. Colette Ysmal, 'Un Colosse aux pieds d'argile: le RPR', *Les Temps Modernes*, 41 (April 1985).
8. Kay Lawson, 'The Impact of Party Reform on Party Systems: The Case of the RPR in France', *Comparative Politics*, 13 (July 1981).
9. Stanley Hoffmann, 'French Politics: June-November 1979', *The Tocqueville Review*, 2 (Winter 1980).
10. Jacques Julliard, 'CFDT: Le salaire de l'angélisme', *Le Nouvel Observateur*, May 11, 1984.
11. René Rémond, 'La Droite d'aujourd'hui ressemble-t-elle à l'idée que s'en fait la gauche?' *Projet*, no. 175 (May 1983).

6. Politics at the margins: The French Communist Party and the National Front*

Martin A. Schain

Introduction

The most important changes in the French party system since the late 1970s have resulted from the emergence of the National Front (FN) on the Right and the decline of the Communist Party (PCF) on the Left. This chapter will focus on the impact of each of these changes on the party system and on the agenda of political issues in France.

We speak of the 'emergence' of the National Front in terms of the party system. The National Front has been a political actor since it was first organized in 1972, but it is only in the 1980s that the party has been what Sartori calls a 'relevant' actor, one that has influenced the organization and behaviour of other actors in the party system.

A party qualifies for relevance whenever its existence or appearance, affects the tactics of party competition and particularly when it alters the direction of the competition — by determining a switch from centripetal to centrifugal either leftward, rightward, or in both directions — of the governing oriented parties.[1]

If we follow Sartori, the National Front has become relevant because of the emergence of its power of intimidation (or 'blackmail potential'), as well as its possible 'coalition potential'. In these same terms, the French Communist Party has become increasingly irrelevant. Thirty years into the Fifth Republic, the PCF has crossed a major threshold. It has virtually lost its blackmail potential, and its coalition potential is minimal, at least for the moment.

Sartori's concepts help us to define and identify the relationship between individual political parties and the party system. However, relevance and irrelevance are processes as well as positions. The process through which both parties have moved, between marginality and

*My thanks to Georges Lavau for his incisive comments on the first version of this chapter.

relevance, has had impact on the political system, quite apart from the position of each party at the end. The process of decline of the PCF, and the process of emergence of the FN, has shaped and constrained the opportunities of other political parties. The way that the PCF has declined has created structural and policy opportunities, while the way that the FN has emerged has restricted others for other party organizations.

Of course, there are important differences between the PCF of thirty years ago and the FN in 1988. Although its organization had declined during the Cold War, the PCF in 1958 was the best (by some lights the only) organized party in France. Its 3.9 million votes (19 per cent of the vote) gave it hegemonic dominance on the Left. Moreover, the anti-regime orientation of the party (the PCF was not alone here thirty years ago), as well as its ideological distance from other parties, helped to create strong centrifugal tendencies within the party system.

The FN cannot claim the organizational strength of the 1958 PCF, and even with 4.4 million votes 14.4 per cent of the vote) in the 1988 presidential elections, it is not electorally dominant within the French Right. Nevertheless, the FN, like the PCF before it, has become increasingly dominant in terms of setting the political agenda for the French Right, and, to some extent, for the party system. Although the National Front is by no means anti-regime, and therefore does not pose centrifugal problems for the party system, it has defined and extended ideological distance further to the Right.

In this chapter we will first analyse the declining relevance of the Communist Party, and the growing relevance of the National Front, for the political system. We will then discuss the importance of the dynamics of this shift for the party system and for the future of politics in France. For our analysis, we will focus on three levels of the party system: electoral politics and competition, organizational strength and the changing political agenda.

The electoral key

The key to relevance in a democracy is the ability of a political party to attract an electoral following. Without significant electoral support, no party can achieve 'blackmail potential', nor can it qualify for 'coalition potential'. In a larger sense, electoral mobilization is the necessary, if not sufficient, key for understanding the ability of a party to affect the tactics and direction of party competition.

The decline of the PCF

The decline of the electoral following of the PCF has been closely monitored for some time.[2] After recovering from the setback of the 1958 legislative election, the PCF attracted a steady 20-22 per cent of the vote in all of the subsequent national elections during the Fifth Republic, until 1981. Then, in the presidential elections of April 1981, Georges Marchais lost 25 per cent of the 'normal' Communist vote (with 15.3 per cent of the vote), and in the legislative elections in June, the party was only able to regain a small piece of what Marchais had lost (0.8 per cent to be exact), confirming the 25 per cent drop. During the years of Socialist government, from 1981 to 1986, the Communist vote was reduced by another 40 per cent (to 9.7 per cent). The shakiness of this remaining vote was revealed by the elections of 1988. The national attractiveness of the PCF was brought into question in the presidential election, when the party's candidate won a mere 6.8 per cent of the vote. However, the locally attractive mayors were largely responsible for almost doubling that score in the legislative elections a month later. Thus, from 1978 to 1988, the PCF vote declined by well over half, from 5.9 million to 2.8 million votes. By 1988, the party no longer had a 'normal' vote, and no longer seemed capable of stabilizing its electoral following.

Indeed, the structure of the lost votes seemed to leave little hope for eventual party recovery. The signs were clear that the party was suffering important electoral losses among the same sectors of the electorate that had formed its historical core vote. The depth of working-class support for the party had always been exaggerated; there is no evidence, for example, that the PCF was ever the party of the majority of the working class (defined as blue-collar workers). Nevertheless, during the Fifth Republic, about a third of the working class normally voted Communist, which gave the PCF a percentage of the working-class vote that was higher than for any other party. This working-class support dropped off sharply in the presidential and legislative elections of 1981, again in the legislative elections of 1986 (to 20–24 per cent — the surveys varied considerably), and more in the elections of 1988 (to about 15–17 per cent).[3]

The loss of the historic core vote is confirmed by the declining ability of the PCF to attract younger voters. 'Normally', 25 per cent or more of voters under the age of 24 voted Communist during the Fifth Republic. The PCF losses in 1981 were reflected in a decline of the youth vote to 18 per cent, but this was still above the national vote. By 1986, this proportion had been reduced to 6 per cent, far below the PCF mean vote for the country.[4] With 5-10 per cent of the youth vote in 1988 (far less than the National Front), the party managed to minimize its relative losses among the youngest voters, but suffered more significant losses among those between the ages of 25 and 50. Clearly, the growing inability of the party to renew its support among the youngest voters in the 1980s is now beginning to feed into the middle-age cohorts. Only among the older *fidèles* does support for the PCF remain above the mean for the country. Thus, the party can no longer count on surviving with its core working-class support, which has been slowly diminishing; nor can it count on the youth vote — another traditional reservoir of support — in order to build its future.[5]

However, perhaps the most important sign of loss has been the electoral decline of the traditional 'bastions' (defined here as the twenty-three large towns that were governed by the PCF between 1947 and 1983) which have been important for symbolic as well as practical reasons since the earliest years of the party's history. The very name 'bastions' conjures up an image of geographic zones of electoral and political strength in which the influence of the PCF is dominant, and in which levels of support for PCF candidates in local elections have exceeded 70 per cent of the vote until recently.[6] Historically, when the party has suffered electoral setbacks nationally, it has been able to maintain its core of representation in these zones of strength. This is no longer the case, in spite of the 'resurgence' in the legislative elections of 1988.

Since 1973, the party has been generally losing electoral support in these areas.[7] Until 1981, these losses were masked largely by gains in other areas where the party was helped by its alliance with the Socialists, and the national level of support remained more or less constant. The problem in the 'bastions' became more evident in 1981, when PCF candidates lost 25 per cent of their vote nationally, but 31 per cent of their electoral support in these zones of strength (compared with 1978). The losses in the 'bastions' were not as severe in 1986 as they were in the rest of the country, but in these towns where they had been dominant since the Second World War, they were supported by only 28 per cent of the electorate. In the presidential election in 1988, mean support in these towns fell to less than 20 per cent, with losses in every town.[8]

Nevertheless, some limits in the electoral decline were indicated by the legislative elections of 1988. A modest increase of electoral strength for the PCF was due largely to increased support in its bastions, where relatively modest electoral increases (over 1986) resulted in significant increases in the number of its deputies. For example, in the Seine-St. Denis department, the PCF share of votes rose from 19 per cent in 1986 to 27 per cent in (the first round in) 1988. However, because of the re-establishment of the single-member districts, the party doubled its number of deputies from three to six. The trade-off appears to be that the party has become increasingly dependent on the popularity of its mayors in order to maintain its areas of strength. Ten of the twelve new Communist deputies, and half of the twenty-four victorious candidates elected in 1988, were mayors, compared with five of the thirty-two incumbents. The resurgence of strength — centred in a handful of bastions — seemed to be due less to the last-gasp effectiveness of the PCF organization than to the attractiveness of its local elected officials.[9] In 1988, there were only four departments where the PCF could still attract its 'normal' 20 per cent of the vote.

The electoral emergence of the National Front

At the same time the Communist Party was suffering electoral collapse, the National Front was emerging as a serious challenge to the established parties of the Right. In none of the elections prior to 1983 did the National Front attract more than 1 per cent of the national vote, and in 1981, Jean-Marie Le Pen was unable to find the necessary 500 'sponsors' for his presidential candidacy. Although, prior to 1981, the FN was unable to mobilize a significant portion of the electorate, the themes and issues that it developed were generally the same as those used after 1981.

By 1983 the ability of the National Front to mobilize and electoral following had improved. Le Pen ran for the city council in the twentieth *arrondissement* of Paris, and gained 11.5 per cent of the vote on the first ballot (compared with 2 per cent by the FN list in 1977). Under the circumstances, this electoral loss was widely perceived as a political victory.

The most portentous electoral contest for the National Front in 1983 occurred in Dreux, where the Socialist mayor, Françoise Gaspard, had been particularly outspoken on behalf of the rights of immigrants. The Left won in March by eight votes in a campaign dominated by anti-immigrant themes fuelled by an alliance between the RPR/UDF opposition and the National Front.[10] Voting irregularities, however, forced a 'third round' in September, which in many ways proved to be a watershed for the acceptance of the National Front, since by then the local election in Dreux had become a test for the national parties.

Under pressure from the national parties, the opposition list refused to cede places this time to the National Front. Nevertheless, the FN list received almost 17 per cent of the vote in the first round of the election, and, as a result, four candidates from the National Front were integrated into the United Opposition list that was victorious in the second round. In return for their collaboration in this significant victory, three of the four National Front candidates were named assistant mayors.

In the June 1984 elections for the European Parliament, the National Front list headed by Le Pen attracted almost 10 per cent of the vote. Five months after the elections, sympathizers had increased from 18 to 26 per cent (31 per cent of those who responded), with 46 per cent of the RPR, 37 per cent of the UDF, 12 per cent of the Socialist and 17 per cent of the Communist identifiers finding sympathy for Le Pen and his ideas.[11]

In 1985, some of the more broad-based support for the National Front began to diminish, and there were signs that the party might suffer a sharp reverse in the legislative elections in March 1986. Le Pen was more broadly perceived as extremist, and less widely accepted 'as part of the opposition in the same way as the leaders of the RPR and the UDF'. Support among those who identified with RPR and UDF for a coalition agreement with the National Front was less than half what it had been in

May 1984. One result of the electoral success, and the political attention that came along with it, was that fewer voters found it possible to remain indifferent to Le Pen and the National Front.[12]

Thus the question for the 1986 election was whether the established parties of the Right would succeed in winning back those voters who had moved to the National Front in 1983–5. The results indicated that the Right was only partially successful. Although about 640,000 of the 1984 FN voters (29 per cent) did in fact return to the established parties of the Right, there was a smaller, but substantial, movement of RPR/UDF voters in the opposite direction (about 434,000 voters), particularly among those most concerned with the problems of immigration and law and order. In addition, the National Front attracted significant number of voters from other parties, including over 200,000 votes from the Left (mostly from the PS).[13] With almost 10 per cent of the vote (and more votes than the PCF in metropolitan France), the National Front was confirmed once again as a substantial political force. The net effect was a solidification of the vote for the National Front nationally, a sharp increase in some areas, and a general validation of the political space within which the party was able to attract support.[14]

The results of the first round of the 1988 presidential elections confirmed an apparent stability of the National Front electorate at the national level. Ninety per cent of the FN voters of 1986 remained loyal to the party candidate, Jean-Marie Le Pen, a proportion that was not matched by any other party. This time the shift from the RPR/UDF was far more substantial than it had been in 1986. About 1.7 million voters of the Right moved from RPR/UDF (15 per cent), which, combined with smaller shifts from the Left (once again, mostly from the PS) and others from smaller parties and new voters, gave Le Pen 4.4 million votes (14.4 per cent), 63 per cent more than the FN had attracted in 1986.[15]

However, in the same way that the local focus of the legislative elections indicated the limits of the decline of the PCF, it also indicated the limits of the electoral attractiveness of the National Front. FN candidates attracted marginally fewer votes (about 1 per cent fewer) in 1988, than had the departmental lists in 1986. The changed electoral system, however, gave a distinct advantage to candidates with strong local roots. In the nine constituencies where the candidates of the National Front 'represented' the parties of the Right in the second round, they should have won in six — if the vote for the Left remained the same, and if all voters who voted for other parties of the Right transferred their votes. However, as a result of a stronger mobilization by the Left of voters who had abstained in the first round, as well as the defection of about 2 per cent of the voters of the Right, only one of the National Front candidates was victorious (Yann Piat, who has now been expelled from the party).

During the last five years, the FN vote has changed in important ways. Sociologically, the 1988 electorate was considerably more *populaire* than that of 1984, with FN attracting almost 20 per cent of the working-class vote in the legislative elections (a higher percentage than in the presidential elections), compared with 10 per cent four years earlier. It was also younger, with 15 per cent of its voters between 18 and 24, compared with 11 per cent in 1984. On the other hand, the partisan self-identification of the FN electorate was further to the Right, compared with voters who supported the two more established parties of the Right. As the self-identified partisanship became more solidified, the sociological make-up of the National Front electorate became increasingly differentiated from that of the traditional Right.[16]

In terms of issue orientations, the commitments of FN voters also became more solidified, and, in significant ways, more differentiated from other parties of the Right. More than voters for any other party, voters were motivated to cast their ballots for FN in 1984 because of the issues of immigration and law and order. This was decidedly more so in 1986 (see Table 6.1), and probably more so in 1988.[17] It was this issue priority that has most clearly and consistently differentiated the FN electorate from the electorates of all parties in every election since 1984.

Table 6.1: The motivations of voters in 1984 and 1986

Percentage voters who voted for	law & order		immigrants		unemployment		the economy		social inequality	
	1984	1986	1984	1986	1984	1986	1984	1986	1984	1986
PCF	9	13	2	7	37	59	14	14	33	30
PS	8	10	3	8	27	40	11	10	24	25
RPR/UDF	17	31	3	16	20	50	11	17	7	8
FN	30	50	26	60	17	35	6	7	10	10
Totals	15	24	6	17	24	46	10	13	16	7

Note: Since several responses were possible, the total across may be more than 100 per cent.
Source: Exit Poll, SOFRES/TFI, 17 June 1984, *Le Nouvel Observateur*, 22 June 1984; and SOFRES, *L'Etat de l'opinion, Clés pour 1987* (Paris: Seuil, 1987), p. 111.

Structure

The process of decline of the PCF and emergence of the FN has had a structural as well as an electoral dimension. In terms of structure, these parties are quite different political actors than they were a decade ago.

1. The PCF: the decline of structure

For the PCF, there has been a complex interaction between the way that electoral decline has taken place and the structure of the party as a political actor. The decline of the working-class vote in support of the PCF has had structural as well as sociological significance. It appears to mark the end of what Robert Lane referred to as 'the breaking effect'.[18] The more concentrated a group (in this case, working-class) is in one area, the more likely its members are to vote, and to vote disproportionately, in the same way. Thus, the vote for the PCF has been most reliable historically in areas of high working-class concentration and/or in areas where the PCF vote has been strongest.[19]

In the 1970s there was evidence that the breaking effect was declining, and that there was diminishing relationship between working-class concentration and the vote for the PCF.[20] By the 1980s, the transfer of the working-class vote to other parties indicates that the Communists are no longer capable of benefiting from working-class concentration.

The effects of the decline in the working-class vote have been most profound in the bastions, which no longer provide an electoral refuge in troubled times. Just a few years ago François Platone and Jean Ranger could write with some confidence of 'a simple rule':

The PC is able to resist [electoral decline] in proportion to its hold on the local political system. When it is electorally well rooted, and above all, when this influence is translated into votes, it can limit electoral losses, and sometimes overcome the crisis ... [21]

This was relatively true through 1981, but was no longer true by 1986. PCF losses in 1986 were greater (compared with their electoral support in 1981) in departments where their electoral support was greatest. While this pattern may have been related to the change in the election law, Platone concluded what is becoming increasingly evident:

The capacity for *encadrement* of the Communist Party is insufficient to reconquer the positions lost in all of the bastions, and the longevity and the initial level of its implantation no longer constitutes in itself a measure of the fidelity of the electorate, above all when the electoral influence is not nurtured by institutional positions — elected office-holders and town governments. We can see here a phenomenon of disaggregation of networks of influence which, on the basis of electoral predominance, make of the PCF the quasi-natural spokesman of social and geographic sectors, carriers of a veritable political sub-culture, in which the communist vote was experienced as a habit ... [22]

Although the results of the 1988 legislative elections highlight the importance of individual Communist mayors, if we consider the gap between the electoral success of the twelve mayors and the poor showing of the PCF presidential candidate in the same constituencies, they do not bring into question the declining viability of local party structures.

Platone raises an important structural issue which has affected the political relevance of the PCF, the ability of the party to survive through *encadrement*. The organizational capacity of the PCF has depended upon its ability to recruit members and on its ability to support its organization with the political and economic resources of a network of local and national office-holders. Party membership reached its peak immediately after the Second World War, and then dropped precipitously (more than 60 per cent) during the height of the Cold War in the 1950s. Membership began to rise again in the 1960s, as the party began to build its strength on a *union de la gauche* position, and then dropped sharply once again after 1978. From 1978 to 1984, membership strength is estimated to have dropped from a high of 520,000 to 380,000.[23] Thus, during the post-war period, there were two important cycles of membership rise and decline, and there is every indication that the present decline is not yet at an end.

However, these two cycles have been quite different in terms of their structural implications. During the post-war period of growth, concentrations of party membership expanded beyond the Paris region, the eastern area of the Mediterranean coast, the Rhône valley and the Nord-Pas-de-Calais. The Cold War contraction left most of these concentrations intact but reduced in levels. The most significant membership losses were outside of the PCF areas of strength.

Although membership increased by 60 per cent during the second cycle, between 1962 and 1978, its distribution was concentrated in smaller areas within the post-war areas of strength. No new important concentrations were established, and the concentrations in the Paris region and the Rhône valley (mostly in the Lyon region) were reduced, according to Philippe Buton.[24]

With slightly higher membership levels in the downturn of the 1980s than in the 1950s (about 380,000 members by 1984), the PCF was unable to stem accelerating massive electoral flight, even in areas where it was organizationally strong. By comparison, although the PCF lost 1.5 million votes in 1958, it maintained its strength in roughly those areas where it was organizationally strong. Part of the problem of the process of decline is clearly what happened during the process of organizational and electoral expansion. Until 1981, the party was losing votes where its implantation was strongest and was gaining votes where its implantation was weak. It was unable to translate organizational expansion into electoral success. Much of its electoral gain can be understood as a result of *union de la gauche* co-operation, rather than the *encadrement* capability of its organization.[25] What is striking about the 1980s, then, is that, in contrast to the 1950s, PCF organization has been surprisingly ineffectual. In the earlier period, electoral expansion (1956) was not entirely dependent on organizational resources, but electoral survival can be explained by organizational implantation. This no longer seems to be the case.

2. FN: the emergence of structure

The initial successes of the National Front were achieved with little organizational support, but this is no longer the case. In a relatively short period of time, the FN has been able to use its growing electoral following to generate a skeletal grassroots organization. The party now claims 60,000 members, to which must be added ten members of the European Assembly, 137 regional councillors, and a network of parallel organizations.[26] After June 1984, the National Front demonstrated a capacity to expand beyond its more traditional front organizations, by creating the association, *Entreprise moderne et libertés,* whose 800 or so members include small businessmen, doctors and lawyers.[27] One sure sign that the organizational expansion of the National Front has had some impact was the priority given by the RPR and the UDF to limit and/or forbid collaboration prior to the 1986 election, and to intensify pressure on militants who may have been thinking of defecting.[28]

Perhaps the most important indication of the expansion of the National Front has been its ability to present large numbers of candidates in 1985, 1986 and 1988. In the cantonal elections of March 1982, the National Front had difficulty finding sixty-five candidates to run in its name. Three years later, 500 candidates ran for the National Front, and in 1986 the lists of the National Front carried over 2,000 names. The FN had no difficulty finding 540 candidates in short order after the dissolution of the National Assembly in 1988. The heads of the departmental lists in 1986 reflected the distance the party had travelled in just a few years. From a party of agitators, it had become coalition of *notables* of the old traditional Right, and Right and extreme Right organizations. Indeed, the party clearly made a strategic choice after 1984 to maximize not only its electoral appeal, but its ability to engage in coalition bargaining.[29]

In the process of expansion, the National Front appears to have attracted a relatively loyal following, who are party and issue voters rather than loyal followers of a single man. In the cantonal elections in 1985, the National Front voters were more likely than the voters of any other party to have voted 'to support the political family to which they feel close', rather than for the personality of a particular candidate.[30] In the presidential elections of 1988, they can be clearly distinguished from other voters of the Right by their commitment to 'ideas' as a motivation for voting for their candidate, rather than 'personality'.[31]

From election to election increasing proportions of them are willing to make a commitment for the next election. In 1984, only 34 per cent of those who voted for the FN identified with the party as such; two years later identification had increased to 57 per cent.[32] This commitment was more or less confirmed by growing voter loyalty. In June 1984, only 45 per cent of those who claimed to have voted for the National Front that month thought that they would vote for the party in the next legislative elections. The exit polls in March 1986 indicated that 67 per cent of the 1984 National Front voters remained loyal in 1986.[33] In 1988, the FN maintained the loyalty of 90 per cent of the its 1986 voters in the presidential elections, a percentage far higher than that of any other party, and 81 per cent in the legislative elections, a percentage about equal to those of other parties.[34]

Thus, in contrast to the PCF, the electoral support for the National Front appears to have a stable core that has not diminished. The second round of the legislative elections certainly probed the weaknesses of the FN local organizations, but the real test will come in the communal elections of March 1989.

Interaction with the party system

What does this electoral and structural change mean, and what will this mean, in terms of the larger party system? On one hand, changes within the system itself have had an important impact on the fortunes of both the PCF and the FN. On the other hand, the changes in these two actors have also changed the more general patterns of interaction within the party system.

1. Systemic Influence on the PCF and FN

Perhaps the most important systemic change that has influenced the changes in the PCF and FN has been the pattern of steadily waning voter confidence in political parties in the 1980s.[35] One aspect of this decline in confidence has been the low integration of supporters into political parties which has, in turn, varied considerably from party to party. Sixty-six per cent of supporters of the PS regarded themselves as 'very close' to the party in 1984, compared with 41 per cent of the supporters of the PCF. Among the established parties of the Right, however, percentages of supporters feeling 'very close' were far lower — 15 per cent for the RPR and only 7 per cent for the UDF. The least integrated voters in all parties have been most electorally volatile. The National Front has drawn its growing electorate, and the PCF has sustained its most severe losses (including losses to the FN), from this group.[36]

A second aspect of this decline of confidence has been the diminishing ability of parties to constrain the left–right dimension of French politics. Voter identification as left or right has remained surprisingly stable during the past twenty years, but a growing proportion of French voters refuse such self-identification.[37] Among voters who identify with a political party, left-right constraints seem to be relatively strong, but among the growing number of voters who do not have strong party identifications, a majority refuse to place themselves on the left–right dimension (see Table 6.2.). On the other hand, as Jean Ranger points out, there does not appear to be any strong tendency for voters to position themselves in the Centre; indeed, positioning on the Centre has diminished during the past twenty years.[38]

Table 6.2. Party identification and Left–Right positioning (per cent)

Party ID:	Left	Cent/ left	Centre	Cent/Rt	Right	NR	
			Left-Right Positioning				
PCF	59	30	6	—	—	5	100 %
PS/MRG	20	51	21	2	—	6	100
UDF	—	1	32	50	9	8	100
RPR	—	2	16	57	18	7	100
FN/CNI	1	5	15	17	54	7	100
No ID	3	8	25	7	3	54	100

Source: 'L'Election Presidentielle de 1988: données de base', *Les Cahiers du CEVIPOF*, no. 1 (Paris: CEVIPOF/FNSP, 1987), p. 24, BVA/OIP, October 1987.

Party constraint, however, varies considerably, and the differences among parties are important. The weakening PCF organization seems to maintain a softened hold on the 'left' pole of French politics — more than a third of its identifiers see themselves 'centre-left' or 'centre', and thus should give pause to a party that is struggling to maintain its identity by emphasizing the hard left alternatives. It is not surprising that 65 per cent of voters who claim to have voted for the PCF in 1986, expressed sympathy for the *rénovateurs* led by Pierre Juquin.[39] The ascendant FN has established a hold on the 'right' pole. Half to two-thirds of its identifiers position themselves as 'right', which gives FN a strong claim on the definition of what is 'right' in French politics in the 1980s.[40] However, the non-identifiers remain a large pool of voters, neither committed to parties nor to the existing definition of Left and Right.

2. PCF and FN Influence on the Party System: Structure

The processes of decline of the PCF and the rise of the FN have also affected the larger party system in several important ways. Perhaps the most important impact has been on the organizational capability of all existing parties. The declining PCF organization has not been replaced, and it is now reasonably clear that this has affected both the ability of the Left to mobilize voters in the poorest areas, and to maintain this potential electorate for the Left (see below). In addition, the functions performed by these PCF structures at the local level — the 'tribune function', the integration of immigrant populations into working-class institutions and ideological and electoral mobilization — have generally not been taken over by other parties.

We are witnessing a complex process of deconstruction of a local hegemonic system, in the course of which the disappearance of a formerly dominant party generates a diffuse modification of political behaviour, the effects of which are felt beyond its own electorate: a fall in electoral participation, the abolition of prohibitions against support for the extreme Right and a tendency to blur the symbolic left-right division, competition for the exercise of the tribune function, until now carried out by the Communist Party.[41]

The system appears to be losing the special role that has long been played by the PCF, especially at the local level.

The network of party structures has also been challenged by the rise of the National Front. For some time before the 1983 take-off, the party had both supporters and sympathizers among the militants and some leaders of the RPR and the more loosely organized UDF. The party also had some militants in small secondary groups, among a wider fellow-travelling audience. Aside from those militants directly associated with the party, probably the largest reservoir of militant strength has been the National Centre of Independents and Peasants (CNIP), which has sometimes run National Front candidates under its label and has served as a party of transition for many ex-militants of the other party of the extreme Right, the New Forces Party (PFN), particularly after 1981.[42]

The process of militant transfer became more visible after the local elections of 1983, with direct transfers of some of the most activist militants.[43] The electoral rise of the National Front has provoked a complex reorganization within the established parties of the Right. Although the National Front has brought some new militants (and candidates) into the party system, much of its organizational expansion can be attributed to defections from the RPR and the UDF.

Finally, the structure of the party system has been altered by the substitution of the FN for the PCF as a symbolic point of reference for the division between left and right, a substitution that has weakened the Left electorally, but weakened the Right ideologically, and in the end, probably electorally as well. The PS has not been able to mobilize for itself all of the votes lost by the PCF in the 1980s, and the result has been a loss for the Left. In the department of St. Denis, for example, the towns where the gap between the Left vote of 1978 and 1986 is the greatest, are the same towns where the FN made its largest electoral gains in 1986. In many of these same areas, voters have also moved towards abstention. In general, the shift within the Left has not been simple, and has produced a crisis of representation for a significant number of voters.[44]

On the other hand, as Duhamel and Jaffré point out, the decline of the PCF means that the Right can no longer effectively run against fear of the Communists, and can no longer attempt to identify the PS and its leaders with the PCF. In the absence of anti-communist glue, the parties of the Right, organizationally and electorally, must find some other source of cohesion.[45] The much heralded 'opening' to the centre of 1988, as limited as it was, could not have taken place without the decline of the PCF.

The debates within the RPR/UDF, and between their central organizations and local organizations around the local elections in Dreux in 1983 and Grasse in 1987, as well as the debate about the proper position to take with regard to the National Front that raged in May–June 1987, are comparable to the long debate about alliances and coalitions with the PCF that dominated the Left until the 1980s. If the Left was both challenged and divided about the PCF, the Right has been tempted, challenged and divided by the FN.

During the debate in 1987, Jean Lecanuet (who has supported coalitions with the National Front) and Claude Malhuret (who has opposed such coalitions) agreed on one thing: that the role of the National Front in the French party system 'resembles a mirror image of [the role] of the Communist Party for the Left. For twenty years, the PC prevented the Socialists from attaining power by frightening centrist electors'. For Lecanuet, the error would be not to recognize the success of the Mitterrand strategy, and accept the support of the National Front. 'We call it national discipline', he argued.[46] For Malhuret, such an alliance would drive the centrist electors to the Left.

If the relationship between the PS and the PCF is to be used as a model, it is clear that the Union de la Gauche worked to the benefit of the PS, particularly in electoral terms. In the process, however, the policy positions of the PS shifted sharply to the Left in the 1970s. If Lecanuet is correct (and his position is close to that of Chirac and especially Pasqua), then the policy positions of the National Front on immigration would be co-opted by the mainstream parties of the Right.

3. The ideological shift and the political agenda

Along with the structural shift within the political system, the decline of the PCF and the rise of the FN has also brought an ideological shift in the political system and a change in the political agenda. Cayrol and Perrineau have argued convincingly that in 1988 there has been both a *recentrage des projets* of the established political parties, with little dividing them except for some details, and a general agreement among the electorate on the key values of the post-war settlement of capitalism and the welfare state.[47] This recentrage is predicated largely on the abandonment of rupture by the Socialists, but more broadly on the quite reasonable assumption that the PCF is no longer capable of exerting pressure on the PS for a Left alternative. The argument also notes the abandonment by the RPR/UDF of the more radical neo-liberal alternatives that were posed and promoted during the last legislature from 1986 to 1988.

However, what is missing from this analysis (and similar ones that have appeared during the past few years), is an incorporation of the impact of the rise of the National Front on the political agenda, as well as a consideration of the issue of immigration. Most French voters do not give priority to the immigration issue, but a growing percentage from all political parties do, and these are the most likely to vote for the National Front (see Table 6.1.).

Moreover, parties are generally most responsible for setting the political agenda, and there is some evidence that the FN has been a pole of attraction for the policy commitments of militants of the RPR. The attraction of the programme of the National Front for many militants of the Right is indicated by a survey of delegates at the RPR national congress in 1984. The survey found that the delegates (from local sections) perceived themselves to be considerably to the right of the party as a whole, and were much further to the right than the delegates at the RPR congress in 1978. The youngest and the most recently recruited militants were those who perceived themselves furthest to the right.[48]

Thus, patterns of commitments within the party system in France have shifted in important ways. Even as the decline of a Left alternative has moved political values towards greater consensus, the commitments of party militants of the Centre-Right have moved to the right as defined by the National Front. This complex change appears to be directly related to the decline of the legitimacy and attraction of the PCF and the rise in the legitimacy and attraction of the FN.

Conclusion

For Sartori, party relevance is directly linked to the tactics and the direction of the pattern of party competition. In these terms, the National Front has become increasingly relevant with each succeeding election, and the Communist Party has become increasing irrelevant. The emergence of the FN can be seen not only in the election results, but also in the party's ability to attract an increasingly loyal electoral following, at least at the national level, and in its organizational capacity. The parallel decline of the PCF is evident not only in its falling electoral support, but also in the structure of its falling support, and its contracting organizational capacity.

In each case, the process of becoming relevant and irrelevant has been affected by larger trends within the party system, and has, in turn, had an impact on the dynamics of the party system. One major impact has been a change in the focus and direction of party competition. Thirty years ago the focus of French politics was the PCF. For all major French political parties, the PCF was a reference point for the right–left division. Since 1978, however, the process of electoral and organizational decline has meant that the PCF is less relevant in defining this division. Its rapid electoral ascendancy, on the other hand, has given the National Front a role in the party system formerly occupied by the PCF. The positioning of parties (and candidates) in relation to the National Front, and the attitudes and policies it has come to represent, has created a new (and different) definition of the left–right division. In this sense, the 'margins' of the far Left and the far Right, far from being marginal, have been at the very centre of determining the direction of the party system.

In terms of orientations towards the regime, the French party system can no longer be characterized as centrifugal, since no party supports an anti-regime position. However, in terms of actual governing, the emergence of the FN can be seen as the emergence of an important centrifugal force that pulls policy-making to the right. Jérôme Jaffré has characterized the 1986 FN electorate as a *force de refus,* opposed to the more consensus-orientated policy positions of the established Right and established Left.[49] It is possible, of course, that agreement among the established parties will exclude the alternatives of the National Front. However, it seems more likely that, because of the new systemic relevance of the National Front, it will continue to exercise a centrifugal influence within the French party system.

Notes

1. Giovanni Sartori, *Parties and Party Systems: A Framework for Analysis* (New York: Cambridge University Press, 1976), p. 123.
2. Three articles have probably best summarized the evolution of the PCF: Jean Ranger, 'Le Déclin du PCF,' *Revue Française de Science Politique*, Vol. 36, no. 1 (February 1986); François Platone and Jean Ranger, 'L'Echec électoral du parti communiste', in Alain Lancelot, *1981: Les Elections de l'alternance* (Paris: Presses de la FNSP, 1986); and François Platone, 'Parti Communiste: sombre dimanche, triste époque', in Elisabeth Dupoirier and Gérard Grunberg, *Mars 1986: la drôle de défaite de la gauche* (Paris: PUF, 1986).
3. Jérôme Jaffré, 'La Défaite de la gauche et les progrès du parti socialiste', *Pouvoirs*, no. 38 (1986), p. 152. Jaffré's figures for 1986 are somewhat lower than those of other surveys. His survey results give the PCF 15 per cent of the working-class vote, compared with 20–24 per cent in other surveys. See the dossier by Frédéric Bon, Eric Dupin, Gérard Grunberg and Béatrice Roy, in *Libération*, 18 March 1986, as well as Nonna Mayer, 'Pas de chrysanthèmes pour les variables sociologiques', in Dupoirier and Grunberg, *Mars 1986: la drôle de défaite de la gauche.* The 1988 results are from a CNRS-BVA survey directed by Gérard Grunberg, Pierre Giacometti, Florence Haegel and Béatrice Roy, 'Trois candidats, trois droites, trois électorats', published in *Le Monde*, 27 April 1988, p. 12; from a CSA survey, reported by Eric Dupin in *Libération*, 27 April 1988, p. 12, and from SOFRES, *Les Elections du printemps 1988* (Paris: SOFRES, 1988).
4. Platone, 'Parti Communiste: sombre dimanche, triste époque', p. 205.
5. For background on the youth vote, see ibid., pp. 205–6. The 1988 figures on the youth vote are taken from the CSA survey published in *Libération*, 27 April 1988, p. 12, and SOFRES, *Les élections du printemps 1988.*
6. I have written about this in greater detail in Martin A. Schain, *French Communism and Local Power* (London: Frances Pinter, 1985), pp. 46–50.

7. Ibid., p. 48. This trend was first reported in the PCF's own analysis of the 1973 elections. See *Bulletin de l'élu communiste*, no. 45–46 (1973), pp. 2–3.

8. More generally, beyond the 'bastions' themselves, the PCF has consistently lost more votes since 1967 in the Paris region than in the remainder of the country. See François Platone, 'Parti Communiste: sombre dimanche, triste époque', p, 196. For a more detailed analysis of the PCF losses in 1981, see Schain, French Communism. The 'bastions' cited here are the twenty-three cities with over 30,000 population that were governed by Communist mayors from 1947 to 1983.

9. See Pascal Perrineau and Colette Ysmal, 'La logique notabiliaire', *Le Figaro*, 8 June 1988.

10. See Françoise Gaspard and Claude Servan-Schreiber, *La Fin des immigrés* (Paris: Editions du Seuil, 1984).

11. See the SOFRES survey for the International League Against Racism and Antisemitism (LICRA), in November 1984, 'L'Electorat de Jean-Marie Le Pen', p. 2.

12. See SOFRES, *Opinion Publique 1985* (Paris: Gallimard, 1985), p. 183, and *Le Monde*, 7 March 1986.

13. These figures were recalculated from tables presented by Elisabeth Dupoirier in 'Chassés-croisés électoraux', in Dupoirier and Grunberg, *Mars 1986: la drôle de défaite*, pp. 172–3, 184–5.

14. See Jérôme Jaffré, 'La relève protestataire', in Dupoirier and Grunberg, *Mars 1986: la drôle de défaite*, and Nonna Mayer, 'De Passy à Barbés: deux visages du vote Le Pen à Paris', *Revue Française de Science Politique*, vol. 37, no. 6 (December 1987).

15. The vote transfers were calculated from tables in *Libération*, 27 April 1988, p. 12, and the results are reported in *Le Monde*, 26 April 1988.

16. Jérôme Jaffré, 'La relève protestataire' p. 227; Grunberg *et al.*, 'Trois candidats', p. 12; and SOFRES, *Les élections du printemps 1988*, pp. 12 and 39. Among voters who stayed loyal to the FN in 1986, over 70 per cent (!) classified themselves as 'extreme right', compared with 24 per cent of those who stayed loyal to the RPR/UDF. See Dupoirier, 'Chassés-croisés électoraux', p. 184.

17. In 1988, the question deals simply with the importance of the problem of immigration. Nevertheless, 74 per cent of the FN voters indicated this as an important problem (up from 60 per cent in 1986), compared with 43 per cent for RPR voters and 28 per cent of UDF voters. See Grunberg *et al.*, 'Trois candidats'.

18. Robert Lane, *Political Life* (New York: The Free Press, 1958), pp. 261–4.

19. See Philippe Ariès, 'La fidélité de la clientèle communiste', *XXème Siècle*, July 1984; 'La Culture des camarades', *Autrement*, March 1986; and Michel Verret, 'Mémoire ouvrière, mémoire communiste', *Revue Française de Science Politique*, vol. 34, no. 3 (June 1984).

20. See Schain, *French Communism*, pp. 46–7.

21. Platone and Ranger, 'L'Echec électoral du parti communiste'. p. 122.

22. Platone, 'Parti communiste: sombre dimanche, triste époque', p. 202.

23. These figures are derived from Philippe Buton, 'Les effectifs du Parti communiste français (1920–1984)', *Communisme*, no. 7, 1985, p. 8.

24. Buton, 'Les effectifs," p. 21.

25. See François Platone, 'Les adhérents de l'apogée: la composition du PCF en 1979', *Communisme*, no. 7, 1985, pp. 36-8. I have examined the expansion of electoral support for the PCF during the 1970s in *French Communism*, Ch. 2.

26. See Nonna Mayer, 'L'Usure de l'effet Le Pen?' *French Politics and Society* (April 1988), p. 17.
27. *Le Monde*, 3 August 1985.
28. Colette Ysmal, 'Le RPR et l'UDF face au Front National: concurrence et connivences', *Revue Politique et Parlementaire*, no. 913 (November–December 1984), pp. 15–16.
29. See Pascal Perrineau, 'Quel avenir pour le Front National?" *Intervention*, no. 15, January–March, 1986, pp. 40–1, and *Le Monde*, 22 October 1985.
30. Pascal Perrineau, 'Le Front National: un électorat autoritaire', *Revue Politique et Parlementaire*, no. 918 (July–August 1985), p. 30.
31. See table in *Le Monde*, 27 April 1988, p. 12.
32. See Jaffré, 'La relève protestataire', p. 226.
33. See *Libération*, 18 March 1988, p. 19. For the results of 1984 and 1985, see Perrineau, 'Le Front National', p. 30 and 'Quel avenir', p. 40.
34. SOFRES, *Les élections du printemps 1988*, pp. 6 and 36.
35. See SOFRES, *L'Etat de l'opinion: clés pour 1987* (Paris: Seuil, 1987), pp. 162–3.
36. SOFRES, *Opinion publique 1985*, pp. 216–27. See also Martin A. Schain, 'Immigration and Changes in the French Party System', *European Journal of Political Research* (1989).
37. The percentage of respondents who refuse to identify themselves on a left–right scale varies enormously with the question asked and the way it is asked. See 'La dimension gauche-droite', *L'Election présidentielle de 1988*, Cahiers du CEVIPOF, no. 1 (Paris: CEVIPOF, 1987), p. 23; and Roland Cayrol and Pascal Perrineau, 'La défaite du politique', in *Le Guide du pouvoir* (Paris: Ed. Jean-Francois Doumic, 1988), p. 45.
38. *L'Election présidentielle de 1988*, p. 22.
39. SOFRES survey reported in *Le Monde*, 10 July 1986.
40. The higher percentage comes from the BVA exit poll in April 1988. See Grunberg *et al.*, 'Trois Candidats', p. 12. A similar percentage is reported by Jaffré in 'La relève protestataire', p. 227.
41. Henri Rey and Jacques Roy, 'Quelques réflexions sur l'évolution électorale d'un département de la banlieue parisienne: la Seine-St. Denis', *Hérodote*, no. 43 (1986), p. 38.
42. Edwy Plenel and Alain Rollat, *L'Effet le Pen* (Paris: Editions de la Découverte, 1984), pp. 63–7 and Chapters 5–7.
43. Ibid., p. 71. For an excellent analysis of the complex relations between the central organization and the local deputies and militants of the RPR, see William Schonfeld, *Ethnographie du PS et du RPR* (Paris: Economica, 1985), Chapter VI.
44. Rey and Roy, 'Quelques réflexions', p. 37; and Henri Rey, 'Les grands ensembles de banlieue', in *L'Election présidentielle de 1988*, pp. 67–70.
45. Olivier Duhamel and Jérôme Jaffré, *Le Nouveau Président* (Paris: Seuil, 1987), pp. 124–6.
46. *Le Monde*, 15 May 1987.
47. Cayrol and Perrineau, 'La défaite du politique', pp. 10–16 and 44–51.
48. My thanks to Georges Lavau for pointing out these findings to me. See *Enquête auprès des délégués aux assises nationales du RPR* (Grenoble: Institut d'Etudes Politiques de Grenoble, 1986), pp. 138–51.
49. Jaffré, 'La relève protestataire', p. 226.

7. Interest groups and politics in the Fifth Republic*

Yves Mény

The aversion of French political culture to interest groups, their organization, and their activities, is a long-established and well-known phenomenon. The Fifth Republic therefore has but perpetuated a Jacobin tradition of rejection that neither the experience of war nor the convulsions of the Fourth Republic could shake. Quite the contrary: the Vichy regime's corporatist values, the spectacle of parliamentary lobbying, and the agitation of the Poujadiste movement could only reinforce General de Gaulle's determination to create a 'state which is one'. One might nevertheless have thought some flexibility possible, in the name of the times, drawing inspiration for example from foreign constitutions, especially those adopted since the Second World War. After all, the critic of the party system did allow 'parties and political groups' — neglected by previous regimes — to be written into the Constitution, as in West Germany or Italy.

Yet the Constitution of the Fifth Republic made no gestures in this direction. Not only was it out of the question to imitate the radicalism of the American Constitution's First Amendment ('Congress shall make no law ... abridging ... the right of the people peaceably to assemble'), but the Constitution makes no mention of the freedom of association, as do the German Basic Law ('All Germans have the right to gather peacefully and without arms, without prior declaration or authorization necessary') and the Italian Constitution ('Citizens have the right to associate freely, without authorization, for purposes not prohibited by criminal law'). The only constitutional reference to groups is very indirect and mentions only trade unions: the Preamble of the 1946 Constitution guaranteed people the right to join them to defend their interests. In fact, the freedom of association recognized by the Law of 1901 would only truly be given constitutional status with the Constitutional Council's decision of 16 July 1971.[1]

*Translated by the editor.

The basic law's failure to recognize groups could be considered secondary were it not the expression of a more fundamental attitude of hostility toward groups' participation in politics. In August 1959, Michel Debré went on the warpath against 'feudal forces', and the Rueff–Armand Report published soon thereafter amounted to what is probably the most vigorous condemnation ever of corporatist groups in France. In 1960, de Gaulle refused to convoke a special session of Parliament requested by a majority of deputies, referring to the 'insistent initiatives' of a 'professional group' (the farmers' Fédération Nationale des Syndicats d'Exploitants' Agricoles (FNSEA]). He declared in a letter to the President of the National Assembly: 'I do not believe that a meeting of Parliament resulting from such 'encouragement', supported by such demonstrations as we have seen, could be considered in keeping with the character of our new institutions'.[2] And who could forget de Gaulle's famous epithet: 'The policies of France are not made on the floor of the stock exchange'.

One could cite many other examples throughout the Fifth Republic, to illustrate a conception of politics which rejects the group as a legitimate actor. As Georges Lavau wrote in 1957, 'The existence and the strategy of groups provoke a moralizing reaction. Above all, they are the source of scandals'.[3] This conception is significant, for it is not limited to the political class. It also permeates the culture of the administrative elites, who, as numerous studies[4] have shown, refer constantly and rhetorically to the notion of the general interest to justify the exclusion of interest groups. One could argue that the same excesses found in the group theory of a Truman or a Bentley, reducing politics to the actions of groups, exist in French legal conceptions, which tend to marginalize groups. Yet, practice appears to contradict this overall attitude of excommunicating, ostracizing groups from politics: illegitimate from the perspective of politics, groups appear 'inevitable' in the management of policies. It is as if political exclusion brought with it — indeed, necessitated — more intensive inclusion in the policy-making process.

Such ambivalence is clearly demonstrated by the Fifth Republic, which, far from challenging the traditional forms of relations between interest groups and the state, simply built on and reinforced firmly rooted habits. This pattern is not the only element of continuity, however: group–state relations continue to be characterized by a variety of configurations which make it difficult, indeed utopian, to seek to construct an overall explanatory and interpretive model.

In the debate between Frank L. Wilson and John T. S. Keeler on the pluralist or corporatist nature of group–state relations in France,[5] what is striking is less the radical divergence between their conclusions than the quality and the rigour of both of their arguments. In my view, what is in question is not the relevance of their analyses, but the effort — which Keeler denies — to draw conclusions about the predominance of the pluralist or the corporatist model from in-depth case studies. In truth,

Keeler's neo-corporatist model is quite far from that originally defined by Schmitter.[6] Adopting a less rigid definition than the founder of the neo-corporatist school, Keeler ends up proposing an analysis in dynamic terms, in which group–state relations are situated along a continuum extending from pure pluralism to complete corporatism. Depending on the political system and especially within the context of public policies specific to each system, variations can thus be discovered and used as indications of the more or less pluralist or corporatist nature of the sector under consideration. While sharing Keeler's prudent and empirical approach, one can only wonder what validity remains in using the neo-corporatist concept, which had a substantially different definition at the outset.

French groups on the continuum

If we adopt Keeler's proposal to place interest group–state relations along a pluralist–corporatist continuum, we can observe in effect wide variations depending on both the policy sectors and the time periods considered.

The pluralist model

The first model, one of nearly ideal pluralism, draws on the thousands of tiny groups created officially each year and whose goals and activities have little consequence for the state. The state's role is minimal, limited to defining a simple and easy-to-use legal framework, the Law of 1901, which grants a convenient and flexible legal status in exchange for a simple statement deposited at the Prefecture and subsequently published in the *Journal Officiel*. Under this law, tens of thousands of groups have been created, some with few members, others (such as trade unions or political parties) constituting authentic mass organizations. Whenever citizens wish to create any kind of group — social club or alumni association, but also a union to defend their interests (against a private or a public organization) — the 1901 Law provides a handy format for their initiatives.

In such a pluralist situation, groups are usually weak, small, and generally have little — or no — role to play in public policy-making. And government officials refrain from intervening in their affairs at any level (national or local), because they do not feel challenged by them.

The dependency model

This situation of distance and ideal pluralism is often limited and precarious, because it presupposes both the state's disinterest and sufficient group autonomy. However, both conditions are hardly tenable. In a system with an interventionist tradition like that of France, there can really be no collective action which leaves the state indifferent, especially if it seems to reflect a social movement or appears capable of impinging in any way on politics or policies. As for interest groups, they are often too weak to be completely insulated or independent from the state. Their feeble capacity to broaden their membership base, the inadequacy of their direct resources (and the difficulty they have in raising them) lead them directly to the public authorities, whether national or local, administrative or political.

This relative dependence on the administration appears whenever a group is not oriented exclusively toward activities of a private nature (like a chess club, for example). Once a group enters into relations with the authorities, it often finds itself in the ambiguous position of being simultaneously protester and supplicant. Without enough members and dues, it must solicit aid from local government or the state, threatening to become a trouble-maker if not given satisfaction: examples range from neighbourhood groups to local defence associations set up to challenge a public works project.

On the other hand, public authorities may find advantage in subsidizing and helping organizations which can, at relatively little expense, complement or substitute for public action; for example, sports clubs, or charitable assistance for the elderly, the poor, or the handicapped. A quick look at the budget of the tiniest commune in France would reveal the existence of a lengthy list of associations benefiting from public subsidies — some large, some small — but which generally seek to guarantee that everyone gets something, even if only symbolically. It would take a more serious study to determine the threshold beyond which the pluralist model becomes substantially watered down, because the list of public aid recipients is heterogeneous: the pluralist model is not invalidated by wide distribution of such assistance, but its size and distribution contribute to altering the relations between groups and the state. In this area, the Fifth Republic has not made any perceptible innovations. There has been, especially at the local level, a substantial increase in the intervention of public authorities; this is explained more, however, by the greater demand from the groups than by offers from the authorities, which have only adapted former practices to the growing number of groups.

The interdependence model

In these first two models, the state intervenes little, or in any case not enough, to structure the groups and their action. If it goes further in pursuing control or organizing strategies, it becomes, to use Keeler's analogy, the architect who designs not only the relations that groups have with him, but who shapes even the existence, the functioning and the strategies of these groups. This particular type of relations is neither specifically French nor a creation of the Fifth Republic. Virtually all the countries of Western Europe since the 1960s have committed themselves to procedures of dialogue and consultation in order to fix economic development in as consensual a base as possible. But the efforts in France, particularly in connection with the economic planning process, were not born with the Fifth Republic; the Fourth Republic had already taken care to open a dialogue with the 'social partners', building on a consultative tradition whose roots go back (for the Right) to Vichy and (for the Left) to the National Economic Council, created in 1925 by the *Cartel des Gauches*.

Here too, the Fifth Republic only took over and extended the practice of institutionalizing groups, which at the end of the Fourth Republic was an often unrecognized phenomenon.[8] For example, Michel Debré de Gaulle's collaborator and Prime Minister between 1958 and 1962 — observed: 'One can no longer consider establishing a governmental system without providing a place for men whose past, profession, and selection make them natural interlocutors of the government'.[8] This institutionalization is simultaneously 'affirmative' and 'negative' in that it proceeds to recognize and approve of groups who draw advantage from this legitimization by the state, while at the same time it tends to marginalize those groups excluded from such a benefit. This unilateral assertion, this princely choice, is certainly supposed to be based on objective criteria such as 'representativeness', but quite a few other, foreign, elements intervene: historical circumstances (the earliest-created group seeks to transform its advantage into a vested right), the political dimension (the group's attitude toward the German occupiers, for example), or just the purely arbitrary decision of the government or the administration.

Once again, the practice of the Fifth Republic perpetuates that of its predecessor: rarely has a previously recognized and integrated group seen its status called into question, whatever regrets this may have caused. For example, no government has felt itself strong enough to challenge the labour unions' monopoly in presenting candidates in works council delegate elections. For the most part, the public authorities have continued the unrelenting creation of committees and commissions of all sorts.

The Fifth Republic has thus pursued and intensified a policy of consulting concerned groups about governmental measures. Generally, the state creates formal commissions or committees in which the interest-group representatives are sometimes appointed by the groups, sometimes chosen by the state itself. However, not all groups have access to these formal consultations. The discourse of the political and administrative

elites distinguishes the 'wheat' from the 'chaff', and the 'valid interlocutors' from the groups considered unrepresentative. For example, following the delegate elections, the administration may refuse to talk with some
minor groups, or it may confer additional legitimacy on others by giving
them official approval or by inviting them into official consultation
despite their weakness, thus helping to reinforce them later *vis-à-vis* their
competitors. In the 1970s, for example, the government set up an
approval procedure for environmental groups; only approved groups
were associated with certain decision-making or consultative processes.

If one had to define the Fifth Republic's originality, it would no doubt
be found in its fondness for 'valid interlocutors' and in the privileged
nature of relations fostered with certain groups. The 'special relations'
with the Farmers' Association (FNSEA) or the Young Farmers' Union
(CNJA), or the virtual merger of public and private in the management of
sectors such as the iron and steel industry, nuclear energy, or data
processing, originate probably in the contradiction between a 'heroic'
style of decision-making (creating 'national champions') and the con-
tingencies and constraints of policy implementation requiring collaboration with the concerned industrial groups and their mandated
representatives. Perhaps one should add that the growing osmosis among
political, administrative and private-sector elites has only favoured
strengthening the privileged links between those groups considered of
strategic importance and the decision-making apparatus of the state.

The corporatist model

The corporatist stage is reached when interest groups are represented as
such in the political institutions: democratic representation on a geographic basis yields to the representation of organized interests. Only
corporatist systems — such as the Vichy regime in France — have gone so
far as to eliminate democratic representation purely and simply. But
there is a permanent corporatist temptation in France, if only in minute
proportions: the creation of an economic council under the Fourth
Republic and its preservation under the Fifth in the form of an Economic
and Social Council, demonstrate both the appeal and the reservations that
such an assembly provokes. Certain of the Fifth Republic's innovations
have gone in this same direction: for example, the creation of Regional
Development Commissions (CODER) in 1964, which became the
Regional Economic and Social Committees in 1972, or the aborted effort
to create a mixed Senate in 1969.

None the less, detecting the corporatist trend does not lift its ambiguity,
for interest-group penetration into politics constitutes a legitimization-
marginalization. Groups are made official, but in order better to be under
state supervision. The political role granted them engenders more

frustration than satisfaction, for the political class has never fully accepted — that is the least one can say — the socio-professional groups. What a curious situation: an institutional sanctioning and a bestowed legitimacy have led to a condition of controlled existence. Despite numerous attempts, the structured representation of interests has never succeeded in displacing classical representative democracy.

An additional step in the policy of group integration is made when groups are vested with the prerogatives of public authorities. This state strategy illustrates clearly the dilemma of a government whose natural bent is to intervene everywhere, but which proves to be incapable of handling overall social demands and needs. This intermediate situation between the marketplace and the omnipotent state is not new either, since the decisive step in this direction was taken during and after the First World War.

The considerable expansion of this original form of managing public policies results less from the deliberate will of the authorities under the Fifth Republic than from the conjunction of several factors: the explosion of social demand (e.g., in social or cultural affairs), the expansion of the welfare state, the tendency in the Council of State to incorporate into public law private agencies responsible for a public service, etc. To a certain extent, these new or old institutions are practising a sort of mixed management or exercise a rule-making or control power delegated by the state. Such is the case of traditional organizations like the Order of Physicians or the Order of Lawyers, of closed and regulated professions like notaries or auction-masters. One also finds this public–private mix in the chambers of commerce, of agriculture, or of artisans, which are not only bodies for defending private interests, but also quasi-public organ- izations responsible for regulating their sector, carrying out public investment (e.g., in ports or airports), replacing the state in certain sectors (professional training), and even collecting mandatory para-fiscal taxes from the members. Finally, many professional organizations in less traditional sectors have also been given regulatory powers: for example, national federations of sports clubs, or various types of civic association.

If the public authorities have found undeniable advantage in this system, which frees the administration from the burden of managing some public policies while rationalizing relationships with its private partners, the groups concerned have readily accepted, indeed sought out, the protection and the blessing of the state. The groups thus vested acquired regulatory capacities (in the fullest sense of the term) whose extent and whose bestowal were inconceivable without the support of the public authorities, and benefited from resources (taxes or subsidies) allowing them not only to implement public policies, but also to perpetuate the group and its organizational monopoly.

In truth, the Fifth Republic has had an ambivalent attitude toward these organized groups: at times it has vilified the corporatist groups which hindered the modernization of the state or of the economy (e.g., the recurrent attacks against the corporatism of the professions or the trade unions), but it never led a head-on battle which would have allowed it to raze bastions and citadels. Not only has the Fifth Republic been unable to transform the closed professions (except for the solicitors) or modify the 'privileges' of the unions, but its leaders have often undertaken policies which contradict their rhetoric. Who would claim for example that the Civil Service has been 'decorporatized'? Who cannot see the increased corporatization of the farm sector? Some might answer these arguments asserting that 'the deregulation of the closed professional systems is an unchallengeable fact'.[9] But this deregulation is the result less of a policy deliberately decided and implemented by the state than of external pressures which make current means of regulation obsolete or counterproductive: the deregulation of commercial navigation, for example, is more the consequence of competition from flags of convenience than from the public authorities, and that of the air transport sector is due to American policies combined with technological advances. From this point of view, the opening of the Common Market in 1958, the economic crisis of the 1970s, or the prospect of the Single Market of 1993, have done more to modify the rules of the game than the government's policy, which has, moreover, not been consistent.

This situation points out the paradox of the so-called 'strong state' in France, particularly under the Fifth Republic. The 'heroic' style of decision-making, the preference for 'big' rather than 'small', and the bombastic discourse have all too often been confused with far more prosaic and modest realities: it is ironic to note that the 465 auction-masters managed to torpedo all reform efforts conceived by the Right or the Left, but were suddenly converted to change by the Single Market of 1993 and the prospect of a British invasion. And what of the venerable stockbrokers' federation, whose status was radically modified, without a stir and in a few weeks ... by the virtues of London's 'Big Bang'![10]

The neo-corporatist model

Can one discern in the development of group–state relations under the Fifth Republic an illustration of the emergence of neo-corporatism? Keeler seems to think so, emphasizing the changes that have taken place concerning both the groups and the state since the Fourth Republic:

> Throughout the Fourth Republic period, the corporatization process was limited by the nature of both the principal interest groups and the State. Compared to those of many other polities, the peak interest groups in most French sectors were relatively weak in terms of resources and capacity to mobilize and discipline their members (and thus facilitate intervention).[11]

Under the Fifth Republic, on the contrary, the corporatist process has been amplified, Keeler stresses, by three factors: the growth of state intervention, the transfer of power from Parliament to the executive and the bureaucracy, and governmental stability. Still, Keeler is the first to emphasize the originality of the French phenomenon. He suggests a corporatism with 'a distinctive French flavour' and notes an 'unbalanced corporatist structure' with considerable variations from one sector to another. In sum, Keeler admits that a Schmitter-style neo-corporatist model is inapplicable, and that, even in the specific sectors which come the closest, considerable adaptations and modifications must be introduced. On balance, Keeler's position is not far from that of Bruno Jobert and Pierre Muller, who prefer to suggest, under the label *corporatisme à la française*, sectoral corporatisms, in the absence of a verified neo-corporatist hypothesis.[12] In other words, the neo-corporatist model could apply to France only with such changes that it would no longer be neo-corporatism. In that case, the model would seem to have little use,[13] except that it has provoked in reaction a better explanation of sectoral corporatism in France.

No model will do

The range of relations between the state and interest groups is far from exhausted by the different hypotheses examined above, for the extensive integration of groups by the public authorities has not eliminated all the problems. In the first place, integration does not mean that groups are entirely dominated and controlled by the state. On the contrary, the government is often at the mercy of groups whose veto power is all the greater because they have penetrated the workings of the state and are indispensable to it. The state itself becomes dependent.

In the second place, as a result of the selection of favoured partners, of 'valid interlocutors', the groups which are considered too weak, too unrepresentative, or too critical of authority, are excluded or marginalized.[14] These groups have no option other than to become respectable on their own, or to use means which are generally disapproved of: physical violence, destroying property, kidnapping public officials, blocking the roads, etc. A detour into the streets is often effective and constitutes an excellent means of access to the ministerial private offices which, until then, might have ignored the groups concerned. The scenario has become classic: after proclaiming that it would never negotiate with the street mob and under threats, the government then opens discussions in order to scale down the conflict and give the demands a fair hearing, promising not to prosecute the perpetrators of destruction or vandalism — surely in order to avoid the famous spiral of protest and repression. The Fifth Republic has become accustomed to such violence, which has never seriously threatened its stability and which has incidentally been perfectly reconciled with voting for the party in power!

(Witness, for example, the contrast between voting patterns and actual behaviour of the farmers from 1958 to 1981)

In the third place, violence is not the exclusive property of marginal groups; it has also been used by those who are thoroughly integrated into the state apparatus. This strange situation — for example, farm leaders going from a road block to the Prime Minister's office — illustrates the difficulty that major organizations in France have in disciplining their troops and forswearing expedient methods, for fear of losing contact with their rank and file. The 'formidable potential for mobilizing against the state' that Suzanne Berger noted among the small merchants and artisans[15] is not specific to them, and no organization leader, even if he is fully integrated into a corporatist type of relationship, can afford to neglect this state of affairs. From this follows the mixture of follow-the-crowd attitude toward the rank-and-file when times are difficult, and aloofness, or even separation, when they return to their apathy.

In conclusion, I shall only try to pick up on the themes woven into this brief presentation: on the one hand, the diversity of situations and cases which make it utopian to seek a single explanatory model;[16] and on the other hand, a great ambivalence which underlines the complex nature of group–state relations in France. Jack Hayward has emphasized this aspect by demonstrating that there exist at least three types of relations:

First there are attempts to persuade, manipulate, cajole or coerce interest groups into conformity with official policy presented as the dictate of the general, national, or public interest. Secondly there are attempts by the interest groups to persuade, manipulate, cajole or coerce the official decision-makers into action or inaction in support of their interest, which may be presented as in conformity with the public interest 'as a whole.' Finally there are attempts to promote cooperation between the interest group spokesmen and the official policy-makers by coordinating or concerting their activities within a formal or informal consultative system so as to achieve a consensus which can be presented as in the public interest. Depending on where the emphasis is placed, the key concept of the 'public interest' assumes a different content and function.[17]

Finally, one observes a great continuity between the Fifth Republic and its predecessors as to the type and style of relations between state and interest groups. Without doubt, the extent of these relations has been modified, and some reorientations have taken place. But on the whole, the Fifth Republic is the product of its long history and cannot break with a culture and practice too well rooted to be swept away by the miracle of a man and a Constitution.

Notes

1. See Alec Stone's Chapter 3 on the Constitutional Council in this volume.

2. Quoted by Raymond Barrillon *et al.*, in *Dictionnaire de la Constitution* (Paris: Cujas, 1986), p. 447.

3. Georges Lavau, 'Political pressures by interest groups in France', in Henry W. Ehrmann (ed.), *Interest Groups on Four Continents* (Pittsburgh: University of Pittsburgh, 1958), p. 57.

4. See, for example, Ezra Suleiman, *Power, Politics and Bureaucracy in France: The Administrative Elite* (Princeton, NJ: Princeton University Press, 1974); Suleiman, *Elites in French Society* (Princeton, NJ: Princeton University Press, 1978); Pierre Birnbaum, *The Heights of Power* (Chicago: University of Chicago Press, 1983); Bertrand Badie and Pierre Birnbaum, *Sociology of the State* (Chicago: University of Chicago Press, 1983); Francis de Baecque and Jean-Louis Quermonne (eds), *Administration et politique sous la Cinquième République* (2nd ed, Paris: Presses de la Fondation Nationale des Sciences Politiques, 1982).

5. See Frank L. Wilson, 'French Interest Group Politics: Pluralist or Neo-corporatist?', *American Political Science Review*, vol. 77, no. 4 (December 1983), and John T. S. Keeler, 'Situating France on the Pluralism Corporatism continuum: A critique of and alternative to the Wilson perspective', *Comparative Politics*, vol. 17, no. 2 (January 1985).

6. Philippe C. Schmitter, 'Modes of Interest Intermediation and Models of Societal Change in Western Europe', *Comparative Political Studies*, vol. 3, no. 2 (April 1977).

7. See Lavau, p. 82.

8. Cited by Jack Hayward, *Private Interest and Public Policy: The experience of the French Economic and Social Council* (New York: Barnes and Noble, 1966), p. 20.

9. Denis Segrestin, *Le phénomène corporatiste* (Paris: Fayard, 1985), p. 77.

10. See Chapter 10 of this volume by Philip G. Cerny.

11. John T. S. Keeler, *The Politics of Neo-corporatism in France* (Oxford: Oxford University Press, 1987), pp. 6–7.

12. See Bruno Jobert and Pierre Muller, *L'Etat en action* (Paris: Presses Universitaires de France, 1987).

13. See Andrew Cox and Jack Hayward, 'The applicability of the corporatist model in Britain and France: the case of labor', *International Political Science Review*, vol. 4, no. 2 (1983).

14. See Yves Mèny, 'La légitimation des groupes par l'administration française', *Revue Française d'Administration Publique*, no. 39 (1986), pp. 483–95.

15. Suzanne Berger (ed.), *Organizing Interests in Western Europe* (Cambridge: Cambridge University Press, 1981), p. 87.

16. For a thorough and systematic analysis of interest groups in France, see Frank L. Wilson, *Interest Group Politics in France* (Cambridge: Cambridge University Press, 1987).

17. Hayward, *Private Interest*, pp. 1–2.

Part III: Economic Policy

8. Industrial policy and the state: from industry to entreprise*

Christian Stoffaës

Introduction: industry, power, and glory

An analysis of the relations between state and industry during the course of the Fifth Republic requires taking the measure of the collective French psychology inherited from history. During the seventeenth and eighteenth centuries, France was the dominant power in Europe in the economic, military, diplomatic and cultural fields. Thereafter, the 'Great Nation' had to give way to the pre-eminence of England during the Industrial Revolution of the steam machine and the weaving loom, and then to Germany and the United States during the steel and mechanical revolution.

This relative decline visible in all fields — demographic, military, geopolitical, economic wealth — was symbolized more than anything else by industrial backwardness. France tried to console herself with the illusions of a rustic equilibrium, a colonial Empire, cultural influence. After the victory of 1918, she attempted naïvely to take over German industrial·might, confiscating patents, moving out machines and whole factories, expropriating foreign-controlled mines, occupying the Ruhr — demonstrating the nature of her 'industrial complex'. Hitting bottom with the defeat of June 1940, France heard General de Gaulle's message from London on 18 June: 'Defeated today by mechanical force, we shall be victorious tomorrow by a superior mechanical force'.

Following the war, and even more with the arrival of the Fifth Republic, when decolonization put an end to the illusory ambitions that the former Great Nation still nourished and cleared the way for new national ambitions, it then appeared natural for industry, as well as economic prosperity, to become the symbol of national redemption. France would undergo what it is not excessive to call an 'industrial miracle', marked by strong growth of manufacturing output, rapid expansion of investment

* Translated by the Editor.

and industrial job creation, a powerful wave of corporate restructuring and concentration, and the reinsertion of French industry into international trade. The rhythm of this development contrasted with the relative pre-war stagnation, and allowed France at the end of the period to be nearly on a par with the more advanced industrialized nations, behind which she had initially been trailing.

Reconstruction: the post-war 'industrial miracle'

At the conclusion of the war, France was in fact lacking in most of the infrastructure and industries characteristic of a modern industrial nation. Thirty-five per cent of her population was still actively employed in agriculture. Reconstruction was, at least partially, simply construction.

Economic planning played a major role in the Reconstruction, giving priority to developing productive investment in basic sectors, and drawing on the analyses of the emerging National Accounts offices and on *concertation* : the Plan's commissions brought together the producer groups (employers, labour), the technical and financial administrations, and the directors of public companies. The diagnoses, the consensuses, and the recommendations worked out by the Plan provided a certain continuity in economic policy, despite the ministerial instability of the Fourth Republic. The Plan's principal means of action were the Marshall Plan funds, deposited in a Treasury account, which allowed, among other things, the purchase of capital goods on credit in the USA, and the public corporations resulting from the pre- and post-war nationalizations (SNCF, EDF, Charbonnages, etc.). The First Plan established six priority sectors: electricity, coal, iron and steel, cement, transportation, and farm machinery. The ECSC Treaty guaranteed the opening up of the European market for coal and steel. Important mergers decided or influenced by the state combined basic sector companies into large public or private groups, facilitating heavy investment.

From the perspective of industrial policy, the Fifth Republic can be divided into two fifteen-year periods.

The years of expansion: 1958–73

International opening

The international economic environment of the 1958–73 period was characterized by the high growth rate of the industrialized countries (4 to 5 per cent on average), achieved at first in stable conditions, with moderate inflation and a fixed exchange rate system under the aegis of the dollar. France benefited from this favourable economic environment;

she entered into a period of accelerated industrialization, with a higher growth rate than that of her industrialized partners. In 1957, the Treaty of Rome paved the way for the integration of the European market, giving new openings to French agriculture and industry, at the same time as it exposed them to the beneficial winds of competition.

The Fifth Republic put an end to the chronic cabinet instability of the Reconstruction years. The Gaullist administration undertook a stable and coherent economic policy led by the goal of industrialization, considered indispensable for improving French standards of living as well as France's international independence and influence. Decolonization freed France from a financial burden and an outdated ambition; energies could turn toward the future. The French economy became international: from 1958 to 1973, exports' share of GNP rose from less than 10 per cent to more than 20 per cent. Foreign trade moved beyond the French franc zone, whose share fell from 40 per cent to less than 10 per cent, while the Common Market countries' share increased to over 50 per cent.

Industrialization

With the solid base developed during Reconstruction, French industry was able to take full advantage of the growth possibilities opened up by the great period of world-wide expansion during the 1960s. Growth was very rapid and very regular, with practically no jolts: the growth rate almost never dipped below 5 per cent, was often around 7 per cent, and averaged nearly 6 per cent. Between 1958 and 1973, agricultural production increased by 70 per cent, industrial production by 120 per cent. Growth was founded on an extremely high rate of savings, around 25 per cent. Investment expanded by 150 per cent. Inflation was moderate in the beginning of the period, developed progressively, and then was brought under control by the 1963 stabilization plan, only to pick up again as of 1969.

Profound structural change accompanied the expansion. The importance of agriculture for the active population declined — the number of farmers fell from 6 million to 2 million in thirty years — despite increases in production due to rationalized land use (regrouped plots, early retirement incentives), increasing use of tractors and farm machines (facilitated by loans from the Crédit Agricole), use of modern techniques (fertilizers, insecticides, etc.), and the Common Agricultural Policy (which guaranteed high prices and markets). At the same time, industry and services gained in importance. The consumer durables sector was created, the capital goods sector expanded, while the relative share of consumer goods (e.g., textiles) and basic industries stagnated or declined.

Industrial productivity increased at the rate of 6.5 per cent a year from 1959 to 1963, compared to 4.5 per cent between 1948 and 1958. During the 1960s and until the early 1970s, the rate of investment reached nearly 30 per cent of GNP; the rate of investment in manufacturing was close to 20 per cent. Among the OECD countries, France became the leader in industrial growth, a little behind Japan, but clearly ahead of the other European countries and the USA.

The rate of growth during the period of expansion was in part a consequence of the features of the world environment, but it was also the result of deliberate economic policy choices made by government. From 1958 to 1969, world-wide growth was both strong and stable, within the framework of an organized international monetary system. The 1963–8 period was marked by a certain deceleration of growth, following the stabilization plan. Between 1969 and 1974, world growth remained strong, but became irregular and inflationary. In settling the labour conflicts and strikes of May 1968, the Grenelle accords granted high salary increases and fringe benefits, which were immediately translated into price rises, bringing on the devaluation of 1969 and a specifically French inflationary cycle, higher than that of other Western countries.

The liberation of the economy

Monetary and fiscal policy encouraged investment, real interest rates were low or negative, and loans were easy to obtain from the banking system or the many existing channels of preferential financing. Industrial *dirigisme* and the role of the Plan declined: price and investment controls were relaxed, as a consequence of the steep devaluation of 1958 and the Pinay–Rueff Plan. The management of the public sector gained greater manoeuvrability (a result of the Nora Report of 1969). The state's attention was drawn in particular towards the social needs raised by growth and by the transformation of economic structures. It thus sought to orientate financial resources towards agriculture (through subsidized loans from the Crédit Agricole), the investment needs of local authorities (through the Caisse des Dépôts et des Consignations, which manages the state savings banks and can thus mobilize a major share of private long-term savings), and housing (through loans from the Crédit Foncier and low-cost housing projects). It also increased considerably the investment and operating budgets of the welfare ministries (Education, Health). Infrastructural development projects were continued: roads and highways, ports and navigable waterways, industrial zones, urban infrastructures.

As concerns industry, the policy of creating investment incentives was mainly of a horizontal nature: favourable tax breaks, implementation of value added tax, or abundant bank financing. The state's selective intervention in industry focused on two types of action: major industrial and technological projects, and incentives for mergers in the major sectors. The former bear the indisputable stamp of de Gaulle's will to national independence; the latter reflect Georges Pompidou's concern for competitive growth.

National industrial independence

In the field of foreign investment, the state adopted a determined policy of discouragement, even opposition, to the introduction of multinationals in France. The 1950s and 1960s were in effect the years of the 'American Challenge': numerous large American firms came to Europe to buy out companies and set up their own commercial networks and factories. This movement had a determining influence on industrial restructuring in most of the European countries, especially Belgium, the United Kingdom, and West Germany. The French government, however, for reasons of national independence, declared its hostility to these takeovers; several 'affairs', such as Poclain–Tenneco and Bull–General Electric, made the headlines. While not always able to block such sales, the government created an unpleasant climate which often did turn American firms away from investing in France.

THE GRANDS PROJETS TECHNOLOGIQUES

The *grands projets* policy was linked either to national defence (nuclear weapons, aeronautics and space, electronics and computers, etc.) or to the secure supply of basic materials (e.g., petroleum, uranium, steel). It was based on a wide variety of means and actors in industrial policy, called the 'national champions'. These could be research laboratories or public agencies, like the Atomic Energy Commission (CEA), the National Centre for Space Studies (CNES), the National Centre for Scientific Research (CNRS), or the National Centre for Ocean Development (CNEXO). Or they could be public corporations, like the arsenals of the Ministerial Delegation for Armament, Nord Aviation or Sud Aviation, the Bureau for Petroleum Research, the Independent Petroleum Agency. Others were private or semi-public companies: Dassault in aeronautics; Thomson CSF and Matra in electronics and missiles; the International Data-Processing Company (CII) in computers; Usinor, Wendel, and Sidélor in steel, for example.

These agencies and companies, the secular arm of the *grands projets* policy, obtained significant financial aid from the state: support for research from the Ministry for Scientific Research or from the Ministry for Atomic and Space Affairs guaranteed procurement from the technical ministries (Defence, Post and Telecommunications, Transportation, Industry, Energy), subsidies for operations and investment from the

Budget Ministry, long-term, low-interest loans from the Treasury. And these *grands projets* could count on human resources as well: the technical teams set up by the state's corps of engineers, people found in both the technical administrations responsible for drawing up the plans and the laboratories and companies responsible for carrying out the programmes.

MAJOR INDUSTRIAL CONCENTRATIONS

Around 1965, industrial concentration became one of the main watch-words of industrial policy. From the late 1940s, French industry strongly expanded investment and production. From the end of the 1950s, it successfully faced the opening of the European market and competition with other industries in the Common Market, although many had feared French inability to meet the challenge. Beginning with the 1960s, improving French industry's competitiveness on international markets became a major objective. And among the different criteria of competi-tiveness, emphasis was especially laid on acquiring critical mass, the minimum turnover necessary to take advantage of economies of scale in production runs, research laboratories and commercial networks, and to be able to export, set up abroad, and gain multinational status.

The 1962 industrial census shows that, of 570,000 industrial firms, 65,000 — just over 10 per cent — had more than ten salaried employees. In 1966, no French company was among the top fifteen firms world-wide in steel, chemicals, pharmaceuticals, paper-making, agricultural products and foodstuffs, textiles, or electrical engineering. Clearly, France was far from her current position as the third or fourth industrial power in the world.

The end of the 1960s and the beginning of the 1970s witnessed significant concentration of French industry, particularly in two fields: basic industries and capital goods. On the other hand, consumer goods and food processing industries were to a certain extent left out of these mergers and are still today somewhat behind their foreign counterparts in this respect. It was during this period that French industrial 'major groups' came into existence: Saint Gobain-Pont à Mousson in building materials; Rhône-Poulenc in chemicals; Pechiney-Ugine-Kuhlmann in non-ferrous metals and chemicals; CGE-Alsthom, Thomson-Brandt in electrical engineering; Berliet-Saviem-Renault in vehicles; and Sacilor in steel.

The awareness of the need to regroup was quite widespread among most of the leaders of industry. In many cases, it was they, or their stockholders, or the investment banks (Paribas, Suez, Lazard, for exam-ple) who took the initiative in mergers. But the state was not just a passive observer in the associations that mark the period; it set up a series of incentives to encourage concentration. To begin with, overall credit policy favoured investment, especially in external growth. The Treasury at times was led to grant state loans or guarantees to facilitate certain mergers: examples are the Plan professionel in the steel industry in 1966 and the Peugeot–Citroën and Berliet-Saviem mergers of 1974. In addition, the government expanded financial aid for exports and encouraged industrial and commercial investments abroad with tax measures aimed particularly at large firms.

Most importantly, a certain number of tax measures gave advantages to companies which merged, and thus swept away the natural resistance to change. For example, a 1965 law created tax agreements which allowed firms to re-evaluate their assets to take inflation into account in the case of mergers; this measure allowed them to set aside greater amounts for depreciation and thus reduce corporate income tax. This was undoubtedly one of the main motivations for industrial concentration.

Elsewhere, the state led the way by undertaking mergers in the nationalized sector or in those sectors which depend heavily on industrial policy: examples are the creation of Elf-Aquitaine, in petroleum; EMC and CDF-Chimie in chemicals; and Aérospatiale in aeronautical construction. It was the government which imposed the mergers of steel firms in the Lorraine: the creation first of Wendel–Sidélor, then Sacilor; and it was the state which sped up the same process in the North around the Usinor concern.

From state financing to bank financing: credit as a 'public service'

The very rapid rate of growth of investment was accompanied by the expansion and profound transformation of means of finance. During the 1960s, the Treasury's role in financing investment declined, compared to its role during the Reconstruction period. The Bourse (stock exchange) witnessed a long period of stagnation. Penalized by the partitioning of the financial markets which favoured non-industrial sectors (agriculture, housing, public works, etc.), business kept up a steady rhythm of investment and expansion by bank borrowing, benefiting from both the lever effect and zero or even negative real interest rates. But bank financing would eventually create inflationary tendencies. The growth of corporate debt during the 1960s was not a purely French phenomenon: it was characteristic of all the industrial economies. French firms were less indebted than the Italian or Japanese, but much more so than the German, British or American.

The crisis years: 1974–88

The turning point of 1974

The year 1974 was marked by major political and economic changes. The election of Valéry Giscard d'Estaing as President signalled the shift of political power from the Gaullist party to a coalition dominated by the Centre-Right. At the same time, the consequences of the oil shock at the end of 1973 struck the French economy at the peak of a period of expansion. The world environment suddenly changed, producing a very strong rise in the price of raw materials, inflation, wide fluctuations of exchange rates, and a deep recession in 1974–5. The international economy would pick up again between 1976 and 1979, but at a growth rate barely half that of the pre-1973 period. Inflationary tensions reappeared and contributed strongly to a second oil shock in 1979, followed, like the first, by a period of deep recession, aggravated by the very restrictive monetary policies implemented in the major countries in order to combat inflation. The recovery was evident as of 1984, but continued to be unstable under the effect of interest rates which remained high, the financial suffocation of the overindebted countries, and the oil counter-shock.

The 'industrial crisis'

The break of 1974 was even more strongly felt in industry than in the economy in general; whereas industry had been, prior to 1974, the principal driving force of the French economy, creating jobs, investment, and earning capacity, it became a sector in difficulty subject to unstable markets, in which sharp depressions alternated with weak rallies. The growth rate of industrial production abandoned its annual growth curve of 6 per cent. Between 1974 and 1988, the average annual rate was only 1 per cent, with very marked fluctuations: +3.6 per cent in 1974, −5.9 per cent in 1975, +0.5 per cent in 1980, −2.8 per cent in 1981, −1 per cent in 1982, and +8 per cent from 1986 to 1988. Industry lost jobs, all together a million and a half between 1974 and 1988, or roughly 30 per cent of all salaried positions. Over fifteen years, therefore, industry regularly lost some 100,000 to 150,000 jobs annually.

The earning capacity of firms collapsed: business profit margins eroded. Industrial concerns' net savings went from an average level of 17 per cent in the early 1970s to 8 per cent in the 1980s. For the hardest hit firms and sectors, profit loss turned into operating deficits, often leading to bankruptcies. A new character appeared on the French economic and political scene: the 'lame duck'. The annual number of failures tripled, especially among the small and medium-sized firms, but affecting also some major groups which went under (e.g., Creusot-Loire in 1984 and Normed in 1986), or were saved only by being nationalized (e.g., Usinor and Sacilor in 1978, Pechiney-Ugine-Kuhlmann in 1982).

Reduced profitability and depressed markets provoked a sharp drop in investment: industrial investment fell by 15 per cent between 1974 and 1977, to reach the level of 1970. The slight rally of 1978–80 was followed by a new drop of 20 per cent between 1980 and 1984. In certain branches, production declined; steel and naval construction, for example, lost money practically every year and their manpower fell respectively from 160,000 to 70,000, and from 25,000 to 7,000. At the same time, employment in the textile/clothing industry fell from 800,000 to 350,000. The impact of the industrial crisis was focused on certain regions: the North (textiles and steel), Lorraine (steel), the Vosges (textiles), the Basse-Loire and along the Mediterranean coast (shipbuilding). The unemployment rate in these areas reached 20 per cent or more.

Despite the slowdown of growth, international trade continued to expand rapidly. Capital goods industries in particular turned increasingly towards exports and would conquer new markets in the OPEC countries and the Third World. At the same time, however, the domestic market increased imports of foreign products.

This maelstrom placed industry at the heart of national interests and made industrial policy a major issue of political debate, one of the principal points of cleavage between political and social forces. As a country of relatively recent industrialization, France had never really experienced an industrial crisis, like the United States, Britain or Germany. It is thus not surprising that waves of imports, deindustrialization, layoffs, industrial restructuring and conversion gave rise to more emotions and impassioned debates than elsewhere, all the more so because, in the Social-Colbertist tradition, recourse to state intervention has always seemed endowed with magical powers.

The economic policies adopted in France in reaction to this entirely new situation were marked by hesitation. At first, between 1974 and 1976, salaries were allowed to rise and a plan was drafted to revive investment and public spending in order to stimulate demand and combat rising unemployment. Some measures were adopted to help those seeking work (longer unemployment compensation), firms in difficulty (a top-level inter-ministerial committee for structural adjustment (CIASI), state loans, etc.), and to limit redundancies in the sectors in difficulty (these required prior administrative approval).

The recession and government's counter-cyclical policies led to increased budget and trade deficits. The Barre Plan of 1976, orientated towards financial rigour, aimed primarily at reducing the budget deficit, balancing external payments, maintaining the franc's value in the European monetary 'snake' (predecessor of the 1978 European Monetary System), slowing down wage increases, and improving business profit margins. At the same time, monetary policy was progressively tightened to increase long-term interest rates as an encouragement to savings, which fiscal incentives sought to orientate towards the stock market.

GISCARD–BARRE: INDUSTRIAL REDEPLOYMENT (1974–81)

The state's direct intervention in investment was motivated by the goal of industrial redeployment: adjusting France's productive capacity to the new international context. It would mean developing exports with the aid of 'industrial diplomacy' and export credits for major contracts, as well as arms sales to OPEC countries and the developing world. It would require a revision of assistance policies to firms in difficulty: for instance, taking control of and restructuring the steel industry, helping industrial development in designated conversion zones, deregulating industrial prices, strengthening competition, protecting the openness to imports. A policy to encourage innovation had to be defined: the National Agency for the Promotion of Innovation (ANVAR) and the Strategic Industries Development Committee (CODIS) were set up. Competition for major public procurement markets was opened up, and a certain distance was taken *vis-à-vis* the 'national champions' policy, allowing challengers to bid. Two major national investment programmes were initiated in the electronuclear and telecommunications sectors. These would henceforth play a driving role in developing productive investment, each representing investments on the order of 1 per cent of GNP. They would thus pick up the investment slack left by other national companies' declining investments (transportation, non-nuclear energy, public works, housing, etc.). As the policy of financial rigour and price deregulation was progressively gaining coherence, the state thus continued to play an important role in the modernization of the economy and the financing of productive investment.

THE CHALLENGE TO REDEPLOYMENT: INDUSTRIAL VOLUNTARISM (1981–3)

In 1981, with the change of political majority, economic policy was once again strongly modified. Austerity and redeployment had been sharply criticized by the Left and by the labour unions, for increasing unemployment and deindustrialization. In contrast, new policy would be based on stimulating growth and employment, restoring domestic demand, setting up *filières*, and voluntarist investment financed by the state budget and the nationalized banks. The state was to provide counter-cyclical stimulation, as long as the 'crisis' and the dictatorship of profit and the international market were stifling investment and modernization. But global economic circumstances from 1980 to 1983 were extremely unfavourable, due as much to the consequences of the second oil shock as to a new American monetary policy.

The nationalization programme of 1981–2 concerned five major conglomerates, two steel firms, two arms producers, three subsidiaries of multinationals, thirty-six commercial banks and two financial companies. Adding to the nationalizations of 1936 and 1946, the state would henceforth control virtually the entire sectors of energy, transportation and communication, basic and capital goods manufacturing industries, and banking. In manufacturing alone, a quarter of the industry, one-half of the major firms — everything considered 'strategic' — came under public control.

With very large budget increases for the Ministries of Industry and Research, and expansion of capital for the nationalized companies, the state acquired the means to stimulate investment and employment in voluntarist manner. Public aid to industry thus increased by 240 per cent between 1981 and 1985, up to 86 billion francs. Capital grants to nationalized firms reached 12 billion francs a year (59 billion between 1982 and 1986). The budget for research grew by 25 per cent annually between 1981 and 1984.

The policy to stimulate industrial investment had several facets. A growing number of plans by sector set production targets for the nationalized companies (steel, coal, electronics, etc.), in which the boundaries between them were significantly reshaped. Restructuring in the nationalized sector was carried out in steel, basic chemistry, electronics, data processing, telecommunications, among others. In addition, sectoral plans were devised for industries in difficulty in those sectors still predominantly private, such as machine-tools, clothing, shipbuilding and paper. Interest subsidies and selective credit orientation were also used.

Overall economic and social policy none the less contributed to reducing once again business profit margins, leading to a reduction of productive investment. Wage increases and the growing burden of social and tax charges, as well as the reduction of the working week, squeezed profits, which fell to their lowest level since 1945. At the same time, the strong rise in interest rates in 1981 increased financial charges considerably for the heavily indebted firms.

The voluntarist sectoral policies succeeded in rescuing 'lame ducks' and in curbing the decline of investment in the sectors in difficulty. However, because of the depressed markets of the moment, firms' financial deficits increased: debts of 95 billion francs accumulated between 1981 and 1985 in the nationalized manufacturing sector, focused essentially in steel, automobiles, and basic chemicals. Still, recapitalization allowed the necessary restructuring in the basic industries, around Pechiney-Ugine-Kuhlmann or Usinor-Sacilor, for example. In the high-technology industries, the results were varied: some firms used public funding to increase investments in technology, while the restructuring around future 'national champions' was more criticized.

SOCIALIST RIGOUR (1983–6)

Introduced in an international environment marked by recession and disinflation, the policy of stimulation and *dirigisme* from 1981 to 1983 had to be modified because of the sharp increases in the budget and balance of payments deficits, which led to inflation and several devaluations. Beginning in mid-1983, a policy of rigour was implemented, based on stabilizing public spending and the budget deficit, increasing interest rates and maintaining the franc in the European Monetary System, the deindexing of wages, the progressive deregulation of industrial prices, the reduction of certain tax charges, and the beginning of deregulation in several state-controlled sectors, such as the financial markets or petroleum. The concept of 'modernization', coined by Prime Minister Laurent Fabius, helped to justify the redeployment of industrial structure. The objectives of the sectoral plans were either reduced or abandoned altogether; that led to radical changes and deep restructuring in the steel, coal and shipbuilding industries. The nationalized firms were granted greater strategic autonomy and were encouraged to restore profitability, even if that meant lowering investment and cutting jobs. Investments in the major electro-nuclear and telecommunications programmes were also cut, largely because the projects were nearly completed. These reversals were a major factor in the split between the Communists and the Socialist government in 1984.

In an international environment now characterized by disinflation and economic recovery, this policy of rigour brought firms back into equilibrium, while aggravating the difficulties in certain areas and sharply increasing unemployment. Industrial investment began to pick up as of mid-1985.

A LIBERAL INDUSTRIAL POLICY (1986–8)

Despite the change of parliamentary majority in March 1986, the policy of budgetary and financial rigour was continued and reinforced. The ideological terrain had been prepared by the revised economic policy undertaken by the Left: a rather broad consensus appeared in support of rigour and a deregulated economy.

The government provided a new framework for the economy with a series of free-market measures of broad scope: corporate tax reductions over two years of nearly 30 billion francs; virtually complete deregulation of prices, including services, and exchange rates; new rules on competition; reduced labour–market rigidities and the abolition of prior administrative approval for lay offs; the elimination of credit volume controls and an accelerated deregulation of the banking system; and deregulation in the fields of transportation, telecommunication, and energy, among others.

An unprecedented privatization programme was undertaken, aimed at sixty-five firms, banks and public concerns. The first privatizations — Saint-Gobain, Paribas, Compagnie Générale d'Electricité, and the Société Générale — brought 3 million new stockholders to the Bourse, in a context very favourable to new issues, at least until the abrupt crash of October 1987.

The budgetary rigour and the policy of disengaging the state produced a clear reduction of public aid to industry. The sectors in difficulty — such as steel, chemistry, the Renault carworks — had to accelerate their strategies of plant rationalization and manpower cutbacks; the most spectacular consequence was seen in shipbuilding, where Normed closed down three sites (La Seyne, La Ciotat, Dunkerque).

Business profitability confirmed and accelerated the recovery begun in 1985: by early 1987, firms' financial situation and profit margins were back to their best pre-1974 levels. Margins reached 30.7 per cent in 1986, after 28.9 per cent in 1985 and a low of 26.1 per cent in 1983. The profit-to-investment ratio rose spectacularly: 68.8 per cent in 1983, 79.5 per cent in 1985, and 83.2 per cent in 1986. The financial markets became active, as the Bourse rose by 60 per cent in 1986, tripling the number of shares traded.

Finally, investment confirmed its recovery, rising in the competitive sector by 5 per cent in 1986 and 1987, and by 13 per cent in 1988. Investment's dynamism was particularly evident among small firms, where it rose by 10 per cent a year, in the creation of new companies (270,000 in 1986, compared to 200,000 in 1983), in commerce and services (up 11 per cent in 1986 and some 7 per cent in 1987), and in the foreign investment of industrial firms (an average 50 billion francs between 1986 and 1988, compared to 25 billion in preceding years). And finally, economic growth was taking off: up 2 per cent in 1986 and 1987, and 3.5 per cent in 1988.

Industrial production, which had stagnated between 1980 and 1986, grew by 8 per cent in 1987–8. Large firms regained their margin of manoeuvre in self-financing, debt liquidation, bonds and share issues, manpower management, international alliances. In this manner, the major French companies were able to participate in the international redistribution of assets during the 1986–8 period, as CGE-Alcatel gained control of ITT, Bull took over Honeywell Information Systems, Thomson obtained RCA and Thorn-EMI, Air Liquide acquired Big-Three, Rhône-Poulenc got Union Carbide fertilizers, and so on.

The Fifth Republic and investment in competitiveness

Having examined the sequence of economic policies pursued since 1974, with their failures and successes, it is useful to re-examine their evolution in the context of the central problem which has emerged: the external constraint and competitiveness, modernization and its financing.

The external constraint: lost competitiveness

Since the mid-1970s, foreign trade has generally been in deficit. The French economy twice ran into external constraint when governments sought to stimulate growth in 1975–6 and in 1981–3, and after several devaluations caused by balance of payments deficits, was obliged to adopt austerity policies. On the contrary, one can consider that, prior to 1974, the French economy was competitive. Between 1963 and 1973, the French growth rate (5.8 per cent a year, on average) was higher than the average of other OECD countries: the European Community showed 4.6 per cent and the USA 4.1 per cent; only Japan fared better (9.7 per cent). The balance of payments and the trade balance were continually favourable, and there was full employment.

Between 1974 and 1979, the growth differential was sharply reduced, but remained positive (3.2 per cent average growth in France, 2.6 per cent in the USA, 3.7 per cent in Japan, 2.4 per cent for the other European Community nations, including West Germany's 1.3 per cent and the UK's 1 per cent). From 1980 to 1985, the differential became negative by about 1 per cent: France's average growth was 1.1 per cent, the USA's 2.3 per cent, Japan's 4.4 per cent, West Germany's 1.3 per cent and the UK's 1 per cent. In 1986 and 1987, French growth barely kept up with the European average (2 per cent) but France did less well than Italy or the UK (3 per cent).

This slowdown in growth was accompanied by a continued rise in unemployment, at a practically constant rate of 200,000 new job-seekers a year. The decline is visible in the trade balance deficit, which became structurally negative (minus $1.6 billion between 1970 and 1974; minus $11 billion between 1975 and 1979; and minus $26.6 billion over 1980 and 1985. By contrast, West Germany and Japan showed regular surpluses. The 'dark years', from the point of view of foreign trade, came immediately after the two oil shocks (1974, 1980) and the two attempted counter-cyclical recoveries (1976, 1982).

French industry's market shares declined in the international marketplace: 7.9 per cent of world industrial exports in 1980, 6.5 per cent in 1985, a loss of nearly one-fifth. Imports of manufactures gained at the same time on the French market: 27.5 per cent in 1980, 33 per cent in 1985, a gain of one-fifth. For example, in the automobile industry, between 1980 and 1985, the French share of the European market fell from 29.5 per cent to 22.1 per cent, and the share of foreign cars on the French market increased from 21 per cent to 36 per cent.

INADEQUATE INVESTMENT: A PROBLEM OF QUALITY, NOT QUANTITY

Insufficient competitiveness is connected to inadequate productive investment. It is because the French economy did not invest properly in response to the new conditions of the international environment that the problem of external constraint appeared. Beginning in 1974, productive investment in France witnessed a situation of global stagnation, marked by the succession of periods of decline (1974–6 and 1980–4) and periods of slowed recovery (1977–9 and 1985–7). But since France had been, until 1973, the country with the highest rate of investment (after Japan), this slowdown simply placed her thereafter in the average among her principal competitors. Investment's share of GDP declined by about one-fifth over a decade, as in Japan, whereas this share remained stable or even increased in other countries. In fact, the rate of productive investment, which was 14.5 per cent between 1970 and 1974, fell to 13.3 per cent between 1975 and 1979 and to 12.4 per cent over 1980–4. The rate in the USA rose from 10.4 per cent in 1970–4 to 11.7 per cent in 1980–4; Japan's fell from 18.9 per cent to 15.4 per cent, West Germany's from 12.9 per cent to 11.7 per cent, and the UK's rose from 9 per cent to 9.9 per cent.

Thus, the generally advanced hypothesis that France suffers from inadequate investment requires some restating. *The problem is not that France did not invest enough, but that she invested badly.* The inappropriateness of French productive capacity for the new international market context and modern technologies seems due more to the distribution of investment among sectors of activity — or the 'quality' of investment — than to a purely quantitative insufficiency. To simplify the analysis, the French economy may have overinvested in steelworks, nuclear generators, or petrochemicals, and not enough in electronic components, video-cassette recorders, machine-tools, household electronics, furniture, and so on.

Strengths and weaknesses of the French industrial structure in the late 1980s

The allocation of investment in the economy suggests inadequate international specialization of the French manufacturing industry to meet the requirements of the world environment: domestic and international demand, international competition, technological evolution, and so on.

The specialization of foreign trade highlights several strong areas which produce nearly constant surpluses. Weapons and high-technology industries and major engineering contractors linked with state purchases, for example, expanded their exports to OPEC and Third World markets, thanks in particular to support from the state. However, success in this area has been threatened by the slump in these markets since 1983, largely because of the Third World's excessive debt and the fall in oil prices. Other areas include luxury consumer goods, an old tradition; agriculture and the food processing industry, protected within the European Community by the Common Agricultural Policy; and the automobile industry, whose competitiveness however has seriously worsened since 1981.

On the other hand, the weak areas are quite pronounced, often rooted in history and tradition. These include industrial capital goods: machinery, industrial vehicles, office equipment, and so on, with a few exceptions like railway equipment or electric construction. Household goods and consumer electronics usually are in deficit, but have seen strong growth in recent years. In consumer goods industries, competitive positions have been declining as a result of competition from low-wage producers in South-East Asia or from more creative producers, like Italy.

It seems that the deficits, like the surpluses, are not big but are widely distributed. The French economy does not have any confirmed sectors of competitiveness — technology–market linkages enjoying a dominant competitive position on the world market — contrary to some other countries: examples are West Germany's mechanical or chemical industries, Japan's automobile and electronics industries, or the USA's high-technology industries.

On a more qualitative level, one can observe that the principal adjustment problems facing France's productive apparatus since 1974 result, in particular, from three factors. First, there was an excessive development during the 1960s of industries based on low-skilled labour, which suffered subsequently from competition with low-wage producers: the textile/clothing and leather/footwear industries, for example, had to cut employment by half, and many investments had to be written off. In the automobile industry, there was too much reliance on manpower with inadequate training and qualification.

Second, there is an insufficient web of high-performance, high-technology medium-sized firms, strongly orientated towards exports, like those found in West Germany or in Italy. And third, the French economy has suffered from overinvestment or delayed adjustment in certain sectors benefiting from protective measures, monopoly situations, or state financial aid, for example, steel, coal, naval construction, electro-nuclear energy, oil refining and automobiles.

THE 'TERTIARIZATION' OF INVESTMENT: FROM HEAVY INDUSTRY TO 'SOFT' INDUSTRY

The concept of immaterial investment encompasses all those expenses considered operating expenses in bookkeeping terms — i.e., not capitalizable as assets — but which contribute to the development of the firm's activity beyond the fiscal year, and thus take on the economic characteristic of an investment. Examples include research and development to perfect new products, marketing, advertising, the establishment of commercial networks, training of personnel, and computer software.

It is a recent concept, but one which has had extraordinary success in recent years. Why? After all, there is nothing new in the fact that what makes firms competitive are technologies and know-how, marketing and 'human resources', that is, the 'soft' before the 'hard'. In West Germany, in Japan, in the USA, enterprises have been stressing the tertiary side of manufacturing industry for a long time. In France, the concept of immaterial investment was probably necessary to exorcize the classic notion of investment, dating from Reconstruction and 'heavy industries', and which is no longer relevant, as we have seen with the failure of the recovery plans for steel, coal and shipbuilding, or as one can observe in the USSR and in Eastern Europe. Modern industry is no longer the factories with smoking chimneys and turning wheels portrayed in pre-war Soviet cinema.

The 'network-based corporation', based on quality products, on technological innovation, on a commercial image, and on human capital, has displaced the 'factory-based corporation' inherited from the nineteenth century. The organization of work, the quality of products and services, and the employees' commitment to the firm's goals, are all part of this notion, which is in fact difficult to isolate from the very substance of the firm and from the socio-cultural context of its national environment. Human resources, investment in intelligence, the tertiary side of industry: more and more frequently cited as sources of competitiveness, these concepts are close to that of immaterial investment.

AREAS OF FRENCH BACKWARDNESS: MARKETING, TRAINING,
INNOVATION, QUALITY

Marketing has traditionally been deficient in French firms, more concerned with producing that with selling. Although overall statistics are rare, one can observe that French concerns have fewer full-time marketing and technico-commercial services abroad than their major international competitors. Often cited weaknesses of French goods on foreign markets include failure to respect delivery dates, inadequate maintenance and repair service; these explain, for example, inadequate French competiveness in industrial capital goods. Advertising, only a part of commercial investment, accounted for 0.8 per cent of GDP in France in 1984, but 2.4 per cent in the USA, 1.3 per cent in the UK, and 1 per cent in Japan.

Manpower training varies according to activity sector and function. The technical quality of French *ingénieurs* is often excellent; the weaknesses appear more among the middle-level executives, technicians and supervisors, office-workers and workers. The famous 'management gap' cited twenty years ago as a weakness now appears to have been absorbed, thanks to the emergence of management schools and ongoing training.

On the other hand, despite the development of professional training, the level of training and the adaptation of qualification to needs are probably still behind, compared with West Germany, where apprenticeships and on-the-job training play a major role (twice as many apprentices as in France), or with Japan, where initial training is very extensive (90 per cent of salaried employees have at least a secondary school diploma).

In research and development, international statistics offer clear comparison: France is somewhat ahead among major industrialized countries in public spending on R&D (1.2 per cent of GDP). She is behind, however, in R&D spending by private firms (1.1 per cent of GDP, compared to 1.8-1.9 per cent in the USA, Japan and West Germany). The public share of national research is 60 per cent in France, but 50 per cent in the USA, 40 per cent in West Germany, 25 per cent in Japan.

Industrial research, moreover, is concentrated in a small number of firms belonging to the high-technology sectors tied to state procurement (aeronautics, arms, nuclear engineering, electronics, telecommunications, etc.). On the other hand, the traditional industries (mechanical, textile, consumer goods) and the small and medium-sized firms often seem to be a 'technological desert': it is estimated, for example, that in France 2,000 firms have access to technological innovation, compared to 10,000 in West Germany. Of course, investment in innovation, essential for competitiveness, cannot be measured by the level of research expenditure alone: patents, imported technologies, spending on market studies, design research, and creativity, are just as essential. Most of these indicators, too, however, show France clearly behind.

The crisis of 'capitalism without capital': the financial revolution

State financing and the large public sector contributed powerfully to the modernization of the French economy from the reconstruction at the end of the 1940s and into the 1950s. Bank financing provided the main external resources needed by business during the period of expansion during the 1960s and into the 1970s; negative real interest rates, inflation being higher in France than in other countries, encouraged firms to borrow. Inflation financing contributed to the creation of overcapacities in certain sectors of production; the slowdown in growth and the appearance of new international competitors in the 1970s highlighted the inadequately competitive nature of these sectors. Bank financing certainly engendered rather lax investment behaviour, favouring material investment, considered as assets on the balance sheet and thus providing 'guarantees' for banks, rather than immaterial investment, which would have required equity financing and venture capital.

The sometimes artificial and hasty manner in which industrial concentrations were carried out worked against the small and medium-sized
firms, allowing, for example, the large groups to keep within their control
activities which would have been more efficiently managed by autonomous structures. The large groups and the 'national champions' thus
hampered at times the high-performance medium-sized firms. They
were also penalized by the quantitative techniques of state-imposed credit
control, which encouraged banks to give preference to their bigger
customers, but did not favour selective approaches in the choice of
investments. Yet it is precisely among the small and medium-sized firms
that the competitiveness of French industry is most lacking.

Finally, the implementation of state-financed investment, far from
extricating the economy and businesses from the vicious circle, served to
delay considerably the adjustment process and the reduction of uncom-
petitive overcapacities in most of those areas subject to sectoral plans:
steel, shipbuilding, coal, electricity generation, Renault, and so on.

Thus, modernization of the French economy and firms' competitiveness seem to have suffered seriously in recent years from an administered
form of investment financing — by state or banks. This type of financing
was preferred to equity financing as much because of economic policy
choices as because of the influence of a collective mentality which, despite
the modernization of France, remained relatively hostile to the accumula-
tion and free disposal of capital in private hands. The complete
nationalization of banks in 1981 and the active involvement of the state
budget in financing productive investment marked the high point of this
attitude. This administrative mode, different from the pre-war 'Malthusian liberalism', was once useful, during the period of reconstruction and
expansion, but it gradually gave rise to unintended consequences, which
developed latently during the second half of the 1970s and then quite
visibly during the first half of the 1980s. The particular features of the
French system of investment financing thus appear, at least partially, as
one explanatory factor, among others, for competitive backwardness.

The change in the nature of investment necessitated a profound
change in the system of financing: reduction of debt and finance charges;
more selective investments, in response to market segmentation; a faster
rate of innovation and product obsolescence; availability of venture
capital for medium-sized, high-performance firms; creation and transfer
of companies; more immaterial investment, based on expanded profit
margins; increased capitalization; and the development of capital markets and shorter circuits between savers and borrowers.

The fundamental transformation that the world's financial system has
undergone in recent years, owing to disinflation and deregulation, has
also affected France. Such a break, although less sharp than in other
countries, is none the less spectacular, given France's deeply embedded
traditions of administered financing. Until the beginning of the 1980s,

the transformation of savings to investment was largely carried out by financial intermediaries: banks lent out their deposits, the state played a direct role in investment, imposed credit volume controls, and set interest rates. Following the financial revolution, the French system is turning toward an economy in which markets are taking over from government agencies.

This transformation took place in several stages. In 1978, the Monory Law granted significant tax advantages to private savings invested in stock, bringing investors back to the Bourse after fifteen years of stagnation. Under the Barre Plan's austerity policy, the sharp increase of bond interest rates, restoring real positive rates, brought about an expansion of issues. In 1983, a second stock market was opened, allowing firms access to capital under less constraining conditions. In 1985, venture-capital companies were given tax status, and a number of other reforms were adopted: certificates of deposit, negotiable short-term bonds, and negotiable futures options were created, as was a forward market for financial instruments.

Conclusion: towards *a politique de l'entreprise*

From the point of view of growth, of industrial competitiveness, and of industrial economic policy, the Fifth Republic can be divided, as we have seen, into two distinct periods. During the 1958–73 period, the economy developed harmoniously, rapid industrialization being the symbol of national redemption and restored prosperity, and a rather broad consensus supported the goals and methods of industrial policy.

During the period 1974–88; on the contrary, the French economy was thrown out of order by the world-wide economic crisis: slowed growth, unemployment, decline of investment, bankruptcies, deindustrialization, regional difficulties. The whole of economic and industrial policy was challenged, and became subject to lively political debates and controversies; the 'French model', the product of the marriage of social Keynesianism and Colbertist traditions, was put in question.

Following fifteen years of trial and error, hesitation and abrupt reversals, a new consensus appears to be emerging around the firm and the *competitive imperative*, illustrated for example by the media success of a new generation of entrepreneurs and by the astonishing appeal of the slogan 'Europe 1992' and the perspective of a more closely integrated European market. To win the long battle to recover competitiveness, France will have to continue the recently begun process of acknowledging the business world. In response to long years of Malthusianism and stagnation, hoarded savings, and collective behaviour unfavorable to business, the France of the reconstruction and expansion considered industrial development and investment financing as a kind of 'public service': business should not be given too much freedom or autonomy, which the 'capitalists' and the 'bosses' might misuse. Consequently, there were nationalizations, price controls, various regulations, the diversion of profit margins to satisfy wage claims, and the financing of investment by the 'public credit service'.

With the decline of the French economy's competitiveness, it became apparent in recent years that elaborating an industrial policy without consulting business could lead to an industrial policy without industry. A profound transformation has thus begun in the financing of firms, in the state's intervention, in mentalities, caused as much by the spread of free-market ideology as by the challenge to the traditional Colbertist/welfare state model.

It is more freely admitted today that firms must be more responsible for their own investment strategies and that, to achieve that end, they must have profit margins and free access to capital. Less of a role for the state, more of a role for business and the financial markets. The conclusion reached for material investment must henceforth apply also to immaterial investment. In research, training, and commercial expansion abroad, France does not do less than her competitors overall; but the distribution of roles between the state and business must change, in order to make these investments more effective for competitiveness. Businesses must attach greater importance to innovation and professional training, and major state agencies like the Ministries of Education and Research must seek more effective means to co–operate with business. After witnessing — and sometimes provoking — the withering away or even the collapse of several of the most central institutions of traditional France — the Church, the army, the universities, agriculture — the Fifth Republic will thus have given birth, following a difficult pregnancy, to the institution of free enterprise, a symbol above all of modernization.

Bibliography

Actes du Colloque 'Politique Industrielle et nationalisations', published as *Socialisme et Industrie* (Paris: Club Socialiste du Livre, 1981).

Adams, James and Christian Stoffaës (eds), *French Industrial Policy* (Washington, DC: The Brookings Institution, 1984).

Les Cahiers Français, *La Planification Française* (Paris: La Documentation Française, 1977).

Cotta, Alain, *La France et l'impératif mondial* (Paris: PUF, 1978).

Estrin, Saul and Peter Holmes, *French Planning in Theory and Practice* (London: Allen & Unwin, 1983).

Le Franc, Jean-Daniel, *Industrie: le péril français* (Paris: Le Seuil, 1982).

McArthur, John and Bruce Scott, *Industrial Planning in France* (Cambridge, MA: Harvard University Press, 1968).

Machin, Howard and Vincent Wright (eds), *Economic Policy and Policy-making under the Mitterrand Presidency, 1981–1984* (London: Frances Pinter, 1985).

Monnet, Jean, *Mémoires* (Paris: Fayard, 1976).

Stoffaës, Christian, *La Grande menace industrielle* (Paris: Calmann-Lévy, 1978).

9. Economic planning: policy-making or policy-preparation?

Howard Machin

'*Quant au plan, ce moyen pour la Nation de ramasser ses forces autour d'objectifs dominants, on lui restituera l'esprit et les moyens de la mission confiée naguère à Jean Monnet par Charles de Gaulle.*'[1]

In 1988, Mitterrand promised, if re-elected, to restore planning to its former glory. The golden age to which he hoped to return was not, however, the status quo ante Chirac, when, in theory, planning had already been 'restored' by Rocard. Nor was it the first decade of the Fifth Republic, when de Gaulle and Debré had declared the Plan to be the *ardente obligation* for the whole nation. Instead, Mitterrand chose the Monnet Plan. Given the campaign theme of 'uniting France' and preparing for the unified market of 1992, references to Monnet, de Gaulle and the heady days of national unity after the Liberation were electorally apposite. None the less, the President was also implying that planning had never been a very effective policy-making process throughout the Fifth Republic, from de Gaulle to cohabitation.

Drawing up such a balance sheet of the last three decades of indicative economic planning in France involves at least three different types of evaluation. The first is that of the Plans themselves, to survey the extent to which the targets set in the seven Plans of the Fifth Republic were actually achieved in practice, to compare the outcomes with the stated policy goals. The problem with this approach, however, is its assumption that chronological coincidence reflects causation, or, as Jacques Rueff warned de Gaulle: 'Planners are like the rooster who believes his crowing causes the sun to rise.'[2] A second approach to evaluation, therefore, is to assess the methods and structures of planning, to analyse whether the planners really made policies, and hence to determine whether or not the outcomes of economic performance have actually been decided through the processes of economic planning. In the third type of evaluation, the indirect effects of the planning process are examined, and in particular those upon industrial relations, on group-state and firm-state linkages and on the general pattern of public policy-making within the state. What emerges from this survey is that Mitterrand was right: during the Fifth Republic, the main impact of planning has been on the frameworks of and approaches to economic policy-making, and only indirectly on the economic policies themselves. In short, French indicative planning has not been a policy-making process, but rather a system for improving policy preparation.

The Monnet model and its transformation

In 1946, shortly before his resignation, de Gaulle appointed Monnet as Commissar to draft a Plan for reconstruction. The approach adopted was highly pragmatic, with limited goals and very slight resources. A four-year flexible programme of development for just six key sectors of the economy — coal, steel electricity, cement, tractors, and transport — was drafted, by a new, participatory method. This involved bringing together in a 'planning commission', for each sector, forecasting experts, civil servants, top industrial managers, and trade-union leaders to exchange information and ideas and thus 'concert' their projects for the future. A number of 'horizontal' or problem-solving commissions were also created. The tasks of organizing the meetings, drafting the reports, and co-ordinating the results was given to a small, 'task force' of committed civil servants, grouped around Monnet — the Planning Commissariat. This body was made directly responsible to the Prime Minister. Despite the Soviet-style titles, the methods were anything but Stalinist. Flexibility was the main characteristic of the First Plan: its length was extended to cover the whole period of Marshall Aid, its scope was broadened by the addition of two more sectors, and its targets were revised. Indeed, its only legal recognition was a governmental decree, for it was believed that the passing of a law might have imposed too much rigidity. In theory, the planners had virtually no formal powers, so the success of the Plan depended on conviction and co-operation.[3]

During the Monnet Plan the war-torn economy was reconstructed and the 5 per cent annual growth rate (which was thereafter maintained almost monotonously until 1975) was first achieved. The Commissariat certainly remained a small, low-key body, a 'cross-roads' rather than a 'power-house', and this was a deliberate tactic for avoiding both conflicts with established ministries and involvement in day-to-day implementation work. But Monnet had a network of pro-planning friends in high places, including such men as François Bloch-Lainé at the head of the Treasury. Thus, while the Plan lacked even an outline financial programme, this planning mafia operated quietly but effectively (and sometimes ruthlessly) to ensure that the resources were made available.

Happily, Marshall Aid provided many of the funds for the investment programmes; this was an essential asset, given the penury of state funds and the ultra-cautious attitudes of many banks, including those recently nationalized. One other advantage for the Commissariat was its new, unknown and temporary nature; the Monnet Plan was widely seen as a one-off operation for reconstruction, and this reputation reduced opposition and facilitated co-operation.[4]

By the end of 1953, the Plan was seen as such a success that it was decided to have another, bigger and better Plan for the next five years, to draft it by the same method of concertation in the commissions, and to continue the existence of the Commissariat as the organizational key stone of the planning process, albeit with a new Commissar, Etienne Hirsch, and a new political overlord, the Minister of Finance. These decisions completely transformed the nature of planning, and represented a very different approach from that of Monnet. The new view was massively ambitious, and ultimately unrealistic.

In this new view, planning represented nothing less than a middle way between the ineffective brutality of coercive Soviet-style central planning and the wastes of Western market capitalism. Hence it was superior not only to traditional market economics but also to short-sighted and often clientelistic politics; it aimed at drawing up a consensual programme of rational medium-term policy strategies for the whole economy. This model of indicative planning involved four conceptually distinct, but closely linked, processes: study and forecasting; concertation and co-ordination; decision-making and implementation.[5]

One basic premise was that the forecasting of major economic variables was not only possible, but also highly accurate if carried out by the state and its technocrats. State agencies, however, do not hold a monopoly on forecasting; all economic actors — firms, trade unions, associations or simple individuals — are constantly involved in similar, if simpler, examinations of the present and speculations about the future. Large business corporations, especially multinationals, often rival the state in the sophistication of their forecasting systems. In this post-Monnet planning model, however, an attempt is made to combine and co-ordinate the individual study-forecasting activities of most key private actors (referred to as the 'social partners of government', but which are, in practice, leading firms and unions) within a collective, economy-wide forecasting process. This concertation and exchange of information and ideas between 'private' and 'public', between society and the state, was not to be limited to a number of sectors, or problems, or years. The concerted economy, in which the state persuades all the main individual or group decision-makers 'to perform together in close harmony' and thus to avoid waste and excess was to complement and thus modify the market. Concertation was hailed as a dynamic process of reducing uncertainties, and intransigence, but also of collective, participatory consensus-building, a new approach, distinct from both pluralist consultative and neo-corporatist techniques. This theory was both ambitious and imaginative, but it was not Monnet-style planning.

Policy goals and outcomes: planning in the Fifth Republic

During the life-span of the Fifth Republic there have been seven official medium-term French Plans. The first of these, the Third Plan, officially covered the period 1957 to 1961 but was only formally approved by decree on 19 March 1959 and so may be considered within the Fifth Republic. The most recent, the Ninth Plan, is still in operation, as it covers the years 1984 to 1988, and any judgements about it, quantitative or qualitative, must be limited and cautious. Its predecessor, the Eighth Plan, intended for the 1981 to 1985 period was stillborn: it was not yet approved when the 1981 presidential election took place, and the new government at once scrapped it and replaced it by an 'Interim Plan' for 1982 and 1983. Our assessment of the 'results' of the Plans is thus limited to five Plans between 1958 and 1988, although a few conclusions may be drawn about the Ninth Plan.[6]

Estrin and Holmes have shown that the 'results' of the Plans are almost impossible to assess by any simplistic formula.[7] The gross domestic product targets of the Third, Fourth and Fifth Plans were achieved or exceeded, and the shortfall began not in 1975 with the Giscardian Seventh Plan, but during the Sixth Plan. For both these Plans the GDP target-result gap was greater than 10 per cent. The pattern is roughly similar for gross fixed capital formation and for total consumption, but for imports and exports the Plan targets were rarely even close to the outcomes. For the Fourth and Fifth Plans, imports exceeded the target by over 30 per cent. While it does appear that the major variables of the economy did fluctuate more or less as the planners had targeted before 1970, the evidence is not conclusive.

An alternative approach to assessing the impact of the Plans is to compare the French economic growth rate to that of other similar economies, for if the Plans influenced business expectations and hence resource allocation, then the growth rate should have been both higher and more stable in France than in countries with no indicative planning. For planners, Britain was an obvious choice for such comparisons (at least until the recent and unplanned boom began). With no indicative planning, British growth between 1957 and 1970 was always lower than in France, but also much less even. Both Italy and West Germany, however, had similar growth rates to France during this period, although in both countries the growth was rather more erratic than in France. It does appear, therefore, that French growth has been more stable than elsewhere, but this does not prove that it was the Plans which provided this stability.[8]

Estrin and Holmes also made an interesting attempt to quantify the impact of the Plans by calculating what they termed 'alternative forecasts' and long-run trends. Their results, show only that the Third and Fourth Plan targets were closer to the outcomes than the predictions of businesses would have been had they been made without the information collected and distributed by the planning process. For the Fifth and Sixth Plans individual firms might have forecast more accurately without the Plan. Their calculations did not cover the Seventh Plan.[9] Once again, therefore, the evidence is unclear.

One problem of this type of evaluation of planning is that even many planners have not considered that the outcomes of economic performance could be used to assess the impact of the Plan with any accuracy. As early as 1969, Pierre Massé (then Planning Commissioner) warned that evaluations based on implementation rates could be misleading.[10] Overachievement may not indicate the irrelevance of the Plan targets, but may point to success in raising the level of confidence among businessmen. Similarly, underachievement might also indicate success — that the Plan targets had in fact raised expectations beyond what they would have been otherwise, and thus saved the economy from a far worse result. This 'wish-fulfillment' approach to planning was seen in the Ninth Plan, when Rocard was instructed to increase the Plan targets, even though this was generally viewed as unrealistic.

A further criticism of 'implementation-rate' evaluations is that they do not take into account the changing nature of planning and hence assess all Plans by criteria relevant only to the Second, Third and Fourth Plans. The objectives of these plans were the reconstruction, modernization and development of the economy to permit France to compete successfully in open European and world markets. By the mid-1960s the internationalization of the French economy was well under way; indeed, as noted above, French trade grew consistently faster than the planners foresaw. By the late 1960s the main aim of the Plan was to steer the growth, not set detailed targets. The economy grew by and through the success of French firms in international trade. This extensive internationalization of firms and the economy as a whole could be seen as an indicator of the success of the early post-Monnet Plans. It was also a portent of doom for this second type of planning, sectoral target setting was no longer possible.[11]

None the less, if macro-economic 'targeting' was of ever-declining relevance (except as a catalogue of hopes and good intentions) there was still a role for planning public spending. According to this view, therefore, the relevant criterion for assessing the effectiveness of Plans since the mid-1960s is state performance: the extent to which the state achieved the targets set for itself in the Plans. Since the Sixth Plan, a distinction has been made between ordinary targets (which ultimately depend on annual budgets and short-term management decisions) and firm commitments or 'priority programmes' (PAPs or PPEs). The Ninth Plan also introduced the idea of 'planning contracts' — between the state and public sector corporations or between the state and regions — and, like the 'priority programmes', they formed part of the core of firm state commitments in the Plan. Some of the outcomes of these programmes and contracts have been surveyed by the Commissariat.[12] Once again, these results present a complex picture: most, but not all, of these targets were substantially, but not completely, attained.

In short, this attempt to assess the achievements of Plan targets leads to few clear conclusions about the changing impact of indicative planning. Our next step, therefore, is to examine the linkages between the Plans and actual performance — by considering the methods and structures of planning.

Structures and methods

By examining both the quality of the forecasting systems and the numbers and identities of those involved in the planning consultations, and by considering the attitudes of businessmen, trade unionists, civil servants and ministers, it is possible to assess whether or not the abstract model has been effectively operationalized in the planning procedures of the Fifth Republic.

One necessary precondition for effective planning is a state research and data collection apparatus of sufficient scale and competence to accumulate and analyse the statistics of thousands of economic indicators over time and space. Detailed statistical analysis of the structures, interrelationships, flows and trends of the economy as a whole and its separate sectors is the starting point for the whole planning process. This 'total market study' is carried out to provide a base for forecasting, and the immediate objectives are the identification — or modelling — of trends and possibilities (or 'projections' and 'scenarios' or 'prospectives' in plannerspeak). The 'construction' of 'scenarios' is itself a complex process involving wide-ranging discussions. Finally, long-term projections and prospectives, as well as short-term problems, cannot be ignored in the forecasting process. The products — five-year forecasts — are thus calculated by sophisticated modelling techniques which include all these elements as well as basic probability factors. As Quinet and Touzery[13] show, the research, study and forecasting mechanisms of the Plan developed substantially in both scope and sophistication after the First Plan.

Not only was much more research carried out and information collected and analysed but forecasting models were greatly refined. The simple input–output models of the 1950s were replaced by a 'physico-financial model' (known appealingly as FIFI) for the Sixth Plan, then by the 'dynamic multi-sectorial model' (or DMS) for the Seventh, Eighth and

Ninth Plans. For the Seventh Plan, two other charmingly acronymed models, MOISE and REGINA, were employed for detailed simulations of international and interregional exchanges respectively.[14]

Ironically, this improvement in the sophistication of planning models coincided with the decline in the predictability of the phenomena to which they were applied. The sheer increase in the complexity of the economy obviously complicated the forecasters' work. But more significant was the growth of international trading, especially during the late 1960s and 1970s when international markets were destabilizing. The oil shocks of 1973 and 1979 confirmed a widely held view that at a time when accurate forecasts would have been most useful they were becoming least reliable. In addition to this international problem there were also specifically French difficulties, of which perhaps the most unpredictable was the 'Events of May 1968'; the wage rises and increases in public spending, notably on education, could not have been foreseen by any agency, however skilled.[15] None the less, there was a demand for an ending of the effective monopoly on forecasting and modelling exercised by INSEE and the Commissariat, and it was largely in response to this dissatisfaction that the creation of such bodies as the BIPE and the Observatoire Français des Conjontures Economiques came about.

Forecasting, however, was not the only element of planning with problems in the late 1970s. The concertation process in the commissions appeared to be losing credibility. The involvement of economic actors in the planning process had begun at a low level with only 500 individuals in ten commissions in the First Plan. The number of participants had quadrupled by the Fifth Plan, and by the Sixth Plan, there were twenty-eight commissions with a total of over 3,000 members. The number of commissions and committees was reduced to nineteen for the Seventh Plan and to fourteen for the stillborn Eighth Plan. For the Ninth Plan new structures were adopted. An eighty-member National Planning Commission, composed of unionists, businessmen and regional council presidents was created to co-ordinate the work of nine 'sub-commissions', and a parallel structure of eleven 'industrial strategy groups' was set up to consider problems of competitivity, new technology, and development possibilities for different industrial sectors. For the Tenth Plan, a mere seven commissions have been established.[16]

The changing structures and numbers of participants reflected a gradual but important change in the contents of the Plans. In the first Plans, the majority of commissions were sectoral (or 'vertical'), and each dealt with one industry or sector. Later 'horizontal' commissions and committees concerned with economy-wide problems (including employment, education and training) appeared as the scope of planning broadened from industrial to economic to social matters. By the Seventh Plan, most commissions were 'horizontal'; only for energy, commerce, transport, agriculture, public works and 'industry' were there sectoral commissions. For the Tenth Plan not a single vertical commission was set up. The ambitions of successive governments to use planning for all kinds of problem-solving inevitably transformed the nature of the Plans. By the 1970s, the Plan was as much a social and regional Plan as an economic one. Even the official title changed: the Third Plan was the last 'modernization and infrastructure Plan', and the Fourth became an 'economic and social development Plan'.

One consequence of these changes was that attempts were made to forecast and to set targets in areas where no sophisticated research, forecasting or model-building services existed to compare with those dealing with economic matters.[17] A second consequence was that the planners became increasingly dependent on the co-operation and good-will of the administrative services and agencies dealing directly with the 'horizontal' problems, and notably, the Ministries of Education, Health, Housing and Labour, and the agencies for research (DGRST) and regional development (DATAR), and the social security system. The Plan was increasingly a state plan, an outline programme for major public capital expenditure. Furthermore, relations between the Planning Commissariat and the budget division of the Finance Ministry were complicated as the planners attempted to secure firm funding commitments for future budgets for social and regional projects.

The evolution towards social planning also made the quasi-absence of trade- union leaders from planning all the more embarrassing. For most of the Fifth Republic, the CGT and FO have refused to take part in the commissions of the Plan, and even the CFDT withdrew during the Sixth and Seventh Plans. Ironically, neither the CGT nor the CFDT was ideologically hostile to the concept of planning, but both condemned French planning practice as serving the interests only of business and the state. After 1976, the unions were also doubtful whether the liberal Barre government was at all serious about planning.[18] As representatives of democratic organizations, trade unionists had difficulties with the idea of concertation (rather than negotiation). With limited research facilities of their own, they had little to contribute to the forecasting process. They did not, however, wish to give any legitimacy to the Plans by their presence in the commissions. None the less, social planning was less than convincing when the key social partner was conspicuously absent from the planning process.

By the late 1970s, however, the doubts of the unions were matched by those of businessmen, at least according to a SOFRES survey conducted for the Commissariat.[19] Amongst the 'heads of firms' questioned, the single most frequently cited cause for this decline was the turbulent international economic environment and the impossibility of making forecasts in such conditions. Some also saw the political liberalism of Giscard's governments as a significant reason for the decline of planning. The SOFRES results showed clearly that the Plan had lost credibility among businessmen: only 9 per cent of the respondents thought the Plan was 'very important'; two-thirds saw the Plan targets as government decisions (rather than as the fruits of concertation); 57 per cent said the government itself was not really committed to its own targets. Even worse, less than 10 per cent of those consulted had ever used planning documents for professional purposes, and two-thirds had never consulted any publication of the Plan. This same survey, however, found that many businessmen actually would have wanted more information from the Commissariat, especially independent forecasts relevant to their firms.

The attitudes of successive governments have inevitably influenced how their social partners reacted, in part because the extent to which the government listens to its planning partners in drawing up the Plan determines whether or not the Plan will be seen as a 'national plan' or as a governmental plan.' Obviously concertation cannot solve all problems. Decisions should certainly be more rational and better informed as a result of the concerting processes, but the need for arbitration, as well as co-ordination, is not removed. There will still be choices, and these choices must ultimately depend on priorities which are set by the government. Hence, the Plan 'targets' will be more or less governmental goals. One of the consistent shortcomings of the planners and their political masters, since the Monnet Plan, has been their inability to present the Plans as real 'national plans.'[20]

There is a second way in which governments and their civil servants have weakened the impact of the Plans. No government of the Fifth Republic, not even under de Gaulle, has an impeccable record of respecting its own planning choices.

The Plans were often displaced as the major policy strategies by short-term packages to meet specific problems including inflation, trade deficit and unemployment. Confusingly these packages were also popularly known as 'plans'. This practice did not begin with the Fifth Republic: the 1952 Pinay 'plan', and the 1957 Gaillard 'plan' had modified the First and Second Plans, respectively. The Third Plan suffered even greater indignities; even before its formal approval it had been downgraded in favour of the Rueff reform package, and an 'Interim Plan' for 1960–1 replaced its last two years. The Fourth Plan (1962–5) had the 1963 Giscard d'Estaing 'stabilization plan', the Fifth Plan (1966–70) faced the post-May 1968 financial measures, the Sixth Plan (1970–5) met the 1974 Chirac 'reflation plan' and the Seventh Plan (1976–80) suffered two Barre 'austerity plans'. Not even the Socialists' 'Interim Plan' was secure; a few months after its inauguration the Delors 'rigour plan' was introduced.

The exceptionally casual treatment of the Seventh Plan reflected the impact of the oil shocks and their side-effects, but also the liberal views of Giscard d'Estaing and his ministers. Giscard did not, however, destroy planning; indeed, there was no serious suggestion of the abolition of the

Commissariat until Chirac returned as Prime Minister in 1986. Under Giscard there were considerable efforts to promote strategic forecasting for the economy. There were also, in the priority programmes (the PAPs and PAPIRs), a real attempt to make the State commitment to its own Plan more serious. None the less, by admitting that only this 'hard core' of the Plans was a real commitment, the Giscardian planners were also acknowledging that the rest of their Plans were little more than catalogues of hopes and good intentions.. In this respect, the Socialists' priority programmes and 'contracts' with regions and public corporations were not only less original than claimed (as they were built on foundations laid by their much-criticized liberal predecessors), but also represented a similar avowal that these were the only serious parts of the Plan.[21]

Furthermore, after the wave of reforms to planning institutions and the drafting of the Interim and Ninth Plans, the Socialists themselves did little to enhance the public prestige of planning. After the transfer of Rocard to the Ministry of Agriculture, the Plan seemed to be almost forgotten. Under Fabius after 1984, planning was rarely mentioned. In practice, therefore, successive governments have paid more attention to short-term problems than to their own long-term promises.

It was not, however, until cohabitation in 1986 that the whole idea of planning was openly challenged. Chirac may have claimed to be de Gaulle's spiritual heir, but freeing the market was his main goal as Prime Minister for two years. It was the Chirac government, which, in heated infatuation with liberal ideas, had briefly considered giving a positive response to Fabra's question:'Faut-il supprimer le Plan?"[22] In 1986, however, caution triumphed and the death sentence was commuted. The lesser penalty of emasculation as the slave of the Economic and Social Council was also rejected. The Planning Commissariat was subjected to a change of leadership, and the Prime Minister called on two civil servants to draft 'full and detailed' reports on planning, a disguised decision to do nothing. The reports both agreed that planning as practised in 1986 posed no challenge to the market, but had a worthwhile role of information-sharing to play.[23] The Commissariat survived to prepare the Tenth Plan.

Whatever his campaign promises, Mitterrand still chose Michel Rocard as Prime Minister after his re-election. Rocard's career includes a celebrated attack on Socialist planning dogmas (at Metz in 1979) and an only partially successful attempt to revive the Plan (as Minister for Planning between 1981 and 1983). The Prime Minister chose a liberal, Lionel Stoléru, as his junior planning minister, and a former adviser of Jacques Delors, Cosse, as the new Planning Commissar to replace Fragonnard, whom Chirac had chosen. It was Rocard himself who wrote the preface for 'first outline' of the Tenth Plan in September 1988. This document bore remarkably little resemblance to the Monnet Plan, since it simply listed ways of solving general problems of the economy before 1993.

In 1988, as in 1981, the Socialists do not appear to have resolved the real dilemma of planning which baffled and bemused all their predecessors — that of linking the macro and the micro, the economy and its component firms and public agencies. In particular, there are major difficulties in dealing with industrial problems within the planning framework. Big firms and especially those in the expanded public sector require special individual treatment, not appropriate even for the sectoral approach of the Third, Fourth and Fifth Plans. Small firms in difficult regions for employment or with special prestige or technologies also often demand or expect individual attention. The main contact point for such firms with the state is the Ministry of Industry (or in some cases the Energy, Transport or Finance Ministries), but not the Plan. In the crisis times of the 1970s and 1980s alike, industrial policy was more concerned with *ad hoc* reactive measures to deal with specific problems (or 'fire-fighting') or with problem prevention by measures to create or refloat national champions. Moreover, normal demarcations of powers and political rivalries between ministers (and especially between Rocard, Delors and Jean-Pierre Chevénement, at Planning, Finance and Industry, respectively) reinforced this trend to keep the Plan out of such key industrial policy areas as restructuring.[24]

What the Socialists, like their predecessors, have discovered is an intractable problem at the heart of the structures and methods of planning — whatever the traditions of *dirigisme*, the economy is essentially a market economy where actors are and must be relatively autonomous and flexible, especially in a dynamic and interdependent world. No state can even give a firm promise about its own budget in four years' time. Furthermore, most planning targets are at a macro-economic, or sectoral, level and certainly cannot determine the investment or employment decisions of individual firms. Only in theory can the concertation process link the forecasting, decision-making and implementation processes: by coming together for collective study, forecasting, and discussive co-ordination firms and state agencies alike should be drawn into common ways of thinking, common assumptions about trends and probabilities and some loyalty towards the achievement of macro-economic targets which have been decided in common. In practice, however, the structures and methods of planning do not appear to have played a very important role in determining the economic performance of the French economy in the last three decades.

The side-effects of planning

The long experience of planning has, in contrast, had a considerable impact on the French system of government. One result was the adoption of the planning model of administrative organization, the single purpose, non-executive task force or *mission*. After the early success of the Planning Commissariat, with less than 200 staff, in 'getting things done', the idea became popular. For encouraging scientific research a task force, the DGRST, was set up in 1958, and a similar type of organization was created for regional policy-making in 1963, the DATAR. The same model has been used for purposes as varied as the coastal development of Languedoc-Roussillon and the adaptation of regional prefectures to their new economic functions after the 1964 reforms. Whatever its policy impact, the planning system clearly had an administrative organization which merited imitation.

Another effect of the experience of nine Plans has been the adoption of the idea of rational forecasting and advance programming throughout the state apparatus. Almost every ministry or agency is concerned with long- and medium-term problems and prospects, and now has its own in-house planning service. While this does not imply that the state as a whole now operates in a much more rational and programmed way than in the past, at least its component agencies and ministries do so in programming their major capital spending.[25]

One real success of the planning experience has been the creation of an impressive research capacity. Economics, econometrics, statistics, computing and business studies have all prospered with the support of and contracts from the Plan. Largely in response to the planners' demands, detailed national income accounting was begun and the statistics service, INSEE and the Forecasting Division of the Finance Ministry were set up, all largely in response to planning requirements. Other specialized study units, including CEPREMAP, CREDOC, CERC and CEPII also began life as part of the planning network. Even political science and sociology were encouraged, especially through the CORDES scheme.[26]

A further consequence of planning, with an impact very difficult to assess, was the creation of a remarkably talented network of planners, whose prestige, national and international, has considerably enhanced the reputation of their Plans. Some observers believe that a gradual change in the attitudes of policy-makers at all levels has taken place under the influence of these planners and their planning approaches when they have moved into key decision-making posts elsewhere in the state.[27]

The normalization of concertation is perhaps the biggest claim for the Plan, and its effect is most difficult to assess. Certainly, in the 1950s the planners were breaking new ground in this respect, and by the 1980s consultations with the social partners had become part of the ordinary policy-making process in most ministries, agencies and local governments. None the less, as the Socialists and Chirac have in turn discovered, protest politics is by no means a thing of the past, and trade unions, far from benefiting by their consultative role or their return to planning in the 1980s, are generally in decline.[28]

Conclusions

We may cast doubts not only on the plausibility and practicality of Mitterrand's promise to return to the planning practices and powers of the Fourth Republic, but also on the desirability of this proposal. The idea of a Plan represents a singular challenge to normal economic and political decision-making processes. A Plan is a massive series of decisions taken in public, but it covers a medium-term (four- or five-year) period, so many of the individual choices are not even intended for implementation until two, three, or even four years after the adoption of the Plan. The indicative planning process may be, in theory, a self-policing cyclical process. Its participants should constantly be involved in studying the present and exchanging information and ideas with others within the commissions. They should be working in a continuous process of implementing and revising the present Plan, but also preparing the next one. This implies that the state's planning agency, the Planning Commissariat, must play a role of animation and another — contradictory — role of control. The planners should be salesmen — enticing, coaxing, persuading, or convincing the social partners into participation in the work of the commissions. But they should also be policemen, cajoling them to respect the provisions of the Plan. Hence, they should be 'honest brokers' outside politics, especially bureaucratic politics. The theory may be splendid, but in practice it does not work.

The basic problem is that a Monnet Plan in an mixed economy which is part of a European market is a contradiction in terms. A five-year macroeconomic strategy, even if limited to a small number of sectors, could only be decided if forecasting were reliable, and implemented by incredibly powerful and effective policing: both conditions imply a suspension of open borders and market economics and a truce in normal competitive politics. Fabra's questions in 1986 may be harsh but are not unreasonable: if it is not a serious strategy, why call it a Plan and oblige Parliament to give it legal recognition by one, or even two, laws?

This is not meant to imply that the planning processes have been futile for the last thirty years or more; on the contrary, they have been very productive and influenced many aspects of politics and economics. The actual drafting of the Plans of the Fifth Republic may, however, have been their least fruitful activity.

Notes

1. François Mitterrand, *Lettre aux Français*, Paris, 1988, p.31.
2. Quoted in *Libération*, 5 August 1986. I wish to express my particular gratitude to B. Cazes and Y. Ullmo for invaluable help and advice. David Cameron, Saul Estrin, Peter Hall, Jean-Marcel Jeanneney and Vincent Wright all made very helpful suggestions which I have followed.

3. P. Mioche, *Le Plan Monnet* (Paris: Sorbonne, 1987); H. Rousso (ed.), *De Monnet à Massé* (Paris: CNRS, 1986); J.F. Picard, A. Beltran, M. Bungener, *Histoires de l'EDF* (Paris: Dunot, 1985), Chapter 7.

4. C. Gruson, *Origines et espoirs de la planification française* (Paris: Dunot, 1968); Rousso, *De Monnet à Massé* ; Peter Hall, *Governing the Economy* (Cambridge: Polity Press, 1986), pp.140–50.

5. Some studies present decision-making and implementation as a single process: E. Quinet and L. Touzery, *Le Plan Français: mythe ou necessité* (Paris: Economica, 1986) and Y. Ullmo *et al.*, *La Planification Française* (cours), (Paris: FNSP, 1986).

6. Results for 1984–6 are presented in *Document d'orientation du 10éme Plan* (Paris: Commissariat Général du Plan, typed copy).

7. Saul Estrin and Peter Holmes, *French Planning in Theory and Practice* (London: Allen & Unwin, 1983), pp. 69–81.

8. Ibid., pp. 84–5.

9. Ibid., pp. 81–4.

10. Pierre Massé, *Le Plan ou l'anti-hasard* (Paris, Gallimard, 1969).

11. S. Estrin and P. Holmes, 'International Trade: The External Constraint', paper presented to the ASMCF Conference, Nottingham, 1984.

12. 'Les Contrats Etat-régions', *La Croix,* 23–4 November 1986; Diana Green, 'The Seventh Plan: the demise of French Planning', *West European Politics* vol. 1, 1978, pp. 60–76.

13. Quinet and Touzery, *Le Plan Français: mythe ou necessité,* Chapter 4.

14. Pierre Bauchet, *Le Plan dans l'économie française* (Paris, FNSP, 1987); Estrin and Holmes, *French Planning* ; and Quinet and Touzery, *Le Plan Français* all provide good accounts of these different models.

15. J.P. Vesperini, *L'Economie de la France de la crise de mai 1968 aux résultats de expèrience socialiste* (Paris: Economica, 1985).

16. Dominique Strauss-Kahn and Michel Ozenda, 'French Planning' (see also 'Comment' by Jack Hayward), in Howard Machin and Vincent Wright (eds), *Economic Policy and Policy-making under the Mitterrand Presidency, 1981–1984* (London: Frances Pinter, 1985); S. Estrin and P. Holmes, 'Planning for modernisation', in J. Gaffney (ed.), *France and Modernisation* (Aldershot: Gower, 1988); *La France, l'Europe: Le Plan 1989–1992, Première Esquisse* (Paris: CG Plan, 29 September 1988), pp. 29–30; Quinet and Touzery, *Le Plan Français*, pp. 38–42, 105–110.

17. Ullmo *et al.*, pp. 66–8; Bruno Jobert, 'Aspects of social planning in France', in J. Hayward and O. Narkiewicz (eds), *Planning in Europe* (London: Croom Helm, 1978); B. Jobert, *Le Social en Plan* (Paris: Editions Ouvriéres, 1981).

18. Jacques Delors, 'The Decline of French Planning' and Jacques Attali, 'Towards Socialist Planning' in S. Holland (ed.), *Beyond Capitalist Planning* (Oxford: Blackwell, 1978); Ullmo *et al.*, pp. 9–10.

19. Quoted in Estrin and Holmes, *French Planning*, pp. 115–18.

20. Pierre Mendès France, *La République Moderne* (Paris: Gallimard, 1966), pp. 43–182.

21. Hall, Governing , pp. 157–158; Diana Green, 'The Budget and the Plan', in Philip G. Cerny and Martin A. Schain (eds), *French Politics and Public Policy* (London: Frances Pinter, 1980).

22. Paul Fabra, *Le Monde,* 8 July 1986.

23. Jean-Pierre Ruault, 'Rapport au Premier Ministre' (Paris: Commissariat Général du Plan, typed copy, 1986); M. Velitchkovitch, 'Rapport au Conseil Economique et Sociale' (Paris: CG Plan, typed copy, 1987); see *Le Monde*, 26 January 1989, for details of the Tenth Plan.
24. 'Introduction', in Machin and Wright, *Economic Policy* ; M. Rhodes, 'Industry and Modernisation: an overview', in Gaffney, *France*, pp. 66–95.
25. 'Débat: le Plan, moteur de l'information économique', in Rousso, *De Monnet à Massé*, pp. 79–85; Charles Debbasch, *L'Administration au pouvoir* (Paris: Calmann-Lévy, 1969), pp. 13–21; for an alternative view, see Louis Nizard, 'Planning as the regulatory reproduction of the status quo', in J. Hayward and M. Watson (eds), *Planning, Politics and Public Policy* (Cambridge: Cambridge University Press, 1976).
26. A. Drouard (ed.), *Le Développement des sciences sociales en France: au tournant des années soixante* (Paris: CNRS, 1983); E. Lisle, H. Machin and S. Yasin, *Traversing the Crisis: the Social Sciences in Britain and France* (London: ESRC, 1984), pp. 151-4, 163-9.
27. Strauss-Kahn and Ozenda, 'French Planning'.
28. Louis Nizard (ed.), *Planification et société* (Grenoble: Presses Universitaires de Grenoble, 1975). See also Stephen Cohen, *Modern Capitalist Planning: the French Model* (2nd edn, Berkeley: University of California Press, 1977); Richard F. Kuisel, *Capitalism and the State in Modern France* (Cambridge: Cambridge University Press, 1981); and V. Lutz, *Central Planning for the Market Economy* (London: Longman, 1969).

10. From *Dirigisme* to Deregulation? The Case of Financial Markets*

Philip G. Cerny

Dirigisme and the State

The French state has often been labelled *dirigiste*, a word which has no straightforward equivalent in English. *Dirigiste* implies that key economic orientations and outcomes, usually (though not exclusively) those of a longer-term strategic or developmental kind, derive not so much from autonomous market forces as from 'state preferences'.[1] *Dirigisme* can take a variety of forms, depending on both state structures and preferences and on socio-economic structural factors.[2] *Dirigisme* in itself is neither favourable nor unfavourable to capitalist development, but must be set in a wider context of the organizational analysis of different 'markets'.[3] Indeed, the *dirigiste* state may even seek to *strengthen* certain market actors and forces in the context of an implicit or explicit economic strategy. Furthermore, any *dirigiste* state exists in the context of the international marketplace, which has no overarching state structure, but a mixture of market forces, transnational structures and 'regimes', and patterns of competition and co-operation between states. Thus debates on *dirigisme* usually concern both the different *forms* found within a particular system and the *effectiveness* of *dirigisme* in controlling market forces and actors in shaping longer-term patterns of economic development.

In the particular case which we are dealing with here, France, analysts have been concerned with whether a long and venerable *dirigiste* tradition dating from the seventeenth century experienced an effective renaissance following the Second World War at several levels: first, the planning system; second, the development of a new technocratic ethos in

*An earlier version of this paper was presented to the Workshop on Deregulation in Western Europe, European Consortium for Political Research, Amsterdam, April 1987. Fieldwork was assisted by a small grant from the Nuffield Foundation and travel funding from the University Association for Contemporary European Studies and the University of York.

the higher reaches of the civil service; third, the *étatiste* policy orientation of the Gaullists and the Fifth Republic; and fourth, the financial system, or how money has been provided to the economy, especially for industrial modernization and development. The most thoroughgoing defence of the *dirigiste* thesis with regard to France is to be found in the work of John Zysman, who emphasizes the fourth set of developments, the financial system.[4] This 'strategic state' thesis has come under fire from those who argue that the French state does not have the co-ordinating capacity or the policy goals necessary for true *dirigisme*.[5] These are mainly differences of degree. But financial deregulation is potentially a difference of kind.

Deregulation, in theory, means more than just the removal of specific government regulations. It implies the removal of restraints on the free play of market forces inside the national economy, as well as opening up the national economy to transitional market forces. The 'strategic state', if it exists, is directly undermined by deregulation — especially if we accept Zysman's argument that the key building block in the French version of the strategic state in recent decades has been the financial system. However, as Moran points out, the state may actually impose deregulation on its own state officials and on state-sponsored corporatist bodies like stock exchanges.[6] Indeed, state officials may impose deregulation on market actors like banks or industrial and commercial firms previously shielded from the full blast of the market — especially the international market. Paradoxically, then, the 'strategic state' may pursue deregulation as a part of an international competitive strategy, to shake up ossified market structures and unadventurous market actors. But does the state thereby undermine its own *modus operandi* and even its *raison d'être* ? Does the very concept of the 'strategic state' lose its plausibility in the era of the international 'financial revolution'? We will look first at the *dirigiste* model and financial markets in France, then at the process of deregulation so far, and finally at the implications of this process both for the French state and public policy, and for economic policy generally.

French *dirigisme* and the Financial System

In the late nineteenth century, the Paris Bourse was the equal of the London Stock Exchange.[7] Its twentieth-century decline reflected France's inability to recover from the First World War, the stagnation of her economy between the wars, and the growing role which the state came to play in providing finance to industry in the post-Second World War period.[8] The development of the new *dirigisme* of the post-war period and, in particular, of the 1960s and 1970s, was mirrored by the stagnation of financial markets, regarded as the outdated and decidedly shady legacy of the Third Republic's *mur d'argent* and also shunned by the 'modernizing' fractions of the Right, who preferred to put their faith in technocratic elitism, indicative planning and state-sponsored industrial development.

Of course, this was not the whole story of France's post-war economic development, which was characterized by increasing demand and reducing factor costs. But this came about in a structural environment in which the role of the state was transformed from defender of financial orthodoxy and provider of protectionism, to innovator and catalyst. Much of this change derived from the pragmatic use of a variety of instruments of control, unified primarily by a widespread elite outlook in favour of economic modernization. Post-war French elites may have differed over party politics and the form of the Republic's constitution, but they agreed on the need for a structural transformation of the French economy.[9]

Four developments in the years immediately after the war are of particular importance here. One of these was the inheritance or establishment of a battery of regulatory economic controls — price controls, credit controls, exchange controls, for example, many of which lasted long after the scarcity of the post-war period had been overcome. A second element was the nationalization not only of certain basic industries, mainly in the energy sector, but also of large parts of the financial system. A third tool of the state was its control of new funds for investment, especially those coming from the American Marshall Plan, in the earlier years, and later through the national *caisses* which are responsible for the investment of funds in the national savings system. And bringing all of these together was, of course, the planning system.

Planning involved several levels of *dirigisme*. It was the core of concertation, mainly through a form of widespread bilateral corporatism. It presented economic policy and growth as a positive-sum game, taking the edge off struggles over turf within the state as well as between public and private sectors. It provided a supply-side macro-economic alternative to Keynesianism. And it created the image, and occasionally the reality, of strategic potential, the material core of which was the direct and indirect capacity to influence and provide flows of credit for investment over and beyond the bounds of self-financing and of the limited resources of the French investment banking system.

With the advent of European Economic Community and the Fifth Republic in 1958 came a new quantum leap for *dirigisme*. Post-war *dirigisme* had mainly pursued the reconstruction and reconversion of the French economy at a national level; now it explicitly took on the objective of making French capital competitive internationally. The most important elements were the use of regulatory controls, subsidies and the control of credit flows to speed economic restructuring and industrial development. Both nationally and at the European levels, subsidies cushioned the growing rural exodus while structural measures such as the Pisani Laws speeded it up further. The miners' strike of 1963 hastened the substitution of imported oil for coal. Defence spending and the development of a nuclear strike force channelled state funds towards sectors such as aeronautics, electronics, civilian nuclear energy and scientific research in general. Government backing for industrial concentration came through subsidies, loans, guarantees, procurement and the like, directed towards particular firms (especially those which remained under French control) or whole sectors, such as, steel, oil, and the Plan Calcul for electronics.[10] The Fifth Plan, while systematizing this new 'industrial imperative', also widened the ambitions of planning in the social field, including education, low-income housing, etc., to deal with some consequences of restructuring. But the government's intentions to end exchange controls and to move towards a more flexible monetary policy were thwarted by the Events of May 1968 and the financial instability which followed.

The 1970s saw a paradoxical set of developments. Planning was overtaken by more short-term macro-economic policy, as economic disruptions falsified forecasts and undermined credibility. But at the same time the state took a stronger role in controlling and targeting the provision of finance to industry. In addition to existing instruments, new financing bodies such as the Institute for Industrial Development (IDI) were established, major state-funded projects extended and more closely targeted micro- and meso-economic policies adopted. Inter-ministerial committees took on a more comprehensive co-ordinating role. But one of the most important innovations arose almost accidentally in 1971, in the context of the international monetary perturbations. This was the establishment of credit ceilings (also adopted briefly by the Heath government in Britain) — the *encadrement du crédit* system.

The system was incrementally extended over time to become not only the main means of quantitative control of the money supply, but also a method of controlling the direction of financial flows. A number of analysts — Zysman in particular — have argued that, given the under-development of alternative sources of finance, especially the small size and stagnation of the financial markets, credit ceilings ensured that there was a shortage of credit for investment purposes which could only be satisfied by selective exemptions from these ceilings. The criteria for granting exemptions were overseen by the Finance Ministry, which ensured overall co-ordination of policy.

When taken together with direct government financing, subsidization of interest rates and other favourable conditions attached to state-controlled credit, the potential for using credit policy as a means to achieve other policy objectives was increased. And when combined with a widespread *Colbertiste* political culture of state promotion of industry, a technocratic civil service interpenetrated with modernizing fractions of capital, and the greater political control of the policy process afforded by the institutional arrangements of the Fifth Republic, Zysman concluded, such a state-led, credit-based supply-side approach put France into the 'strategic state' category.

Other writers have perhaps not seen the *encadrement* system as quite so coherent as Zysman has. What they do suggest, however, is that the French state may be characterized by competing policy networks and therefore lack the co-ordinating capacity to be a strategic state like, for example, Japan.[11] In this context, a number of intra-state cleavages become more significant, especially that between those ministries, state agencies and *grands corps* whose outlook tends to be characterized by what might be called an 'industrial logic' and those characterized by a 'financial logic'. The first would perhaps better represent the *Colbertiste* tradition of state promotion of industry, infrastructure, and so on, which today would be reflected in a priority for modernization, the growth of production, research and development, and technology. Its institutional base would have been in the planning system in the post-war period, but this would have shifted to the Ministry of Industry (the Defence Ministry and the Ministry of Foreign Trade might be in this category also); and its *grands corps* association would be in the Corps des Mines, the Corps des Ponts et Chaussées, the prefects and civil administrators.

The second would represent what in Britain would be called the 'Treasury view', giving priority to the control of government expenditure and its effects on the *grands équilibres* — inflation, the balance of payments, the government budget deficit, the percentage of GDP taken in tax and compulsory contributions, and so on. This outlook would be found in the Ministry of Finance, the Trésor in particular; and its corporate identity would be firmly rooted in that most prestigious of *grands corps,* the Inspecteurs des Finances. Now these contrasting logics are no less *dirigiste* for their competition; state elites are still dominant in their narrower spheres of competence; the private sector of industry and commerce is still enmeshed in a series of special relationships of a quasi-corporatist nature, while the public sector is still seen as playing a leading role in restructuring and modernization; and the system of provision of finance for economic development is still as predominantly state-controlled and credit-based. But the implications for financial market reform are widespread.

The developments of the 1980s have only partly undermined this paradigmatic image of state intervention. Socialist policy after May 1981 did not dismantle existing instruments, but sought to reinforce and complement them in several ways — through increased state funding of economic modernization, more direct control of major sectors through nationalization, an expansion of the planning system, and a number of reflationary social measures, all of which were intended to set off a virtuous circle of growth and restructuring.[12] The residual consequences of the second oil shock, plus the deep international recession of 1982, however, undermined the French state's capacity to pursue its full range of goals. The consequent shake-out of 1982–3 led to a new austerity ('socialist rigour') and a new emphasis on managerial autonomy and the profitability of firms in both public and private sectors. Private investment continued to stagnate, and only state-funded investment prevented a more precipitous fall. In what was then seen as an apparent paradox, Socialist governments took measures to strengthen private capital markets. With the coming into office of the Fabius government in July 1984, the policy of deregulation, led by Finance Minister Pierre Bérégovoy, took a quantum leap forward — although the consequences were not fully visible until 1986. After a cautious start, the Chirac government continued along lines previously traced, adding elements such as privatization, which will be considered below.

The state and the financial markets, 1978–84

The objective of any policy of deregulation is to increase the efficiency of markets by reducing barriers to exchange and widening the range of both goods and market factors involved. This does not, however, necessarily entail a reduction in the role of the state. Indeed, the expansion and increased efficiency of markets may actually require the expansion of the role of the state.[13] Historically, this is quite characteristic of financial markets, which have frequently been established and developed not to respond to private demand for capital but to government demand for borrowing, as in seventeenth-century France and nineteenth-century Britain. Furthermore, promotion of market expansion in general does not necessarily entail the expansion of private capital markets at the core. It has been argued that predominance of private capital markets leads to a preponderance in allocation decisions of a short-term perspective on profit and loss which hinders the longer-term development and efficiency of other markets (product markets or labour markets) in wider production and distribution processes. Such has been the foundation for the argument in favour of financial *dirigisme* and the 'strategic state' in Imperial Germany, Japan and Gaullist France.

The analysis of deregulation policy, therefore, must concern not only the question of whether the impetus for that policy derives from 'state references' or from market demand, a question noted at the beginning of this chapter, but also the question of whether the impact of that policy actually works to promote market efficiency and expansion compared with other systems of capital allocation. In analysing the French financial market reforms of recent years, the first question can be answered more readily than the second. Paradoxically, those reforms quite clearly derive from 'state preferences': domestic market forces provided little impetus for change, and international market forces in the financial field seem to have had a more direct impact on state policy than they did on domestic capital markets.[14] At the same time, however, the content of state preferences is still at issue. Do these reforms reflect a shift, within the French state, from an industrial logic to a financial logic?

This, of course, leads to the second question. If the financial logic of ascendant groups of state actors, influenced by global market forces, is leading to the replacement of the state-led, credit-based supply-side financial system with a system based on private and open capital markets, what will this mean for *dirigisme* itself? Must deregulation be pursued to some logical conclusion, or could the state attempt to turn back the clock — unlikely as it may seem?[15] There is a third possible set of issues, however: whether financial deregulation may provide opportunities for rethinking the 'fault line' of contemporary state/economy relations, reflecting the blurring of the distinction between public and private sectors found in the contemporary 'competition state'.[16] This can be seen at two levels in the French case: the difficulty of undermining *dirigisme* sufficiently to lead into a genuinely 'arms-length' financial market system; and the elusive objective of turning Paris into a competitive financial centre in the integrated, twenty-four-hour global financial marketplace of the late 1980s.

French financial markets in the post-war period must therefore be seen in the context of the development of the French financial system as a whole. From 1961 until 1982, the Bourse was stagnant or worse. This stagnation paralleled the development of the state-led, credit-based financial system which the Fifth Republic evolved on top of the post-war controls and the planning system. In 1972, one government loan mopped up three times the entire amount of new issues on the Bourse for the year.[17] In 1976, the major institutional investors (primarily the state *caisses*) represented 80 per cent of daily business.[18] In 1977, the state, through the Caisse des Dépôts et Consignations, the *caisses d'épargne* and other public establishments held 55 per cent of French shares.[19] Bond markets, though scarcely more active, were better capitalized and had significant tax advantages.

From a structural point of view, then, the Bourse was fairly irrelevant to French economic development in this period. Indeed, broadly-based private sources of capital for industry were crowded out at a number of levels. Capital and investment funds, especially for expansion and restructuring, were more readily available from the state, and on favourable terms, too, for both public and private sectors, despite the 'queuing' system created by credit controls. The investment banking system was limited in its resources, and the interbank market was closely controlled by the *encadrement* system. French commercial banks, the biggest of which were nationalized, and which attracted the lion's share of deposits, concentrated on extending their branch networks to become the largest per capita in the world; overhead costs were high and they made inefficient sources of capital. The private bond market was a better bet than the share market, partly due to preferential treatment from the state, but this only reflected the weight of state issues and institutions. Exchange controls limited the interpenetration of the French financial system with foreign finance, and the structure of the Bourse itself was an obstacle.

The Bourse was run in a *étatiste* manner, reflecting French traditions. The main actors were much more than mere stockbrokers. They were (and still are) *agents de change,* positions first established as venal offices of state under Louis XIV to raise the huge borrowings required to finance seventeenth-century wars. Subjected to the vicissitudes of state fortunes under the *ancien régime* and temporarily abolished after 1789, they were given a monopoly over exchange transactions by Napoleon I, a monopoly which, while having lost its functions on the interbank market, remained intact in the securities field until the establishment of the 'new money market' in 1985 and subsequent reforms. They were, and are, a public body, but in effect with quasi-private status — the other side of the traditional corporatist token. The regulations of their corporate body, the Chambre Syndicale des Agents de Change or CAC (whence the index), have had the status of regulations issued by the Ministry of Finance, and require Ministry approval. And yet their activities have been significantly more restricted than those which have been available to investors in other major stock markets. *Charges* have remained artisanal, often family, firms, passed down through generations, while outsiders have faced a corporate veto. More importantly, however, *agents de change* were not permitted to trade in the market on their own account. Thus the Bourse has had, in effect, only half of a system of dual capacity — brokers trading directly on others' accounts, but no jobbers or market makers. And as *charges* have not been highly capitalized in the past, the development of specialization, research, and so on, has been limited. This has also placed severe physical constraints on the volume and composition of trading, seriously restricting the liquidity of the markets, limiting economic efficiency.

Deregulation has therefore come as a major structural shock. The most visible change occurred in the equities sector; average share prices quadrupled over five years, while West German prices trebled and New York and London prices little more than doubled. Total transactions of shares rose from 26 billion francs in 1976 (62.8 billion in 1982) to 411.2 billion in 1986; bond transactions rose from 28.2 billion francs in 1976 (151.3 billion in 1982) to 1.673 *trillion* francs in 1986. Stock market capitalization rose from 9 per cent of Gross Domestic Product in 1978 to 13 per cent in 1985 and 25 per cent in 1986, putting it in the same league as other major industrial economies.[20] Privatization greatly inflated some of these numbers in 1987 prior to the October crash. Less visible changes, including the introduction of new financial instruments, the ending of the *agents de change* monopoly, banking reform, and the end of the *encadrement* system, will have an important long-term structural impact, even after the crash.

Before 1976 the revival of the Bourse was not a major issue; the policy legacies of the Gaullist years were not easily dismantled. But the first oil shock of 1973–4 exposed the inflationary potential in the financial system. Planning was left to decline, undermined by the volatility of the period;[21] and in 1976 the new Prime Minister, Raymond Barre, pushed the freeing of market forces to the forefront of political debate, although *de facto* state micro-economic interventionism continued to grow.[22] In 1978, Economics Minister René Monory introduced the measure which is now seen as the beginning of the process of financial market reform — an income tax deduction of 5,000 francs for new purchases of French shares. This measure proved immensely popular. Banks responded with new SICAVs (mutual funds or unit trusts) designed to conform with the act. Share transactions doubled in 1978, partly because the Right's electoral victory reversed a flight of capital, and partly because of the Monory Law.[23]

The 1981 elections revived splits in the Right and the Socialist challenge overshadowed market reform. After the Socialist victories, shares lost about one-sixth of their value despite an end-of-year recovery, both share and bond issues stagnated, and market capitalization fell.[24] Although share markets were relatively stagnant in 1982, bond transactions, in contrast, rose 83 per cent. More important, however, were shifts within the government in 1982 and the start of deeper change in financial policy. Paradoxically, policies adopted during the 'honeymoon' period in 1981, along with changes in the market environment, cast a new spotlight on the Bourse.[25] The nationalization programme, approved in early 1982, was the main spur. 'Nationalizable' firms had made large losses in 1981 and the Constitutional Council's decision to increase compensation terms seemed a bit of a windfall; their shares rose dramatically. Even once the shares had been withdrawn from the markets, trading in the firms' indemnity bonds proceeded at a lively pace.

Nationalization thus had the unintended consequence of stimulating the Bourse: despite a reduction of 30 per cent in share capitalization, new capital was attracted; and, after compensation, existing capital was redistributed to other outlets on the exchange. New 'glamour stocks' emerged from the pack. Other investments became less attractive: gold prices fell, and the government lifted the rule permitting anonymity on gold transactions; property markets were in disorder and savings accounts showed little return. Securities also became more attractive. Shorter-term and floating rate bonds attracted a new clientele. The secondary bond market flourished, too. The Monory reforms were still working. But the closed nature of the Bourse and the unfavourable economic climate still dissuaded unquoted firms from applying for listing.

Rising inflation and pressure on the franc led to drastic measures in June 1982, depressing the markets and wiping out most of the year's gains. Shares stagnated, but bond markets improved, thanks mainly to increased government borrowing and new short-term and floating rate issues.[26] And a new tone was reflected in Mitterrand's 1983 New Year message: it was necessary to restore profitability in industry; management, whether in the private sector or the public sector, had to be given the necessary autonomy; and only when financial balances had been restored — including the *grands équilibres* — could expansion safely proceed. The Mitterrand Presidency Mark I was over. A new package of financial mechanisms — tax-free savings accounts whose funds would go into subsidized loans to high-technology industries — and more market-oriented measures, from authorization for public sector firms to issue new hybrid debenture stocks (*titres participatifs*) and non-priority non-voting shares (*certificats d'investissement*) which counted as capital, to setting up a new Second Marché or unsolicited securities market. Both nationalized firms and smaller businesses were brought into the private capital markets. Continuing austerity, falling inflation, the bottoming-out of the recession and the new measures together set off a long-term upward trend in the markets.

A further element was the government's changing relationship with the banks, 75 per cent of which had been in the public sector since 1945. Bank nationalization failed to expand the state-led, credit-based financial system. Some ministers had wanted a new national investment bank to co-ordinate expansion, but this was vetoed. However, measures to stimulate the development of private capital markets were maintained, and reform proposals brought out of desk drawers. Rules were simplified for new flotations, new financial instruments authorized, the 'monthly settlement' market reformed, securities 'dematerialized' — no more bond and share certificates by the end of 1984, only computerized records — and financial market authorities' powers strengthened.[27] The bond markets were stimulated by public sector deficits — a new structural factor in France after 1981 and often a major forcce in stimulating financial markets elsewhere. By 1984 French financial markets were poised to make a structural breakthrough as domestic and international trends converged.

The 'Financial Revolution' and the Emerging Momentum of Reform

In 1984, two elements predominated. First, there was an even more important change of government. Laurent Fabius, the new Prime Minister and long a close adviser to Mitterrand, had been Budget Minister and a rationalizing Industry Minister. The new Minister of Finance was Pierre Bérégovoy, who as Social Affairs Minister had presided over the 'pause' in social reforms. The Communists, who supported social reforms and industrial expansion to combat unemployment, withdrew. In the second place, however, Europe was becoming aware of changes in the world financial system. In 1981–2, European finance ministers had attempted to deal with capital flight and high interest rates by calling for concerted action by the major industrial countries to reduce rates and for a more managed exchange rate system. But volatility was increasing with First World recession and the Third World debt crisis, and the Reagan administration was even more opposed to such measures than the Carter administration had been.

Following the move to floating exchange rates in 1973, the United States had begun deregulating its financial markets. Under Reagan, financial deregulation and the growth and diversification of American financial institutions were bound up with the more freewheeling environment created by broader deregulation and extensive tax cuts. Furthermore, tax cuts created budget and trade deficits which required financing. High interest rates were the key to financing the deficits out of capital

..ows from abroad. But European policy-makers saw their lack of sufficient investment capital as the main obstacle to recovery. Europe was seen to have a major financial supply-side problem. Capital market deregulation would be necessary to compete with the USA for international funds. In 1983 Britain started the process which would lead to the Big Bang three years later.

American pressure on Japan in the same year to open its financial markets faced strong opposition at first, until Japan began to adopt its own strategy to take advantage of deregulation elsewhere in order to benefit Japanese institutions. Other countries, too, experimented with financial deregulation. International capital flows were increasing (and increasingly volatile), while new negotiable instruments were successfully competing on a large scale with credit finance. A state which wished both to retain a sufficient share of domestic capital for investment and to attract foreign capital would have to enable its public and private sectors alike to compete for funds in rapidly integrating global securities markets.

The unregulated Eurobond market, for floating-rate notes in particular, was growing rapidly in the wake of the collapse of Eurodollar loan markets with the Third World debt crisis. New instruments for currency and interest rate hedging and speculation — US Treasury bills, futures, options, commercial paper, swaps, etc. — began to be widely copied as bank intermediation came under pressure. High real interest rates — growing as inflation fell — made hedging through securitization an ever more crucial tool of the company treasurer's trade. At the same time, nominal interest rates began to fall, prices of securities rose, and the secondary market became more attractive and competitive.

Indeed, the whole structure of profitability from financial transactions was changing. To reduce costs, the burden was shifting from interest income to commissions (to the detriment of bank loans). Pressure increased from large issuers and investors to shave commissions. Arbitrage between increasingly interpenetrated markets made it impossible for financial institutions to stay aloof. Disintermediation and securitization gained an international momentum and created an appetite for more and more new instruments. These external pressures converged with the aims of French policy-makers, making financial market deregulation seem not only an attractive alternative to the credit-based system, but also the only alternative to a siege economy. But the situation was full of pitfalls. However, once the French state became interested in the markets, it was characteristic that policy-makers should attempt to marshal state authority in favour of reform. Thus the objectives of state actors came to define the parameters of reform.

It is clearly critical that 'financial logic' had already won the day in government and civil service circles through what were widely perceived as the 'lessons' of trying to pursue 'socialism in one country' in 1981–2.[28] But industrial logic also played an interesting role. The rationale presented by Bérégovoy for deregulation was that it would reduce interest rates charged to industry for investment and modernization.[29] His claim to have reduced interest rates by 2 per cent as a result is widely accepted. This convergence of the two logics enabled the authoritative resources of the state to be effectively mobilized, through the Ministry of Finance, in favour of financial market reform — first under the Socialists, and eventually under the 'neo-liberal' Right too. Rather than setting the markets a task and simply overseeing their attempts to fulfil it, as in the classic self-regulatory mode, the French state has imposed reform in a step-by-step manner.

The reform process, 1984–7

In November 1984, in order to focus public attention on the new policy direction, Bérégovoy became the first Minister of Finance to visit to the Bourse since 1962. Reforms introduced since 1983 fall into six major categories: authorization of new financial instruments and decompartmentalization of various capital markets; extension of the negotiability of commissions; tightening of regulatory supervision; privatization; modifying the role of the *agents de change;* and attempts to start a process of internationalization.[30]

The introduction of new financial instruments was the first major step. At first these were mainly longer-term;[31] the next stage, in line with trends abroad, was a range of more flexible medium- and short-term instruments which could be freely traded by banks and other institutions as well. A key innovation was the introduction of negotiable bank certificates of deposit.[32] More new instruments were to follow in rapid succession.[33] The market for new short-term instruments (including CDs and commercial paper) rose from 31 billion francs at the end of December 1985 to 255 billion by 30 September 1986, with the lion's share (75 per cent) taken up by negotiable Treasury bills.[34] New instruments for interest rate and currency hedging were copied from international markets; swaps are an example. A new *caisse* for mortgage refinancing was set up.[35] And a variety of new banking institutions emerged to operate in the 'new money market' which, although outside both the Bourse and the old interbank market, was open to actors from both.[36]

Probably the most important structural breakthrough was the 1986 opening of the Paris financial futures market — the Marché à Terme des Instruments Financiers, or MATIF. The *Journal des Finances* headlined its opening 'When Pierre Bérégovoy gets his inspiration from Chicago', with the apparent paradox that 'Under a Socialist government, and with elections just three weeks away, Paris sees the opening of a futures market: the last word in capitalism'.[37] Although real competition with Chicago is not feasible, the MATIF' main contract quickly became competitive with its London equivalent.[38] The new exchange soon had to move to new and more spacious quarters. Most importantly, with only half of the seats reserved to the *agents de change*, the MATIF represented the first major breach of the brokers' monopoly in an integral part of the Bourse itself — and the reverberations have been felt all around the financial system. The establishment of a traded options market in 1987 has continued the process.

The second major set of reforms concerned the fixing of commissions for financial services. This has been a key structural issue in the reform of other securities markets.[39] Fixed commissions have not been eliminated in France, but were negotiable first for the private sector in March 1985, then for the public sector in December. Brokerage commissions are still fixed on smaller transactions, but on larger transactions they are freely negotiable on the entire transaction. This attests to the tendency of deregulated markets to favour the largest (and highest-rated) borrowers and investors. The third major set of reforms involved the extension of the powers of the main regulatory body, the Commission des Opérations de Bourse, (as well as the Commission Bancaire and the Conseil de la Concurrence). Its brief has widened with the new financial market reform act (Law of 22 January 1988). As for other regulatory bodies, the Commission Bancaire was revamped in the 1984 banking reforms, and the powers and remit of the Conseil de la Concurrence are being extended in the areas of price fixing, information and control of takeovers.[40]

A fourth major change has been to privatize public sector firms. The first privatizations, of the Saint-Gobain conglomerate and the Banque Paribas, were very successful, with the former attracting 1.5 million shareholders and the latter 3.8 million. But the October 1987 crash and the 1988 elections have halted the privatization programme. The main impact of the privatizations on the Bourse was that the markets could not cope with the volume of early trading, with brokers unable to make a price in the new shares. Indeed, it was estimated 'that as much as 15 per cent of the daily turnover in French stocks now takes place in London, where six houses make a market in leading French shares without transactions passing through the Paris stock exchange',[41] and it is likely that over half of the turnover of the biggest French stocks takes place in London.

This leads us to consider the fifth major set of reforms.[42] The brokers' monopoly has been the main obstacle to opening market structures. A protected profession, well off but not particularly dynamic — there is only one *agent de change* in *L'Expansion's* 1987 list of the 100 richest people in France — is faced not only with adaptation and expansion but also a major shake-out of firms. There has always been a significant minority prepared to adapt, but many existing positions have been undermined because the *charges* are so undercapitalized. The banks have long been pushing to play a greater role in the markets, but while the main competition was merely the French commercial banks, with their own problems of competitiveness, brokers were able to resist.

Again, it was state pressure, combined with international market forces, which hastened the pace. The flood of new financial instruments and decompartmentalization of markets have led to a search for greater competitiveness, which means a need for larger firms and higher capitalization. The reduction of commissions and the sheer number of markets to deal with all the time require higher turnover, and this means more personnel, more highly qualified personnel (with higher salaries) and investment in computerization. Particularly significant for brokerage methods has been the development of continuous trading on the Bourse. And expanding market activities will eventually require participants to make markets themselves — a very underdeveloped activity in Paris — and to engage in arbitrage.

This leads to the final factor, the lack of international competitiveness of, and foreign participation in, the French markets. There were over 100 official positions of *agent de change* in 1988, and until quite recently they maintained individual practices. However, mergers among *charges* have been increasing in pace, the number of firms falling to sixty-one; only a small number, perhaps ten, carry out the majority of business, although statistics are not available. But by 1986 it had become clear that *agents de change* were facing serious difficulties with new challenges even in their own bailiwick, the share market. Restructuring became imperative.

Indeed, an end to the *agents de change* monopoly seemed inevitable. The reform announced by Finance Minister Edouard Balladur in March 1987 — later to become the Law of 22 January 1988 — was intended to do just this, but in a gradual way. Since 1 January 1988, 30 per cent of the capital of a *charge* may be owned by outsiders; from 1 January 1989, up to 49 per cent; and from 1 January 1990, 100 per cent. Outsiders, French or foreign, will be vetted by the new Stock Exchange Council (Conseil des Bourses) — which along with a new clearing house has replaced the CAC — and the Treasury. *Charges* can expand in the money market, and can register under the Banking Act to provide a full range of investment banking services. A small percentage of the firms' capital can be floated publicly.

The monopoly will formally end on 1 January 1993, at the same time as the European Community's 'single market', which includes financial services, is due to come into effect. *Agents* who find it impossible to adapt will eventually be indemnified by the new authority. The reform has been compared with the British Goodison–Parkinson agreement of 1983, although there are significant differences. The final stage is to promote internationalization of French financial markets in the future, but there is a long way to go.[43] The most important direct step, however, was the agreement by EEC finance ministers in 1986 on a package of liberalization measures in the context of the 'single market' to remove exchange controls on long-term credit and on buying and selling unlisted securities, unit trusts, and so on; new financial instruments are to be included. M. Delors, now President of the Commission, also proposed that all transactions on EEC money markets be freed from control — not just those related to commercial transactions.[44] This is particularly important in the light of proposals, taken seriously by French brokers and bankers, for setting up a computerized continental European market, possibly centred on Paris, linking all existing major European exchanges, in order to rival London in the global marketplace. Such a market would have an advantage in relaying trading from the Far East, as it would be able to open an hour ahead of London, but at the moment it is still a gleam in the eye of the French.

Concomitant changes have also been taking place since 1984 outside the financial markets. The international French banking network, the world's second largest until 1985 when it was overtaken by the Japanese, has had to be rationalized as well; it too was based on extensive branch networks and volume of business rather than on high capitalization and profitability. At the same time, the state-sponsored credit system has changed. The key has been a cutback in subsidized loans. In 1979, three-quarters of all loans to business came from state or para-state institutions, including nationalized banks and subsidiaries; 43 per cent were subsidized by the state. Most state support came through direct subsidies and privileged refinancing arrangements. In 1982–3, the government began to 'banalize' these loans as market rates fell.[45] Total subsidized loans dropped by about a quarter from 1983 to 1986, while budget costs fell from 45 billion francs in 1985 to only 16 billion in 1986. Support for exports has shifted from subsidized loans to direct subsidies and pure guarantees.[46] Thus the extension of the financial markets has paralleled the decline of the credit system. However, cuts in direct subsidies have been difficult to make.[47] Exchange controls have been all but lifted since 1985. And perhaps the most crucial component of that *dirigiste* strategy in the 1970s, the *encadrement du crédit* system, was phased out between 1985 and 1987.

The crash and the future of *Dirigisme*

All of these changes have the potential to undermine the *dirigisme* of the French state. There are two major questions, however. The first is whether the reforms themselves will stick. The second is whether they will alter *dirigiste* state-economy relationships in any quasi-paradigmatic way. The financial market boom in France between 1982 and 1986 was more fragile than in the major internationalized marketplaces. The CAC index peaked in March 1987; its decline began more than six months before the crash. A bear market in bonds, noted in the United States as a sign that a stock market crash might be coming, started earlier and was more severe in France than elsewhere. With a fall of over a third from its peak, and over a quarter from its pre-crash level, the Bourse was hit far harder than New York or London, but about the same as other major continental markets such as Milan, Frankfurt and Zurich.[48] Foreign interest in buying into French brokers was already declining before the crash, but the process is likely to accelerate as the European 'single market' approaches. And the Bourse has been hit by the world-wide post-crash syndrome of 'coming home', which in the French case means that foreign investors, so recently won by the reforms, have cut their holdings from an estimated 25 per cent to around 14 per cent of share capital. Nevertheless, share prices stabilized after the elections in May and June 1988, and have risen strongly since August.

The MATIF and the more recent traded options market have stabilized after some serious difficulties.[49] The bond market has been the strongest, having benefited, like bond markets elsewhere, from a 'flight to quality' since October and from the small downward trend in interest rates since then. The biggest victim was privatization. Suspicions remain that privatization, rather than bringing cash to the markets, also had the perverse effect of soaking up existing liquidity, crowding out other market activity — contributing to the severity of the crash when it came. Finally, the reforms so far have been gradual, step-by-step ones. Trading is still limited to the exchanges during opening hours (the 'single price' policy), which further limits any embryonic market-making. And the brokers' monopoly will not be lifted until 1993, despite provisions for wider ownership. Thus although the state has reaffirmed its commitment to reform, the future is uncertain.

But what will happen to the French economy — and to *dirigisme?* There will be advantages for firms which are in a position to raise funds on the capital markets. However, debate is fierce among economists as to whether expansion of financial markets actually helps or hinders, the 'real economy', and the manufacturing base in particular. It is often said that financial markets reinforce tendencies towards 'short-termism'. And it has been argued that open financial markets privilege the 'best risks' — big firms with high ratings. Brokers and bankers require high turnover to make profits while large borrowers can negotiate low commissions on big transactions. This may lead to a 'dual market' mentality, where the markets engage in securities transactions with multinational firms and large banks, while other borrowers are required to find loans from hard-pressed banks (which would themselves prefer to move 'up-market' — or queue for state subsidies). World markets would seem to be going in this direction. Finally, it is often said that the best risks — the big borrowers — are more interested in recycling old debt through hedging than raising new investment capital.

Dirigisme, in this context, loses its macro-economic function. What would be left would be a mixture of indirect, open market instruments, middle-level clientelism and micro-economic policies for small and medium-sized firms. But financial markets provide opportunities for new forms of state–economy concertation, too. Indeed, one of the main beneficiaries may be public sector firms. On bond markets, the most favoured borrowers are sovereigns and public sector firms with a state guarantee. Prior to privatization in France, the Socialists seemed to see financial market reform as compatible with a dynamic public sector which would no longer be a burden on the state. The British Labour Party seems to have adopted a similar approach to public sector funding in its industrial strategy in the mid-1980s.

At this stage, then, France seems to be replacing 'strategic' *dirigisme* with 'tactical' *dirigisme* — or what might be called 'arms-length *dirigisme'*.[50] Of course, such tactical *dirigisme* has probably been more characteristic of state-economy relations through French history than the strategic pretensions of neo-*Colbertisme* would admit. In the future, the more dynamic sectors of French industry, whether purely through market forces or in conjunction with particular state agencies on a corporatist or clientelist basis (the 'competition state'), will form the core of the search for competitive advantage, whether successfully or unsuccessfully.[51]

But in a world context where even Japan is experimenting with deregulation, this reflects international constraints rather than domestic choice. On that level, the French government sees international policy co-operation, on the quasi-Gaullist model of the Louvre Accords, as the model for future intervention. It is for international reasons, more than any other, that the period when the choice was between 'la Bourse ou l'emploi '[52] is over. Traditional conceptions of state intervention on both Left and Right are already changing.[53] The financial revolution is here to stay, and the state will inevitably adjust its line of fire, even if it has itself to evolve in order to do so.

Notes

1. Eric A. Nordlinger, *On the Autonomy of the Democratic State* (Cambridge, MASS.: Harvard University Press, 1981), p. 15.
2. For a more elaborate consideration of the theoretical problems of *dirigisme,* see Philip G. Cerny, *The Financial Revolution and the State* (Oxford: Oxford University Press, forthcoming).
3. Peter A. Hall, *Governing the Economy: The Politics of State Intervention in France and Britain* (Oxford: Polity Press, 1986).
4. John Zysman, *Governments, Markets and Growth: Financial Systems and the Politics of Industrial Change* (Ithaca, NY: Cornell University Press, 1983).
5. Howard Machin and Vincent Wright (eds), *Economic Policy and Policy-making under the Mitterrand Presidency, 1981–84* (London: Frances Pinter, 1985); J. E.

S. Hayward, *The State and the Market Economy: Industrial Patriotism and Economic Intervention in France* (Brighton: Wheatsheaf, 1986); S. Estrin and P. Holmes, *French Planning in Theory and Practice* (London: Allen & Unwin, 1982); Douglas E. Ashford, *British Dogmatism and French Pragmatism; Central-Local Policymaking in the Welfare State* (London: Allen & Unwin, 1982); Frank L. Wilson, 'French Interest Group Politics: Pluralist or Neocorporatist?', *American Political Science Review*, vol. 77, no. 4 (December 1983); Irene B. Wilson, 'Decentralising or Recentralising the State? Urban Planning and Centre-Periphery Relations' in P.G. Cerny and M.A. Schain (eds), *Socialism, the State and Public Policy in France* (London: Frances Pinter, 1985).

6. Michael Moran, 'Deregulating Britain, Deregulating America: The Case of the Securities Industry', paper presented to the Workshop on Deregulation in Western Europe, European Consortium for Political Research, Amsterdam (10–15 April 1987).

7. P. Sassier and F. de Witt, *Les Français à la corbeille* (Paris: Robert Laffont, 1986).

8. See Richard F. Kuisel, *Capitalism and the State in Modern France: Renovation and Economic Management in the Twentieth Century* (Cambridge: Cambridge University Press, 1981).

9. J.-P. Rioux, 'A Changing of the Guard? Old and New Elites at the Liberation', tr. P.G. Cerny, in Jolyon Howorth and P.G. Cerny (eds), *Elites in France* (London: Frances Pinter, 1981).

10. John Zysman, *Political Strategies for Industrial Order: State, Market and Industry in France* (Berkeley: University of California Press, 1977); and Suzanne Berger, 'Lame Ducks and National Champions: Industrial Policy in the Fifth Republic', in William G. Andrews and Stanley Hoffmann (eds), *The Fifth Republic at Twenty* (Brockport, NY: State University of New York Press, 1981).

11. See Hayward, *The State* ; and Machin and Wright, *Economic Policy*.

12. See Peter A. Hall, 'Socialism in One Country: Mitterrand and the Struggle to Define a New Economic Policy for France'; and Philip G. Cerny, 'State Capitalism in France and Britain and the International Economic Order' in Cerny and Schain (eds), *Socialism, the State and Public Policy in France*.

13. See D. North, *Structure and Change in Economic History* (New York: Norton, 1981), for a 'neo-classical' argument in this vein.

14. See P.G. Cerny, 'The "Little Big Bang" in Paris: Financial Market Deregulation in a dirigiste system', *European Journal of Political Research* (1989) and Cerny, The Financial Revolution and the State.

15. See Susan Strange, *Casino Capitalism* (Oxford: Basil Blackwell, 1986).

16. See Cerny, *The Financial Revolution and the State*.

17. *Financial Times*, 26 January 1973.

18. *Le Point*, 18 October 1976.

19. *L'Unité, 3 June 1977.*

20. *Financial Times*, 11 March 1987; 'CSFB Annual Financing Report', *Euromoney* supplement, March 1987.

21. Diana M. Green, 'The Seventh Plan — The Demise of French Planning?', *West European Politics*, vol. 1, no. 1 (February 1978), pp. 60–70.

22. Diana M. Green, with P.G. Cerny, 'Economic Policy and the Governing Coalition' in Cerny and Schain, *French Politics and Public Policy*.

23. *Le Monde*, 2 January 1979.

24. *Les Echos*, 31 December 1981.

160   *Economic Policy*

25. *Le Monde*, 9 February and 9 March 1982; *Le Matin*, 6 February and 25 May 1982.
26. *Les Echos*, 3 January 1983.
27. *Journal des Finances*, numerous articles, February–July 1984; *Le Monde*, 16–17 October 1983.
28. Hall, 'Socialism in One Country'.
29. See his preface to the *Livre blanc sur la réforme du financement de l'économie* (Paris: Documentation Française, 1986); interview, December 1986.
30. For more details, see Cerny, 'The "Little Big Bang" in Paris'.
31. See the *Revue Banque*, 1984.
32. C. Noyer, 'Les certificats de dépot', *Revue Banque* (July 1985), pp. 693–8.
33. See J.-P. Guimbert, 'Exploitants et nouvelles techniques de marchés',*Revue Banque* (March 1987), pp. 224-33.
34. L. Marchetti, 'Les titres de créances négotiables à court terme', *Revue Banque* (December 1986), pp. 1100–4.
35. D. Saglio, 'La réforme du marché hypothécaire', *Revue Banque* (January 1986), pp. 31–4.
36. See *International Financing Review*, 8 April 1986; E. Bertier, 'Drôle de banques', *L'Expansion* (7–20 November 1986), pp. 106–13; and B. Beaufils, G. Py, B. Richard, B. Thiry, and J.-P. Guimbert, *La Banque et les nouveaux instruments financiers: la pratique des marchés* (Paris: la Revue Banque, Editeur, 1986).
37. 22–28 February 1986.
38. G. de la Martiniére, 'Le Matif aprés quatre mois', *Revue Banque* (October 1986), pp. 839–46; *Financial Times*, 27 January 1987.
39. Moran, 'Deregulating'.
40. *Le Monde*, 5 November 1986.
41. *Financial Times*, 11 March 1987.
42. This section has benefited greatly from interviews with MM, Xavier Dupont, President of the Chambre Syndicale des Agents de Change, Jean-Jacques Burgard, Délégué Général of the Association Française des Banques, and Jacques Moreau, President of the Crédit Cooperatif, December 1986.
43. A. Fourcans, V. Hubert, and D. Pène, 'Paris: la grande place financière de demain?', *Revue Banque* (May 1987), pp. 438–43; Xavier Dupont, 'La réforme de la Bourse', *Revue Banque* (November 1987), pp. 1042–4; C. de Gournay, 'Paris, place financière européenne pour vos placements monétaires et obligataires', *Revue Banque* (March 1988), pp. 290–4.
44. *Financial Times*, 18 November 1986.
45. *Les Echos*, 10 October 1982 and 22 September 1983.
46. *Revue Banque*, November 1986 and March 1987.
47. E. Bertier, 'Couper les aides? Pas si facile ...', *L'Expansion*, (20 March – 2 April 1987), pp. 84–91.
48. *The Banker*, January 1988; *Euromoney*, January 1988; *Le Monde*, 29 December 1987 and 9 January 1988.
49. *Financial Times*, 10 March 1988.
50. Interview with M. Jean-Marcel Jeanneney, Director of the Observatoire Français des Conjonctures Economiques, December 1986.
51. I am grateful to Professor Jack Hayward for focusing my attention on this point.
52. *L'Humanité*, 14 February 1986.

53. P.G. Cerny, 'From the Welfare State to the Competition State: British and French Industrial Policy in Perspective', in C. Farrands (ed.), *Industrial Intervention in France and Britain* (London: University Association for Contemporary European Studies, 1988).

Part IV: Social Policy

11. The new shape of French Labour and industrial relations: *Ce n'est plus la même chose*

Mark Kesselman

Like many features of the Fifth Republic, within the area of organized labour and industrial relations it is time to abandon the old saw that *plus ça change, plus c'est la même chose*. There have been more extensive changes in industrial relations and organized labour in the past decade than in the entire post-war period through the 1970s.

In reviewing the period from the Liberation until the present, one can discern a relatively stable pattern of industrial relations that prevailed in France from the end of the Second World War until the late 1960s. The real divide, thus, occurred not from the Fourth to the Fifth Republic but within the Fifth Republic. Four phases in the evolution of organized labour and industrial relations in the post-war period can be identified.

1947–68: CGT maximalism versus other unions' accommodation

Workers have typically been a relatively marginalized and excluded class within French politics and society. Despite the fact that organized labour and the Left emerged from the Second World War in a powerful position, as a result of the discredit of the bourgeoisie and the Right, the situation quickly changed. By contrast to the nations of Northern Europe, the Cold War divided and weakened the French working class, as workers split their support between political parties and unions fundamentally opposed regarding their international stance. Thus, organized labour was fragmented among several unions, each seeking to recruit among the same potential constituency. Organizational rivalry weakened every union and meant that the whole labour movement was less than the sum of its parts. By pursuing divergent ideological goals, unions were less able to achieve any.

If French unions were entirely separate, they were far from equal. The Confédération Générale du Travail (CGT) was hegemonic within the labour movement, with greater organizational reach and more members than all other unions combined. The CGT contributed to centrifugal pressures within the labour movement by its close ties to the Communist Party, noisy opposition to the existing political and economic system, and willingness to engage in direct protest to pursue its goals. The CGT's maximalist strategy and confrontational tactics set the tone for the entire labour movement and the industrial system.

Given organized labour's weaknesses and divisions, as well as CGT dominance, it is hardly surprising that industrial relations were highly conflictual in France. Employers were reluctant to bargain and compromise, both because the CGT insistently demanded *toujours plus* and because neither the balance of class forces nor legal compulsion obliged employers to adopt a conciliatory stance. The result was that industrial relations consisted of a relatively unmediated class struggle.

The legal framework of industrial relations contributed importantly to this result. On the one hand, there was no legal compulsion for employers to engage in collective bargaining, and little in fact occurred, especially at lower (enterprise) levels. (Not until 1982 were employers required to bargain collectively.) Indeed, labour unions had an uncertain legal existence — dating back to the *loi Le Chapellier* — and did not gain legal protection at the enterprise level until after the May 1968 uprising. As a result, shop-floor relations in France were tense, chaotic and conflictual. Management enjoyed little legitimacy or support, discipline was severe, and strikes frequent. In brief, the industrial relations system displayed little capacity to regulate conflict privately.

On the other hand, or rather in symbiotic relationship with extensive class conflict at lower levels, class relations were politicized and extremely regulated at higher levels. Union and employer federations frequently bargained on an industry-wide basis, and the state intervened extensively to regulate wages, hours and working conditions - the stuff of (private) collective bargaining elsewhere.

The picture closely resembles the classic model of French authority relations first suggested by de Tocqueville and elaborated by Michel Crozier and Stanley Hoffmann. The key element was the extensive distance and antagonism between opponents at the face-to-face level, with conflict 'exported' outwards from civil society to the political sphere and channelled upward to the centralized state.

A key to the traditional model was CGT dominance of the trade union movement. The CGT's stance within the sphere of industrial relations paralleled that of the PCF in the political sphere: total opposition. In practice, because the CGT adopted the traditional syndicalist position of opposing power-sharing arrangements which might integrate workers within the firm, it placed major priority on maximizing wage gains. Given rapid economic growth and virtually full employment during the period, the CGT's productivist approach seemed a plausible and effective strategy. After 1964, however, CGT hegemony within the labour movement was challenged by the newly secularized and radicalized Confédération Démocratique du Travail (CFDT). (The third major union, Force Ouvrière [FO] has followed a quite constant strategy of espousing bread and butter demands.) The CFDT became the vehicle for representing grievances that the CGT neglected: non-productivist 'qualitative' demands linked to the ravages produced by forced-march industrialization, including occupational hazards, rigid hierarchy in the workplace, urban depredation and inadequate social facilities.

1968-74

The force of the May movement derived, it should be recalled, not primarily from student strikes which immobilized universities but from workers' strikes which immoblilized factories and offices. The uprising challenged not only the Gaullist regime, but the CGT as well, because of its economism.

The May movement induced the Gaullist state to seek ways to integrate workers and the CGT to radicalize its agenda. Both failed in the short run, although eventually workers became far more integrated within the firm.

For a brief period after 1968, the state partially succeeded in institutionalizing capital–labour relations at the national and industry-wide levels. Whereas five national-level collective bargaining agreements were concluded between the employers association (the CNPF) and unions in the ten years prior to 1968, the number increased to sixty-seven in the following ten years. National-level collective-bargaining agreements were negotiated on a wide variety of layoff, sick-leave and unemployment insurance. Collective bargaining agreements were concluded regulating minimum-wage levels, working conditions and skill classifications in important sectors, including petroleum, chemicals and textiles.

In 1969–71, as part of his New Society plan for easing class tensions in France, Prime Minister Chaban-Delmas sought to stabilize labour relations within the state bureaucracy and provide a model for private industry to emulate. Management–union agreements were concluded in many administrative agencies and nationalized industries. With the onset of the economic crisis after 1974, however, negotiations languished; when Prime Minister Raymond Barre froze wages in the state sector in 1976, the rationale for collective bargaining crumbled altogether. Moreover, even during the most intense period of collective bargaining within the state and private sector, the practice never took root at lower levels.

Benefiting from the new militancy that persisted after May 1968, the CFDT posed a radical challenge to CGT control by championing *autogestion* and participating in factory occupations (including the sequestering of managers). The CGT responded by broadening its own agenda. An even more important impetus than CFDT pressure for the CGT to modify its traditional practice was the economic crisis beginning in 1974, which jeopardized full employment and steady wage gains—the fundaments of the CGT's maximalist stance. At the same time, the two major unions began to accord priority to an electoral victory of the Left, which promised the possibility of widespread changes occurring through friendly state intervention.

1974-81

Following the 1974 oil shock and the ensuing international recession, for the first time in decades full employment and steady wage gains could no longer be taken for granted. As factories closed, unemployment began to creep up, and the CFDT scored important advances, the CGT was forced to modify its policy of placing highest priority on wage gains as the 'universal equivalent'. Such goals as regulating conditions of layoffs and providing unemployment insurance assumed growing importance.

When the CGT modified its stance to accommodate CFDT demands, the groundwork was laid for a period of unity in action between the two unions. The unions developed a new 'offensive strategy', which aimed to give unions a voice in economic decision-making and also sought to achieve an electoral victory of the Left in order to gain support from a sympathetic state. However, the dual strategy was a total failure: the state and employers rejected the unions' initiative and the unions' hopes of a political victory of the Left were dashed. After the Union of the Left shattered and the Left lost the 1978 parliamentary elections, the union movement was forced again to modify its strategy.

The failure of the policies pursued in the 1970s drove the CGT and CFDT apart. The CGT moved back toward a maximalism, although now it broadened its demands to include *autogestion*. The CGT occupied a central position in the PCF's plan to supplement (and eventually replace) capitalist profit-making with new, socially desirable criteria for managerial decision-making, such as maximizing employment and halting deindustrialization in France. In the revised approach, the CGT would guide workers to intervene more effectively within their firm.

The CFDT moved in an opposite direction. Calculating that its previous strategy of relying on a political solution to the crisis was mistaken, and that declining worker militancy (the strike rate began to plummet in 1979) precluded change through confrontation, the CFDT adopted a policy of *recentrage* and *resyndicalisation*. The new approach emphasized concrete union actions at the grassroots level. However, in total contrast to its radicalized policy of the early 1970s, the CFDT's recentred strategy consisted of seeking to negotiate realistic solutions to concrete problems within management. The distance between the CGT and CFDT could not have been greater. Although events were apparently to arbitrate in the CFDT's favour, neither approach has resolved growing problems within the labour movement that have reached crisis proportions.

1981 to present

The election of a left-wing government in 1981 helped tip the balance towards the CFDT's post-1978 approach, in which the unions' primary task was to negotiate the terms of industrial adaptation and modernization. The CFDT's new realism seemed plausible both because the Socialist government sponsored policies to institutionalize industrial relations and because the period revealed the limits of what might be expected from even a friendly government. The traditional confrontational model of industrial relations in France is in the process of being replaced by a model involving negotiations, consultation, and integration of workers within the firm. At the same time, there has been a recomposition of the labour movement, with CGT hegemony replaced by an alliance of moderate unions.

The new situation is linked to a key paradox: at the same time as organized labour is experiencing a severe crisis, unions (and other representative mechanisms) have assumed an expanded role as a major legitimate participant within economic and social institutions. Unions have suffered heavy membership losses and severe setbacks in face of state and business initiatives; the labour movement is more divided than ever. Yet, within the past decade organized labour has achieved an important position in corporatist mechanisms and there has been an enormous increase in collective bargaining, especially at the firm level: the balance has shifted within the union movement from class confrontation to moderation.

The crisis of French labour: four elements

The depleted ranks of organized labour. Trade unions organize an increasingly small proportion of workers — by latest estimates a paltry 15-18 per cent of the labour force. According to some estimates, the CGT has lost fully half its members since the mid-1970s; and the CFDT officially admitted to losing nearly one-fifth of its members between 1976 and 1983. These losses are in part a result of the economic crisis: the most extensive layoffs have occurred in basic industries: steel, automobiles, shipbuilding, and textiles, where unions are strongest, as well as in industrialized regions where unions were traditionally based (notably, the North). Additionally, the economic crisis has deprived unions of a growth dividend, the principal object of union activity in the past. Given the open shop in most French industries, workers see little benefit in union membership.

A crisis of tactics: the strike as an archaic weapon? In the past, French unions generally achieved gains through actual or threatened confrontation rather than collective bargaining. Unions were weakly established within the workplace and collective bargaining at the plant level was unusual. Instead, unions applied pressure through mobilization: the strike was the pre-eminent means of demonstrating union strength. A dramatic decline in the strike rate suggests the new vulnerability of organized labour. Between 1973 and 1982, the monthly average of days lost from strikes was 230,000. The comparable figure was 110,000 in 1983–4, with another precipitous decline (to 60,000) in 1985. After a modest rise in 1986, it declined again in 1987.

Strategic crisis: the domestication of organized labour. Within the union movement, there has been a shift toward greater moderation. But in a period of economic crisis and adaptation, it is not clear how the new moderation will generate benefits for union members. The new stance is linked to a recomposition of the trade union movement.

Until the 1970s, CGT strength, measured by size of membership, performance in professional elections, and organizational reach, rivalled that of all other union confederations combined. At present, the CGT is merely first among two other equals (the CFDT and FO), and the fact that it often confronts a united front of these and other unions further seals its decline. In a similar although less extreme fashion to that of the PCF in the political sphere, the CGT has sought to preserve its dominance by defiantly espousing a hard-line attitude. The CGT opposes negotiating concessions in the social or economic realm which would sanction layoffs, weaken employment guarantees, and reduce workers' purchasing power. In the CGT's view, union demands must not be confined to defending past gains but should advance new solutions to the crisis. Three key elements include an alternative pattern of growth, based on increased employment and collective consumption, new criteria of decision-making in production consistent with the first goal, and expanding, strengthening and democratizing the public sector.[1] The CGT's brave new rhetoric has failed to convince workers; although the union's decline is far less steep than that of the PCF, it follows a similar curve.

The fact that FO has made substantial inroads into CGT support is especially noteworthy, for FO has been disdainful of revolutionary slogans or structural reforms and is often regarded as the archetype of a business union. (However, FO has at times been quite militant on wage issues.) In one recent poll soliciting workers' preferences, FO outranked the CGT.[2] In elections to the *comités d'entreprise* (works committees) in the private sector, CGT support declined from 38.6 per cent to 29.3 per cent between 1978 and 1984, while FO increased substantially, from 10.0 per cent to 13.9 per cent. (The other large shift, which bodes badly for organized labour as a whole, was the increase in votes for candidates not members of any unions: from 16.3 per cent to 19.7 per cent.) In elections to the *conseils de prud'hommes* (labour mediation tribunals) in December 1987, FO support increased from 17.4 per cent to 20.5 per cent.

Within the CFDT, all traces of new Left feistiness have disappeared. The CFDT has completely abandoned its previous strategy, which sought to achieve democratic planning, social appropriation of means of production, and *autogestion*. Its new strategy accepts and praises market mechanisms while seeking a greater voice for organized labour in negotiating the terms of economic modernization. In 1984 Edmond Maire presented a report to the Conseil National of the CFDT denouncing the Marxist vestiges within the CFDT's ideology. *Autogestion,* formerly the CFDT's ideological anchor, is now considered merely one among several legitimate approaches. Maire went further in 1986. In an article in the CFDT's theoretical journal, he discerned two logics within the firm: that of management (whose main goals are financial gain and a favourable competitive position for the firm within the market), and that of workers (who seek employment security, adequate wages, improved working conditions, and challenging work). Both logics (and hence both social forces) are legitimate; their interrelationship is one of 'conflictual co-operation': the two logics should 'function together, each with its own legitimacy and according to its own perspective'.[3] Maire praised the market as a 'factor of modernization, adaptation, and ultimate guarantor of individual choices'. He denounced the strike as an outmoded instrument, and suggested that 'class struggle is part of a Manichean vocabulary that obscures more than it describes (clarifies)'.

Yet whether unions have become intransigent (the CGT), more moderate (the CFDT), or pursued their traditional course (FO), they have proved unable to revitalize the labour movement. All have failed to organize major new elements within the working class, notably women, immigrant workers, youth, and the unemployed.

Union membership and collective identity. Perhaps most troubling of all is that unions appear unable to redefine an appropriate identity as a collective actor in the present period. Traditionally, unions symbolized the solidarity of the working class in its confrontation with management. Implicitly, the class model which informed their activity was that of a homogeneous, male, native, industrial proletariat: the 'man of iron'. This was never an accurate picture of the French working class — but never less so than currently, when women, immigrants, and technical and service sector workers are key elements of the working class. The fragmentation and internationalization of the working class means that workers have increasingly diverse situations within production. Moreover, the very concepts of class solidarity and consciousness are questionable in the new situation.

The new mode of union-busting

Part of the explanation for labour's difficulties is that management has been highly successful in using the economic crisis to pursue anti-union strategies. In the past, the French *patronat's* patriarchal and repressive stance nourished class confrontation. In the current period, management has become more sophisticated, notably by responding more effectively than unions to the widespread desire for individual expression, autonomy, flexibility, and participation. Examples include awarding wage gains on an individualized 'merit' basis, hiring part-time workers, and introducing new consultative mechanisms wholly under management control. The foremost example of the latter is quality circles, whose importance can be gauged by their phenomenal growth in France: from fewer than 500 in May 1981 to 3,000 in 1983, 10,000 in 1984, and 30,000 in 1986. The firms belonging to the French Association for Quality Circles claim to employ 40 per cent of the workforce.[4]

Another reason why unions have encountered difficulty representing workers' grievances is that Socialist government industrial relations reforms (the Auroux laws, to be reviewed below) sponsored in the early 1980s strengthened non-union channels of consultation and representation. Although union militants often play key roles in these organizations, participation further stretches the unions' already thin resources. Moreover, the existence of other channels of representation may undermine the rationale for unions.

Unions as partners

Yet unions have not simply declined in importance; they have assumed important new responsibilities, which they exercise through collective bargaining rather than confrontation. The Socialist government (1981–6) played a key role in transforming the labour movement.

The Socialist government sought, in its words, to 'contractualize' social relations through collective bargaining and worker consultation. Its not-so-hidden agenda in this sphere was to weaken the CGT's dominance within the labour movement and to replace confrontation by co-operation between management and labour. The government was highly successful in achieving these aims. It was less successful in unifying organized labour and mobilizing union support for the Socialist party.

The Auroux laws were the major mechanism intended to modify industrial relations. The reform packages strengthened unions, works committees, and health and safety committees, required employers to engage in collective bargaining at the plant and higher levels, and granted workers the right to discuss working conditions and other aspects of production in company time. The shift affecting unions most directly was the expansion of collective bargaining. Employers are now required to negotiate with unions at firm and industry-wide levels on wages, hours, working conditions, job classifications, vocational training and technological innovations.

The reforms have had an important impact on French industrial relations. Take wage determination. Prior to passage of the Auroux laws, there were only a few hundred company-level collective bargaining agreements in effect throughout France involving wage levels. In 1983, the first year in which the collective bargaining requirement was applied, negotiations on effective wages, hours of work and working conditions took place in 42 per cent of the 12,000 firms with union representation; agreements were concluded in nearly 2,000 firms. In 1985, the proportion of firms where negotiations occurred nearly doubled to 71.5 per cent, and agreements were reached in 5,000 firms.[5] Other bargaining and consultative procedures have also flourished within recent years, including works committees, health and safety committees, and expression groups.

The state has increasingly renounced direct responsibility for regulating industrial conflict. Instead, it has sought to privatize industrial relations by mandating collective bargaining at all levels. For example, rather than simply abolishing the requirement for administrative authorization for layoffs, the Chirac government enjoined representatives of management and labour to negotiate the conditions by which management could lay off workers. Another example: management must consult with a firm's works committees before introducing important technological innovations and the works committee can hire an expert, at company expense, to advise it in this area.[6]

Recent collective bargaining agreements suggest tendencies towards institutionalizing class relations. Several industry-wide agreements regulate the introduction of new technology. In the metallurgy industry, a key sector, management agreed to encourage the creation of collective work teams, which would permit workers to acquire new skills, and to increase workers' autonomy and decision-making power. The aim was to improve product quality, reliability of production, and flexibility.

Representatives of management and labour have gone even further to develop an agenda for negotiations. In June 1987, the principal employers' organization, the CNPF, signed an agreement on vocational training with all unions except the CGT, which also provided for lower-level negotiations on this issue. In May 1988, the CNPF agreed with all major unions except the CGT to designate five major issue areas as the focus of future negotiations: the organization of work time, mobility,

equal pay for men and women, working conditions, and occupational
hazards.

The past several years have produced a fundamental shift in production relations in France. Given the range of topics subject to collective
bargaining and consultation, and the greater integration of workers
within the firm, the traditional pattern of class confrontation is
increasingly exceptional. Yet one should not equate the tendency towards
more extensive collective bargaining with increased union strength. For
one thing, participation has increased the gulf between leaders and union
members.[7] Further, management has often seized the opportunity
offered by negotiations to increase its power in a period of economic
crisis, often gaining union support for industrial reorganization which
curtails workers' past gains. For example, Segrestin reports that the
ordonnance of January 1982, which reduced the work week from 40 to 39
hours, called for peak-level negotiations to decide on the new scheduling
of work-time. The *ordonnance* also authorized employers to abrogate
existing labour law if a collective bargaining agreement was reached with
union locals. Soon after, collective bargaining agreements in 600 firms
diluted workers' rights.[8]

The key to explaining the paradox

How can one explain the paradox of declining union militancy and
increasing union participation and legitimacy? I suggest that the two
trends are complementary, not divergent; they are linked by the
recomposition of the labour movement, notably the CGT's decline. When
the CGT was the hegemonic force within organized labour, union
participation was not a surrogate for *contestation* but a means to pursue it
more effectively. The weakening of the union movement, its growing
moderation, and particularly the CGT's loss of dominance mean that the
state and management have less to fear from union participation.

Without seeking to provide a full explanation for the deradicalization
of the French labour movement (which parallels a similar change in the
political sphere), I would emphasize the importance of the international
arena. The Socialist attempt in the early 1980s to sponsor a Keynesian
expansion (based on the attempt to 'reconquer the French domestic
market') foundered on the international economic recession. In an even
more pronounced fashion, the attempts by the PCF and CGT to pursue a
policy of economic nationalism in conflict with dominant trends internationally has substantially eroded the credibility of the two organizations.
All unions but the CGT — which has paid a heavy price for its
intransigence — have adapted to the new trends by accepting the need for
organized labour to co-operate in improving the flexibility and com-
petitivness of French firms.[9] Whether an alternative exists to unions

accepting dominant trends or pursuing economic nationalism cannot be said with certainty; in any event, it has not yet been devised. One requirement, especially with the fateful date of 1992 looming, would doubtless be for unions to co-ordinate efforts internationally. That prospect, however, appears slim. Rather than speculate about future developments, it is preferable to conclude by emphasizing the extent of change that has occurred within French industrial relations and organized labour in the past decade. The old order has passed; yet the contours of the new one are far from clear.

Notes

1. This paragraph draws heavily on René Mouriaux, *Le Syndicalisme face à la crise* (Paris: La Découverte, 1986).
2. Henri Gibier, 'Syndicats: La contestation respectueuse', *Le Nouvel Economiste,* no. 568 (28 November 1968), p. 54.
3. Edmond Maire, 'Interrogations sur l'entreprise et l'anticapitalisme, l'individu et l'action syndicale', *CFDT aujourd'hui,* no. 78 (March–April 1986), p. 48. The following two quotations by Maire are from this article.
4. These statistics are presented and analysed by Guy Groux, 'De l'interventionnisme étatique au "Nouvel échange politique"', paper delivered to the Conference 'A France of Pluralism and Consensus? Changing Balances in State and Society', sponsored by Columbia University and New York University, 9–11 October 1987.
5. Denis Segrestin, 'Changements et crise du système français de relations industrielles: une évaluation de l'effet politique depuis dix ans', paper delivered to the Conference, 'A France of Pluralism and Consensus?'
6. For a study of this issue, see Jean-Daniel Reynaud, 'La négociation des nouvelles technologies: une transformation des règles du jeu?' *Revue Française de Science Politique,* vol. 38, no. 1 (February 1988).
7. For evidence on this point, see W. Rand Smith, *Crisis in the French Labor Movement: A Grassroots' Perspective* (New York: St Martin's Press, 1987).
8. Segrestin, 'Changements', p. 6.
9. For an analysis of the impact of international economic integration on French unions, see Michael Rose, 'The Decline of the Solution Franco-Française: Economic Nationalism and the Unions' in Jolyon Howorth and George Ross (eds), *Contemporary France* (London: Frances Pinter, 1988).

12. Minorities, ethnics, and aliens: pluralist politics in the Fifth Republic

*William Safran**

For many years, French politics and society were viewed in the context of a myth about 'France: one and indivisible'. That myth was reflected in the political structures and regnant ideologies of the country from the Revolution of 1789 to the Fifth Republic. Institutionally, France rejected both the vertical and horizontal expressions of the polyarchic model.[1] Subnational government remained underdeveloped, and the participation of interest groups in politics was not considered fully legitimate. That situation was accompanied by a monistic view of French culture. The concept of a French society based on common descent and a common faith was largely displaced by a cultural definition of commonality: that of language and way of life. Under that definition, 'minorities' were no more than backward communities in the process of assimilation into French society. Such an ideology was so effectively mirrored in public policy that it became a self-fulfilling prophecy. Most members of ethnic minorities were absorbed into the majority culture by means of a national school system, the banning of any public use of minority idioms, the draft, and the co-optative impact of economic development. The integration was so successful that France was touted as the ideal type of nation-state in which polity, society, and culture were virtually congruent.

Pluralism and plural society

In the past decade discussions of pluralism have burgeoned, focusing on decision-making power, the role of Parliament, the involvement of interest groups, competing systems of education, and the relationship between the state and the market. Calls for a revision of the Jacobin centralizing ideology have been heard, but relatively little attention has

*I wish to thank Dominique Schnapper and Catherine Wihtol de Wenden for their useful comments and suggestions.

been paid to the emerging pluralism within society and its implications for policy — except within the narrow confines of 'the problem of immigrants'.[2]

Immediately after the Second World War the government was little preoccupied with ethnic minorities, except that — as a reaction to the 'autonomist' behaviour of a few collaborationist Bretons, Alsatians and Flemings during the Occupation — official policy forbade the public teaching of their languages. Later, the Deixonne Law of 1951[3] allowed the teaching of Breton, Basque, Catalan and Occitan from kindergarten to university. However, that law had mostly symbolic meaning: the government did little to promote the teaching of these languages.

Between early 1958 and the end of 1980, some twenty-five bills were introduced in the Assembly, mostly by deputies from ethnic constituencies, to extend the application of the Deixonne Law to Alsatian, Corsican and Flemish and to allow minority languages on radio and television. A result of these efforts was the passage of the Haby Law in 1975.[4] It reaffirmed the intentions of the Deixonne Law and provided that 'the teaching of regional languages and cultures may be dispensed through all [public school] levels'.[5] The Haby Law was followed by a series of circulars enabling teachers' colleges to offer ethnic languages as electives and permitting *lycée* students to take *baccalauréat* exams in these languages. These measures, however, had little practical effect: The government made few extra funds available to schools, so that the ethnic languages were taught after school hours by unpaid teachers.

After the mid-1960s, and particularly during the presidency of Giscard d'Estaing, some additional progress was made in the promotion of ethnic culture when news broadcasts in Breton, and subsequently in Alsatian, were introduced. In 1975, the national government signed a 'cultural charter' with regional authorities in Alsace that committed it to the subvention of Alsatian music festivals, university courses on Alsatian literature and history, and television broadcasts on Alsatian cultural themes. In 1977, a parallel cultural charter was agreed upon by the national government and Breton local authorities and voluntary organizations. But these actions had little practical impact. Although Giscard publicly admitted that France had become a 'pluralistic society', he and his government still had difficulty in acknowledging the reality or the policy implications of the presence of ethnic minorities. This difficulty was clearly expressed by a French official in testimony before a United Nations committee on minority rights:

[France] cannot acknowledge the existence of ethnic groups, whether minority or not. As far as religion and language [other than the national one] are concerned, the French government recalls to mind that these two domains are not matters of public law but of the citizens' private exercise of their public liberties. The government limits its role to assuring [the citizens] of the full and free use [of these liberties] within the framework defined by the law...[6]

At the same time, citizenship laws were liberalized — not in order to further the development of a plural society but to speed the process of transforming immigrants into French men and women.

The recognition of the ethnopluralistic reality of French society was sharpened in the late 1960s because of the massive influx of immigrants who stood out sharply from the 'natives'; a growing interest in administrative decentralization, an interest that brought with it a new appreciation of the distinct cultural landscapes of Brittany, Corsica, Occitania and other regions; a questioning of the excessively centralizing and homogenizing state; and a quest for greater individual, local and group autonomy.

These developments, which were sparked by the events of 1968, were reflected in the varied policy pronouncements of several political groups. President de Gaulle and his supporters had no use for cultural pluralism, but they prepared the groundwork by calling for regionalization. The Giscardian, too, were culturally Jacobin, but their emphasis on socio-economic pluralism and their fostering of a stronger associational politics led to a readiness to question the cultural monopoly of an all-powerful state. The democratic Left, however, went much further. The position papers issued (between 1969 and 1981) by the PSU and later, the PS, called for a recognition of the ethnic pluralism of French society.[7] Indicative of the emerging orientation of the PS were the following remarks of François Mitterrand during the presidential election campaign of 1974:

The Socialist Party has always decided to choose the development of the personality. And when one considers Brittany, Corsica, the Basque country, and the Languedoc region, too, it is true that the attempt to suffocate all the means of expression of original languages — for the structures of languages are also the deeper structures of the brain, touching the very essence of being — it is true that economic colonialism ... and a certain reflex of centralistic domination of a colonialist nature — all that should be corrected ... At one time the kings of France, the Jacobins, Bonaparte ... were right ... in their efforts to [fight] centrifugal tendencies ... Very well, it was necessary to make France. But the necessary unity has become uniformity, in which individual being is stamped out ... [Now we must respect] the right to be different.[8]

In its *Projet socialiste* of 1980, the PS advocated policies aimed at 'a flowering of regional languages and cultures' and promised that these languages would be taught in public schools and used in the media.[9] These promises were repeated in the *110 Propositions pour la France* (especially no. 56), in party tracts, and in speeches by Mitterrand during the election campaign of 1981.

After the presidential elections, the Socialist governments of Pierre Mauroy and Laurent Fabius introduced measures that exemplified a growing commitment to ethnocultural pluralism: the expansion of teaching of minority languages; their public use, even in official dealings;

more television and radio programmes on ethnic themes; the sponsorship of publications on ethnic languages and literatures, of projects in ethnomusicology, and of ethnic film festivals; the financing of ethnic-language teacher training; the introduction of the CAPES teaching certificate for teachers of Breton; and the maintenance of ethnic culture centres. These measures cost several hundred million francs and involved the Ministries of Education, Culture, Social Affairs, Decentralization and Interior, National Solidarity, and Immigration, and newly established government agencies. They also involved new patterns of relationship between the national government, subnational public authorities, and voluntary associations.

Administrative and ethnocultural decentralization: a confusing relationship

The relationship between policies of administrative decentralization and 'cultural decentralization' on an ethnic basis is a matter of controversy. It may be assumed that the motive behind the creation of more autonomous regional units was not to transform France into a 'plural society' but to foster grassroots participation and local democracy that would result in more effective and realistic policy-making and administration. Nevertheless, administrative and cultural decentralization soon came to be entangled. As the rationale of rigid centralizers was questioned so also was 'the postulate of the homogeneity of social forces' on which it was based. It was recalled that even under the Third and Fourth Republics, national policy-makers, while continuing to adhere to the principle of administrative uniformity, chose divergent approaches to the management of areas with special characteristics: Alsace-Lorraine; the city of Paris; the overseas departments and territories; and Algeria (after the Second World War).[10] These approaches — in addition to the creation of social security regions and school districts — were regarded as possible prototypes for other kinds of functional subdivisions (or centre–periphery rearrangements), including ethnic ones.

The Defferre Law of 1982 bestowed upon regional councils the power 'to assure to the region the preservation of [its] identity' without indicating any specifically ethnolinguistic criteria for that identity. However, many spokesmen of minorities hoped that such criteria would be taken into account: that regional cultural policies would lead to ethnocultural pluralism. They came to regard the autonomy statute for Corsica, passed in 1982, as a model. That statute had provided for a regional legislature empowered to pass laws pertaining to secondary school curricula and to 'determine complementary educational activities aimed at preserving the Corsican language and culture'.

The direction of the government's policy discussions seemed to suggest that administrative decentralization could not be neatly separated from cultural decentralization and that measures aimed at economic democracy, the regulation of the labour market, and the economic integration of repatriates and immigrants would have to take into account the reality of ethnic cultural diversity. These interrelationships were recognized by several study commissions. The Giordan Commission report,[11] submitted to the Minister of Culture early in 1982, is the most radical public document as far as ethnic minorities are concerned. It enumerates the various indigenous ethnic regions and cultural-linguistic communities in metropolitan France. It argues that France is in fact a 'plural society' culturally and that the notion of a monolithic French national culture is a myth whose construction involved a systematic suppression of minority cultures, a 'historic injustice' that the government must repair. Such reparation required not only an official affirmation of the pluralistic character of France and of the legitimacy of minority languages and cultures but also their active promotion, by means of budgetary outlays and appropriate administrative structures. These latter would include divisions within the Ministry of Culture for clientelistic relationships with ethnic communities; regional directorates for ethnic cultural matters; and a national advisory council for minority cultures.

A significant feature of the Giordan report, which reflected the minorities' own input, was the recognition of the territorially dispersed minorities with specific cultures. These *cultures communautaires* should be supported because of their intrinsic values and because, as expressions of people who had become rooted in France, they formed a part of the country's cultural patrimony. The report did not deal with communities of immigrants who arrived after the Second World War, notably the North African Muslims (Maghrebis), but it implied that some of its proposals might apply to them as well.

The Queyranne report,[12] issued in July 1982, focused on regional cultural projects promoted jointly by the national, regional and local authorities and reaffirmed existing contractual relationships, such as the *conventions culturelles Etat-région*, that had been signed earlier with Alsace and Brittany.

Although both the Giordan and Queyranne reports refer to subnational bureaucratic arrangements, the reports have not really clarified the relationship between administrative and cultural decentralization. Both reports eschew strictly ethno-regional solutions and assign a large role in promoting minority cultures to the national government, not only because it had always been actively involved in cultural matters, but also because there are ethnic regions with their own minorities — e.g., Gallicans in Brittany and Corsicans in Provence — whose culture might be discriminated against if left to regional authorities.

The Defferre law, while giving local communities the power to initiate supplementary cultural programmes, also refers to the need to safeguard the unity of the nation and reaffirms the traditional tutelle of the Ministry of Education over local educational institutions and curricula. Moreover, in the view of many observers, 'cultural decentralization' has had — or should have — little to do with ethnic minorities. At a symposium in January 1985 on 'Culture and Democracy Today', many references were made to the need to bring national culture to the provinces, to recognize the 'cultural personalities' of communes, to take inventories of local conditions, to create a balance between low (or popular) and high (or Parisian elite) culture, to guard against an excessive politicization of culture, to improve local and regional libraries, to preserve the local architectural patrimony, and to rely, whenever possible, on local voluntary associations — but no reference at all was made to ethnic minority (or even regional) cultures.[13]

What policies, and for whom?

The public policies that followed the Giordan and Queyranne reports could be divided into these categories: *ad hoc* measures, often circulars of the Ministries of Education and Culture and other agencies that dealt with the specific needs of ethnic communities, in particular, language instruction; assigning 'ethnocultural' tasks to existing bodies concerned with culture and education, such as regional commissions and endowment funds for ethnological, archaeological, and artistic matters; creating new agencies to promote ethnic programmes, including the six Directions Régionales des Affaires Culturelles; supporting the cultural programmes of ethnic voluntary associations; initiating or encouraging new legislation to provide a firmer basis for culturally pluralistic programmes; and measures that affect ethnocultural pluralism indirectly, such as those on immigration, the rights of aliens, and the acquisition of citizenship.

One of the first actions of the Socialist government was to ratify the International Human Rights Convention of 1966, which obliges states to protect the rights of minorities to maintain their cultural life, to practice their religion, or to use their language. A law enacted in October 1981 gave aliens the right to form associations;[14] and the Auroux laws passed in 1982 stipulated that union members could not be deprived of the right to be elected to labour relations tribunals because of lack of fluency in French.

An important effort at strengthening the legal foundation for an ethnic cultural policy was the 'Bill Concerning the Promotion of the Languages and Cultures of France'. The bill, introduced in the Assembly by Socialist J.-P. Destrade in 1984 and supported by the entire PS contingent in the chamber, guaranteed the right of each minority group to speak its language and use it in its dealings with the public authorities; banned discrimination against ethnic groups for using their language; called for the establishment of regional audiovisual centres charged with the use of minority languages in the media; and provided for a national consultative council that would protect and promote ethnic cultures and languages. The bill did not obtain support by the government and was withdrawn. While the government subscribed to the aims of the bill, it was apprehensive that a full debate on the matter would reveal opposition to ethnocultural pluralism within the ranks of the PS, that it would be exploited by hard-line Gaullist Jacobins as well as the National Front for budgetary as well as ideological reasons, and that it would interfere with ongoing efforts at protecting the French language and promoting its use outside of France. Instead, the government thought it wiser to advance ethnocultural pluralism by administrative means.

A principal agent in this approach was the Ministry of Culture, which, during the first two years of the Socialist government, signed more than a hundred *conventions de développement culturel* with regional, departmental and municipal authorities; allocated funds to several Directions Régionales des Affaires Culturelles for ethnic programmes; and undertook projects with selected cities. It also provided seed money and subsidies for a plethora of ethnic cultural projects: theatres, art exhibitions, music and film festivals; museums; the publication of poetry, dictionaries and translations; and the support of documentation centres and libraries — not only of indigenous languages and cultures but also of those of immigrants.

At the end of 1985, the government decreed the formation of a national consultative organ that would be a clearing house for future ethnocultural projects: the Conseil National des Langues et Cultures Régionales. That body, composed of some forty personalities (members of ethnic communities, politicians, and 'independent' academic experts) met in early 1986 for two full sessions. There a welter of suggestions was made, ranging from the inclusion of ethnic languages in the regular public school curriculum to the promotion of bilingualism in regions where ethnic minorities were heavily settled. Nothing came of these ideas, not only because they were considered utopian, but also because there was discord about which cultures were most deserving of support: the spokesmen of indigenous ethnics — for example, the Catalans — did not like the idea of 'foreign' (i.e. immigrant) cultures being subsidized. Among the indigenous minorities, there was uncertainty about whether the 'high' literary culture of the Catalans should have priority over the 'low' peasant dialects of the Bretons; and among the immigrants, which language or which aspect of culture should be supported.

After the elections of 1986 such arguments became moot because under the Gaullist government of Jacques Chirac, the Conseil held only one further meeting (at which little of substance was discussed), the (Socialist) *chargé de mission* for ethnocultural affairs was not replaced, and (except for already mandated programmes, such as the teaching of regional languages) no budgetary lines were provided for the promotion of minority cultures. When François Léotard, the new Minister of Culture, revised the budget for cultural projects in favour of the provinces, it was to promote not ethnic culture but regional archaeological and architectural projects (*patrimoine monumental*).[15] And although Chirac made speeches before minority audiences about 'the precious contributions' of their cultures to France and about his commitment to cultural pluralism,[16] he promoted a policy of constricting actual outlays not merely for ethnocultural projects, but for culture and the arts *tout court*. This was in line with his conversion to neo-liberalism, one of the aspects of which was the idea of the *mécénat* : the effort at encouraging private patrons to support — as they do in the United States — libraries, museums, theatres, symphonies, and components of education.[17] Unfortunately, the private patronage of literature and the arts cannot be a reliable substitute for a public ethnocultural policy, for private patrons will tend to underwrite projects with a general appeal rather than a narrowly ethnic one.

The impact of the privatization of the electronic media on ethnic culture has been especially uncertain. On the one hand, the legalization of *radios libres* has already resulted in the founding of many private stations that broadcast programmes on ethnic culture and in ethnic languages; on the other hand, the dependence of such stations on private funds must inevitably subject them to pressures of the marketplace. That is why the privatization of the television networks — and even the spread of 'regional' networks — will do little for the promotion of ethnic minority cultures. Moreover, even when private or regional authorities manage to retain a significant ethnic content in their television or radio programmes, the national government may intervene if the programmes go beyond the expression of ethnic cultural themes and cross politically permissible boundaries. Thus in October 1987 the prefect of police in Corsica forbade the broadcast on FR-3 of an interview with members of the Corsican National Liberation Front because it might threaten public order. In the same month, the administrative council of FR-3 transferred control over regional Corsican programmes to Marseilles.

The slackening interest of the Chirac government in the pursuit of ethnocultural policies occurred despite the attenuation of orthodox Gaullism, with its rigid views on the political and cultural indivisibility of the nation. In part, such policies ceded to a growing concern among wide strata of French society with security, unemployment, AIDS and drugs — problems that were relentlessly exploited by the National Front. Even before the Assembly elections that brought the Gaullists to power, the Socialists' reformist zeal had diminished, despite the fact that the hold of orthodox Marxism — with its dogmatic view of ethnic consciousness as a false one — had weakened. Their dalliance with cultural pluralism was gradually ending and was replaced by the conviction that the interests of efficiency, equality, and social justice would best be served by a campaign against racism and by the complete economic, political, and cultural integration of the immigrants. The shift from an emphasis on ethnic cultures as permanent features of the French cultural landscape to a stress on individuals of ethnic origin as valuable constituents of an enlarged French society, with its homogenized culture, was reflected in the following remark by President Mitterrand: 'We are French and our ancestors [were] Gauls — [and] Romans, and a little German, a little Jewish, a little Italian, a little Spanish, increasingly Portuguese...and I ask myself if we are already a little Arab [as well]'.[18]

The ambiguities of Chirac's government reflected the diversity of pressures aimed at him: from the market-orientated liberals (especially in the UDF) who wanted to hold the line on expenditures; from Gaullists like Michel Debré and Michel Hannoun (a deputy of Jewish ancestry born in Algeria) who held to a vision of a culturally if not racially homogeneous French nation;[19] from Jean-Marie Le Pen and his National Front, who objected to the presence of masses of 'Arabs' and other non-Europeans on French soil and, a fortiori, to the support of their cultures; from politicians of various sorts, who feared that a sustenance of the cultures of ethnic minority groups might interfere with the protection of the rights of individuals; and finally, from minorities themselves, who were becoming aware of their electoral weight. This was particularly true of the 'Beurs', some of whose leaders began a systematic campaign under the auspices of the *Association France Plus* to register Beur voters for the elections of 1988 and who were hoping to put up their own candidates in future elections. One of the first responses to these efforts was a circular sent by the Interior Minister to mayors calling upon them to listen to the demands of the Beurs.[20] The precise nature of these demands, however, remained unclear: While some Maghrebis wanted the government to commit itself more fully to the promotion of an Arab Muslim culture, others asked merely that they be fully integrated into French society and treated equally with other residents of France.

One attempt at responding to these cross-pressures was the Hannoun Report,[21] submitted to the Prime Minister in November 1987. The Report recommended, *inter alia,* the strengthening of anti-racist legislation, including severe penalties for incitement to hatred; an active policy of integrating minorities, especially immigrants, into the French economy and society; the treatment of Islam like other religions; the establishment of a 'high council on immigration' in which immigrant communities would be represented; the strengthening of methods of teaching 'French as a second language'; the creation of an Islamic representative council in order to facilitate a dialogue with the government; and an expansion of Islamic television programmes. While admitting that 'the openness of French society towards [cultural] diversity would make the process of integrating foreigners easier',[22] the report recommended nothing specifically to encourage ethnocultural pluralism. The integration of the

Maghrebis remained controversial because Islam, to which most of them subscribed at least nominally, was considered by many as more than a religion: It was regarded as turning toward Mecca and as being sustained by help, often officially sanctioned, from Algerian and other foreign Muslim establishments.

In any case, most of the recommendations were too liberal to be welcomed by many RPR leaders, especially in view of the presidential election campaign, during which Chirac did all he could to avoid passing gratuitous ammunition to the National Front. Therefore the report became a dead letter with Chirac's defeat in May 1988 and the poor performance of the RPR in the subsequent parliamentary elections (in which Hannoun himself lost his Assembly seat).

The installation of a (more or less) Socialist government and the reappointment of Jack Lang as Minister of Culture brought little hope to those who favoured an ethnoculturally pluralistic France. The teaching of Breton and other regional minority languages was continued, and the most recent official proposals even provided for an expansion of instruction in these languages in the last three years of the *lycée*[23] — perhaps because it involved a pitifully small clientele of fewer than 30,000 primary and secondary school pupils. However, the office of *chargé de mission* for minority cultures was not likely to be restored, and for a variety of reasons little more could be expected in terms of an activist government policy: the overriding priority of integrating the unemployed, from the ranks of both the majoritarian 'natives' and the (immigrant and other) minorities, into the economy; the desire to do nothing that would interfere with the process of *ouverture* towards the political centre; and the stress on the political and cultural unity of France as it prepared for the celebration of the bicentennial of the Revolution.

Immigrants: future Frenchmen or unassimilable aliens?

The promotion of ethnoculturally orientated public policies was constrained both by surviving Jacobinism and the newly emergent neo-liberal orientation. Nevertheless, the government might have expanded the support of minority cultures if these had concerned merely the Bretons, Alsatians, Occitans and other 'native' minorities, whose cultures and languages were expected to disappear sooner or later in the face of urbanization and the pressures the more useful French language. However, it was clear that such policies would inevitably have to apply to the more than 2 million Maghrebis as well. It was argued that, whereas the cultures of the Bretons and other indigenous Christian ethnics (and even of the older immigrant communities of Jews) were part of Christian (or 'Judeo-Christian') civilization and hence complementary to the culture of the majority, that of the Maghrebis was not. Their experiences, language, folkways, social conventions, and the 'fundamentalist' nature of their Islamic religion were such as to maintain them as a 'counter-society' whose assimilation was impeded also by its rapid natural increase and its relative poverty. Moreover, even if assimilation succeeded, it would so transform society and dilute (or 'corrupt') culture in France that these would no longer be French.[24]

The presence of the Maghrebi immigrant community has highlighted the ethnic question and caused politicians and academics to make a variety of proposals, each with its own drawbacks. (1) Assimilation — the public school system and the economic system would transform the Maghrebis into French men and women just as surely as these systems once transformed Italian and Polish immigrants. But given the large number of Maghrebis, such a process would be slower and costlier. (2) Mass expulsion — often suggested by Le Pen. But even if such a policy were economically feasible (which is doubtful), it would be incompatible with France's democratic values. (3) True ethnic pluralism — minority languages would have the same status as French in the schools and other public institutions.[25] Or a somewhat narrower bilingualism — Arabic would be widely taught as complementary to French.[26] But these approaches would be offensive to the majority whose very conception of Frenchness is bound up with the primacy of the French language. (4) Emphasis on the 'insertion' of immigrants into the economy, rather than on a systematic cultural assimilation. Proposals embodying such an emphasis were contained in the Marangé–Lebon Report, which was submitted to the Ministry of Labour in 1982.[27] The report argued in favour of teaching occupational skills and the languages of the immigrants' countries of origin — if necessary in co-operation with the governments of those countries — as well as French. These proposals were criticized on a number of grounds: the cost of teaching two or more languages to masses of aliens would be prohibitive; a reliance on the help of foreign governments would infringe on France's sovereignty in matters of education; an inadequate cultural adaptation would keep immigrants in economic ghettos; and an insertion into mere production slots would reduce their incentive to adapt to the French way of life and increase the likelihood of their leaving France.

Citizenship and nationality

It was logical that the debate about ethnic pluralism should touch upon the question of naturalization and the meaning of citizenship. The criterion of *jus soli*, under which a person born on French soil to foreign parents has the right to opt for French citizenship, goes back to 1851. Laws enacted since then specified the period of residency — five years under a law of 1927, as updated in 1973 — required for applying for citizenship. Since the end of the Second World War, citizenship laws were progressively liberalized, and elements of second-class citizenship were slowly eliminated.[28] A law passed in 1973 did away with the waiting period of five years before a naturalized citizen could vote; and in 1983, a law was enacted that abolished the ten-year waiting period for a naturalized citizen before running for public office (including the presidency of the Republic).

Nationalistic Gaullists and xenophobic conservatives felt that the existing laws made it too easy for residents to become citizens. Early in 1987 Premier Chirac, under pressure from these critics and from the National Front, introduced a bill to correct this. Citizenship would no longer be awarded automatically at age 18 to children born in France of foreign parents; it would be based on a formal request, on proof of the applicant's knowledge of French, law-abiding behaviour, and other evidence that citizenship was merited. The impact of the bill itself would not be particularly severe, for the children of parents born in Algeria (who constituted the largest group of immigrants) would retain the right of automatic naturalization upon reaching majority.[29] But the bill was withdrawn in response to protests from human rights organizations, church groups, and immigrant associations, who viewed it as a symbol of racism. In mid-1987 Chirac appointed a *Comité des Sages* to make recommendations on the reform of the nationality code. The commission's report — based on the input of numerous lobbies, politicians, and experts — was substantially finished at the end of the year.[30] The report rejected a forcible approach to cultural homogenization and deplored the very use of the terms 'politics of assimilation';[31] however, it also rejected an ethnopluralistic approach to education, not so much because it would endanger national political unity but because it would lead to discrimination.[32] The report proposed that citizenship be formally applied for after a minimum of five years' residency. But it did not suggest such prerequisites as a mastery of the French language or even proof of law-abiding behaviour. Although the proposals were widely approved (except by the National Front), they were not submitted to Parliament before the presidential elections of 1988.

A number of questions remained concerning the meaning of citizenship, the quality of Frenchness, and the very nature of French society as it sought to accommodate itself to the growing presence of alien elements. One of the foci of the debate was the relationship between the state and society, and between citizenship and nationality. Some intellectuals and politicians (among them Mitterrand[33]) have proposed a functionally selective approach to citizenship, under which a non-naturalized resident (as a taxpayer) might have the 'civic' right to vote in municipal elections; others have advocated a clear distinction between citizenship and nationality — the former referring to purely political rights, duties, and loyalties (e.g., voting in national elections or serving in the army), and the latter referring to ethnic origins and cultural identities.[34] Gaullist as well as progressive Jacobins reject both approaches because these would cheapen the meaning of citizenship and reduce the alien's incentive to strive for full national integration.[35] In the eyes of the critics, the disjunction of nationality and citizenship is based on a romanticized view of the American model (with its 'hyphenated American'), which cannot apply to France, for in a country where the state has always taken culture and language as a policy domain it is impossible to separate political from cultural loyalty.

Conclusion

What the election results of 1988 presage for the future of ethnoplural society in France is hard to say. The re-election of Mitterrand and the Socialists' recapture of a dominant position in the Assembly — outcomes to which ethnic minority voters probably contributed significantly — might be seen as imposing a moral obligation on the government to continue where it had left off in 1986. The electoral mobilization of Maghrebis in particular, which is continuing apace, may force the government, the major republican parties, and the public to respond to the desires of that community as much as they would respond to those of other ethnic communities: the desire, on the one hand, to be given the same rights as other inhabitants of the Hexagon — *a droit à la ressemblance*[36] — and the desire, on the other, for a public recognition of the special needs of minorities. These responses might involve: a wider and more systematic instruction in ethnic languages and cultures at *lycées* and universities; a more reliable ethnic programming in the electronic media; bilingual streets signs and public notices where appropriate; a more flexible approach to the use of minority languages in commercial and public institutions; a greater readiness to accord legitimacy to ethnic lobbies; and more substantial efforts at sensitizing the majority to the cultural achievements of minority groups and of their contributions to France.

Some of these undertakings lend themselves to formal policy measures; others must come about through exhortation, examples set by elites, and the creation of an atmosphere of tolerance and cultural openness. It is unlikely that the mobilization of the 'collective identity' of Maghrebis and other minorities within French society[37] will express itself in such 'American' terms as ethnic political parties, ethnically 'balanced tickets', bilingual ballots, or candidates for public office addressing their local electorates in Arabic or Breton. However, a growing political participation of the ethnic minorities in France, whatever form it is likely to take, will inevitably hasten their *francisation* and reduce their own interest in the maintenance of cultures and languages that will be increasingly less relevant for them — and hence, reduce the pressures for ethnopluralist public policies.

Notes

1. See, for example, Robert A. Dahl, *Polyarchy* (New Haven, Conn., and London: Yale University Press, 1971).
2. See 'Dossiers et Documents, Bilan du septennat', *Le Monde*, March 1988, pp. 106–7.
3. Law no. 51–46, 11 January 1951.
4. Law no. 75.620, 11 July 1975.
5. Richard Grau, *Les Langues et les cultures minoritaires en France: une approche juridique contemporaine* (Quebec: Conseil de la langue française, 1985), p. 53.
6. Francesco Capotorti, *Etudes des droits des personnes* (Geneva: United Nations, 1979), p. 13.
7. See William Safran, 'The French Left and Ethnic Pluralism', *Ethnic and Racial Studies*, vol. 7, no. 4 (October 1984), pp. 447–61; and Safran, 'The Mitterrand Regime and Its Policies of Ethnocultural Accommodation', *Comparative Politics*, vol. 18, no. 1 (October 1985), pp. 41–63.
8. Claude Manceron and Bernard Pingaud, *François Mitterrand: L'Homme, les idées, le programme* (Paris: Flammarion, 1981), p. 114.
9. *Projet socialiste* (Paris: Club Socialiste du Livre, 1980), pp. 56, 252–8.
10. Thierry Michalon, 'La République française: une fédération qui s'ignore?' *Revue de droit public* (May–June 1982), pp. 623–88.
11. Henri Giordan, *Démocratie culturelle et droit à la différence: Rapport au Ministre de la Culture* (Paris: La Documentation Française, February 1982).
12. Jean-Jack Queyranne, *Les Régions et la décentralisation: Rapport au Ministre de la Culture* (Paris: La Documentation Française, July 1982).
13. 'Perspectives de la décentralisation culturelle', *France-Forum*, no. 221-222 (July-September 1985), pp. 3–29.
14. For a discussion of the law and its effects, see Manuel Dias, 'La Vie culturelle et associative des immigrés', *Projet* no. 199 (May–June 1986), pp. 61–6.
15. Emmanuel de Roux, 'Le budget de la culture', *Le Monde*, 10 October 1987.
16. *Le Monde*, 15 September 1987.
17. See 'Le Grand air du mécénat', *Le Point*, 30 March 1987, pp. 136–7.
18. Robert Solé, 'Mettre les beurs à la table d'honneur', *Le Monde*, 20 May 1987.
19. See, for example, Michel Hannoun, *L'Autre cohabitation* (Paris: L'Harmattan, 1986).
20. 'Mobilisation à la carte', *Le Point*, 18 January 1988, p. 31.
21. Michel Hannoun, *L'Homme est l'espérance de l'homme: Rapport sur le racisme et les discriminations en France au Secrétaire d'Etat auprès du Premier Ministre chargé des droits de l'homme (Paris: La Documentation Française, November 1987).*
22. *Ibid., p. 137.*
23. *Le Monde*, 3 September 1988.
24. For typical arguments, see Alain Griotteray, *Les Immigrés: Le choc* (Paris: Plon, 1984); Jean-Yves LeGallou et le Club de l'Horloge, *La Préférence nationale* (Paris: Albin Michel, 1985); and Gérard-François Dumont, *La France ridée* (Paris: Editions Pluriel, 1986).

25. See Jean-Pierre Colin, 'Les cultures minoritaires face à l'état', *Change International deux*, no. 2 (May 1984), pp. 106-12.
26. See Jacques Berque, *L'Immigration à l'école de la République* (Paris: La Documentation Française, 1985).
27. James Marangé and André Lebon, *L'Insertion des jeunes d'origine étrangère dans la société française* (Paris: Documentation Française, 1982).
28. See Catherine de Wenden, *Citoyenneté, nationalité, et immigration* (Paris: Arcantère Editions, 1987), pp. 50–1.
29. See William Safran, 'Rights and Liberties Under the Mitterrand Presidency: Socialist Innovations and Post-Socialist Revisions', *Contemporary French Civilization*, vol. 12, no. 1 (Winter–Spring 1988), p. 20.
30. *Etre Français aujourd'hui et demain. Rapport au Premier Ministre par Marceau Long* (2 vols, Paris: La Documentation Française, 1988).
31. Ibid., vol. I, p. 24.
32. Ibid., vol. II, p. 88.
33. On Mitterrand's statement of support for this idea during a speech before the Council of Europe, see *Le Monde*, 30 December 1987; and on his reaffirmation before the elections of 1988, see *Le Point*, 25 April 1988, p. 36.
34. See Nacer Kettane, *Droit de réponse à la démocratie française* (Paris: Editions de la Découverte, 1986); and René Gallissot, 'Nationalité et citoyenneté', *Après-Demain*, no. 286 (July–September 1986), pp. 8–15; and Catherine de Wenden, 'Questions sur la citoyenneté', *Esprit*, no. 102 (June 1985), pp. 24–28.
35. 'Vote des immigrés, *Le Point*, 25 April 1988, pp. 36–37.
36. Cercle Pierre Mendès France, 'Un nouveau regard sur l'immigration', *Projet*, no. 210 (March–April 1988), pp. 59–66.
37. See de Wenden, *Citoyenneté, nationalité et immigration*, p. 15.

13. Health care: the political economy of social policy*

Paul Godt

The French state developed a role in social policy only slowly and reluctantly in the twentieth century, largely because of an inherited dual cultural legacy. On the one hand, the liberal, individualist values of the nineteenth century, combined with slow industrialization which retarded demand for public action, made the state an unwilling accomplice in the development of a socially inequitable distribution of health care; on the other hand, in the name of solidarity, the state was promoting the proliferation of public and private systems of protection for certain designated groups in society.[1]

The delicate balance between the conflicting values of liberalism and national solidarity was disturbed by the return of Alsace-Lorraine to France after the First World War. Unable for evident political reasons to discontinue the advantageous Bismarckian system of compulsory workers' insurance, the government was obliged to adopt it for the rest of France, thus involving the state for the first time in the definition of systematic coverage of health risks.

The proposals in the 1920s to create collective contracts between physicians' associations and sickness funds sparked adamant resistance and organized pressure from the profession. Doctors had long harboured ambivalent attitudes towards the state, at once seeking public health campaigns and protection of corporatist privilege, and yet fearing state intervention in the practice of their arts. Responding to the challenge, they restructured their disparate and decentralized organizations into a single national professional union, the Confédération des Syndicats Médicaux Français (CSMF). In its first national congress in

*An earlier version of parts of this chapter appeared in *Public Administration*, vol.63, no.2 (Summer 1985); the latter sections draw on my 'The Revival of Neo-liberal Doctrine and French Health Care Policy', paper presented at the International Political Science Association meetings in Washington, DC, 1988. I am indebted to Stuart Haywood for his useful critical comments.

1927, the CSMF approved a medical charter in which the doctors cast the defence of their corporate interests in terms of general principles to which they still ascribe transcending social values: the right of the patient and the doctor to choose one another freely and agree on a fee; the responsibility of the patient to pay the doctor directly for his services; the doctor's freedom of diagnosis and prescription; and the guarantee of professional confidentiality.

These principles are what the French call *la médecine libérale* and form the dominant ideology of the medical profession. As a statement of professional concern, these principles are not only self-serving: in the physicians' view they also assure responsible, high-quality medical care for the patient. By thus associating the medical profession's interests in preserving its autonomy with the patient's interest in preserving his health, the principles of *médecine libérale* established a solid rampart against state interference.

The health insurance legislation that eventually emerged in 1930 perpetuated the doctor's freedom to set and collect fees, but introduced the first breach in the doctor–patient relationship with collective financing: the sickness funds as third-party payers would inevitably seek to reduce their members' out-of-pocket expenses, as these limited access to health care. Whenever they raised the reimbursement schedules, however, the doctors increased their fees correspondingly. Since only a small part of the population was covered, there was no great pressure for the state to intervene, and the doctors had demonstrated their influence and capacity to ward off incursions into their professional autonomy.

In the progressive political context of the Liberation, the groundbreaking Social Security Ordinance of 1945 defined a new scheme of comprehensive coverage of health and old-age insurance and family assistance, made compulsory for salaried employees. The Social Security system, however, was designed to be insulated from state control: contributors (employers and employees) would both finance and operate it. Authority to manage the funds fell to private-law Social Security boards which they elected, a striking anomaly in France's legendary centralized administration.

The health insurance scheme thereby acquired the ambiguous authority pattern that would plague it in later years. The state was by no means absent, but collective agreements were negotiated locally between the Social Security boards and CSMF local unions, setting maximum fees for medical services, 80 per cent of which would be refunded to patients by their Social Security fund. Where agreements could not be reached, patients were reimbursed a fixed sum, usually a small portion of the fees actually charged. Despite several attempts during the 1950s to generalize contractual relations to the entire country in order to assure equality of benefits, persistent lobbying efforts blocked any legislation: as powerful notables in the party-dominated, clientelist politics of the Fourth

Republic, doctors were still able to protect their freedom to determine fees.

The medical profession had succeeded for more than thirty years in preserving its autonomy, but the writing was clearly on the wall. The rapid unfolding of a modern industrial society was fostering new needs which France's existing system of social services was poorly equipped to meet. The supply of medical services was proving inadequate to growing demands, and it would be the task of the Fifth Republic to reconcile its economic and social ambitions; in the process, the state acquired major new responsibilities, some of which would conflict with its more traditional roles.

The Fifth Republic

With the establishment of the Fifth Republic came a substantial and abrupt change in the context, focal point, and rationale of policy-making. The Gaullists sought to erect the state as the aggregator of national interest, and this meant remodelling civil society. Economic modernization, an essential element in this pursuit, called for an autonomous executive authority capable of breaking the grip of the special interests which had long colonized entire fields of policy. In order to liberate the policy-making process from their negative and self-serving influence, the Fifth Republic's constitution granted new independent powers to the government and considerably restrained Parliament's ability to hamper its action.

Social policy *per se* was evidently not de Gaulle's primary concern in the early years, but it had clear implications for other Gaullist goals. In terms of purely practical politics, bringing inaccessible social benefits to larger numbers of citizens, especially the working class, would serve to marginalize the class-conflict theme de Gaulle disdained. In health care, as we have seen, the doctors were the major obstacle to uniform benefits.

Macro-economic concerns also called for state action. Although the financial equilibrium was not (yet) endangered, the acceleration of health costs was already noticeable. From 3 per cent of GDP in 1950, they had grown to 4 per cent in 1960; per capita expenses in constant francs had more than doubled.[2] The Rueff-Pinay stabilization reforms of 1958 would necessitate imposing some control mechanism on this increasingly important sector of the expanding economy.

Using its newly acquired powers, the Debré government chose to circumvent Parliament and issue a decree to break the logjam in health care and deliver at the same time a devastating blow to physician trade unionism. State intervention in a formerly two-way dialogue obliged both doctors and the Social Security boards to adopt new strategies, which in turn compelled new state action. This new pattern of tripartite relations developed in several stages.

The Statist approach

The May 1960 decree, drawn up rapidly to prevent organized resistance, perpetuated the local accord as the basic bargaining instrument, but any negotiated fee schedules had to obtain the approval of a state inter-ministerial committee before implementation. The blow to the physicians' union resulted from the option for *individual* doctors to conclude an agreement when the local CSMF chapter refused the collective accord. The CSMF's fragile unity was broken, and the union split along its fault lines: the more affluent, urban physicians, particularly specialists, feared the loss of status as independent professionals and remained die-hard opponents; their less well-off colleagues in rural areas, mainly general practitioners, hoped to increase their clientele and agreed to work with the government on elaborating a nation-wide contract, winning in fact a number of significant concessions.

During the 1960s, most doctors came to recognize that, although they had lost the right to set fees freely, there were compensatory advantages. The recalcitrants left the CSMF and formed a separate union, later recognized as the Fédération des Médecins de France (FMF). The new strategy of the CSMF leadership was to forge an alliance with the Social Security boards to control the substance and process of change; both the union and the boards had reached the conclusion that the state — and especially the Ministry of Finance — was pre-empting the health policy field. They took advantage of the heavily politicized atmosphere reigning between the presidential elections of 1965 and the legislative elections of 1967 to work out a new national accord.

The government, however, had good reason to consolidate its control over the health sector. As a consequence of policies designed to expand coverage, health care costs had doubled between 1960 and 1965, accounting for nearly 5 per cent of a growing GDP. Critical reports from public and private sources suggested that enormous deficits would soon threaten the self-financed system's viability if radical measures were not taken. The Social Security Reform of 1967 (the Jeanneney Ordinances) created distinct national agencies for each 'risk' (health, pensions, family allowances), mandating balanced budgets. Management structure was also modified: the state would appoint a national director for each agency, and employer representation on the boards was increased to one-half of the seats. Given the divisions in the ranks of labour, especially between the Leftist CGT and CFDT unions, on the one hand, and the more moderate Force Ouvrière (FO), an alliance between the employers' association (CNPF) and the FO assumed effective leadership.

In charge of managing health risks, the new National Health Insurance Fund (CNAMTS) is a quasi-public institution under the dual *tutelle* of the Ministries of Health and Finance; two officials are ex-officio members of the administrative board. The CNAMTS is now the principal payer of health services in France, financing more than 70 per cent of all health care costs, although it exercises only partial control over its revenues and expenditures: the government fixes the levels of both the payroll taxes and the tax base, regulates the patient's share of costs, and determines the rates and method of hospital charges. The doctors, of course, decide the type and quantity of medical service through hospitalization and pre-scription of medication, analyses, and auxiliary services. With the CNAMTS, the Gaullists had established a strong, centralized authority to supervise the health sector, under government surveillance; the CNAMTS became the 'countervailing power that the physicians' unions feared most', a monopsony facing a monopoly.[3]

Despite widespread criticism from the labour unions and parties of the Left that the '*Sécu*' was being dismantled, a growing consensus appeared during the preparatory discussions for the Sixth Plan that more effective measures were needed to contain health costs: these had again doubled in five years, now reaching 5.7 per cent of GDP, with no signs of deceleration. The image of the physician was rapidly evolving from that of the disinterested healer to that of just another actor in the economy: the doctors' freedom of prescription and fee-for-service payment gave them seemingly uncontrolled access to collective funds.

Sensing the threat to *médecine libérale*, the CSMF proposed to negotiate with the CNAMTS a new nation-wide contract to replace the local contracts of 1960. By taking the initiative, the CSMF leadership hoped to demonstrate doctors' concern over rising health costs and reassert the union's influence in defining the conditions of medical practice, and thus to forestall more authoritarian measures.

The socio-political context had also evolved. In the wake of the May 1968 social explosion and the subsequent retirement of de Gaulle, Georges Pompidou had assumed the presidency, with his own aspirations and temperament. Committed to making France a modern industrial power, Pompidou foresaw that imposing the *impératif industriel* on a profoundly conservative society would create shocks, which increased social benefits might cushion. Linking social benefits to economic growth required a new type of contractual relations between the state and the various social partners.

The state as mediator: *la politique contractuelle*

The choice of Jacques Chaban-Delmas as Prime Minister signalled the shift in attitude. His 'New Society' programme sought to transform the role of the state from aggregator to interested mediator. The government was responsive to the CSMF initiative, and a negotiated framework was reached in early 1971, after more than a year of discussions between the CNAMTS and the CSMF. The new agreement differed from the 1960 contracts in significant ways. As a national contract, it became binding on all office practitioners; individual doctors could opt out of the agreement, but they would forfeit all fringe benefits (generous tax deductions, medical insurance and pension premiums) and probably lose clients (their patients would get practically no reimbursement). The new agreement re-established the CSMF as the doctors' bargaining agent and portrayed it as a responsible social partner.

The rationale behind the contractual process was to organize a system of co-operation between the payers (the CNAMTS) and the providers (the doctors) of health care. Heretofore the principal objective had been to assure that medical care would be accessible: uniform fee schedules and substantial patient reimbursement were to remove financial barriers. The 1971 agreement shifted the emphasis to developing concerted means of cost containment, which implied, among other things, focusing on physicians' activities. Office consultations, house calls, and prescriptions then accounted for more than half of overall health costs. The real challenge to the medical profession, therefore, was to demonstrate that private office-based practice was not incompatible with a socially financed national health insurance scheme. In order to reconcile cost containment and *médecine libérale,* the CNAMTS and the physicians' unions were to collaborate on defining instruments to control the prices and volume of medical activity.

The new agreement called for perfecting the fee schedule as a mechanism for assigning relative values to various medical procedures. By separating medical activity into categories (office visits, house calls, surgery, radiology, etc.) and attributing coefficients according to technical criteria, the schedule theoretically allows a more accurate, although imperfect, system of weighing fees and services. The fee schedules are a major determinant of both physicians' incomes and health insurance expenditures, and also constitute an important factor in the consumer price index, which the government cannot neglect. The annual bargaining, moreover, invariably touches sensitive nerves within the medical profession, requiring careful balancing of interests among general practitioners and various groups of specialists.

Despite the opposition of the minority medical union (FMF), the labour unions and the parties of the Left, the 1971 agreement met the approval of the doctors, nearly all (97.4 per cent) of whom were covered by 1980. The government was satisfied to have established a new legal framework for ongoing collective bargaining, while preserving the essential interests of providers, payers, and consumers of health care. It was considered axiomatic that continued economic growth would finance the development of a modern health system worthy of a modern industrial society. Government policy therefore focused on expanding the supply and accessibility of medical services, building new hospitals with the most sophisticated equipment, and training more physicians. The concurrent rise of the Left, united behind a Common Programme which promised even more benefits, meant that cost containment policies were not given further consideration, despite dire warnings in 1970 of enormous deficits looming ahead.

The oil crisis of 1974 produced shock tremors felt throughout the economy. The combined effects of inflation and unemployment severely strained the financing of social policy by reducing available resources while simultaneously increasing demand for benefits. Since health protection could not be curtailed, it was inevitable that the CNAMTS would seek to control costs; it was required by law to balance its books. The annual fee schedule negotiations became difficult encounters as of 1975, poisoning the atmosphere of discussions to renew the basic agreement. The CSMF alternated between boycotts and obstructive participation over a three-year period, but eventually a new contract was reached. That the unions' power was waning was made evident when the 1977 fee schedule failed to keep up with inflation; for the first time, doctors' real income declined.

Neo-liberalism and *médecine libérale*

Although health care costs continued to grow at an average of 16 per cent a year, the government adopted several measures (increased payroll taxes, reduced reimbursement for non-essential drugs) which averted deficits until the latter part of 1978, when a huge shortfall forced a reappraisal of policy. For twenty years, the dispersal of authority over health care among several ministries (Health, Finance, Social Security), the CNAMTS, and the doctors, had produced a series of partial and sometimes contradictory reforms. As a result, a host of interrelated problems had accumulated which the government now needed to address.

The 1958 Debré Hospital Law, for example, which had merged regional hospitals with the medical schools, offered privileged positions to those physicians who would accept salaried employment, combining clinical service, teaching and research in the public hospitals. To attract the top physicians, the Law offered them high salaries, control over their service units, and the right to receive and hospitalize their private patients (for high fees) separately in the public hospital, where they had access to the sophisticated equipment. In effect, the Law transformed the traditional 'charity institutions' into modern, high-technology hospitals, but left the physicians in full control.[4] Even the efforts of the 1970 Hospital Reform to rationalize resource allocation did not succeed in slowing down the excessive growth in the number of hospital beds.[5] By 1980, hospital care accounted for roughly half of overall costs.

Moreover, hospital management methods created disincentives to cost control. In order to obtain public capital investment, service directors were encouraged to maintain high occupancy rates.[6] The payment method was also highly inflationary: as government tried to hold down the patient/day rate (based on general operating expenses), the hospital compensated by prolonging the patient's stay. Since laboratory tests and technical procedures are paid separately, the multiplication of their use brought the hospitals added revenue.

The dramatic forward strides of technology in health care also posed problems. State-financed research kept France in the forefront of biomedical science, and the state-financed hospitals purchased the most advanced equipment. As medical care became increasingly technically orientated, the hospital-based physician had neither utility criteria nor financial incentives to seek the least costly procedures in diagnosis or treatment.[7]

Profound social changes long under way were also having a major impact on health care: an aging population, rapid industrialization, the shift from an agrarian to an industrial and service economy, the growing 'medicalization' of social problems (alcoholism, tobacco consumption, institutional care for the aged) produced not only greater demand for medical services, but also an increasing concentration of consumption. By 1980, 10 per cent of the population accounted for 70 per cent of health expenditures; 4 per cent generated fully half the costs.

Another consequence of the health policies of the 1960s was the rapid expansion of the supply of licensed physicians. Between 1960 and 1978, the number of annual medical school graduates tripled to nearly 12,000, twice the comparable figure for Great Britain.[8] Although the exact nature of the relationship is disputed, it is generally recognized that a greater supply of doctors induces a greater demand for their services.[9] The CSMF initially rejected this charge, arguing that patients determine medical demand; it is none the less clear that patients are directed to secondary services (specialists, laboratory tests, prescriptions, etc.) by their family doctors.

Fee-for-service payment of private physicians, the quintessential principle of *médecine libérale*, is another element generating high health care expenses. The collective agreements applied since 1960 had succeeded in bringing nearly all office practitioners under uniform fee schedules, determined through negotiations between the doctors' union and the CNAMTS, under government control. The doctors' response, however, to fixed fees was simply to increase the volume of their activity.

The 1971 and 1976 agreements created another problem by placing the doctors' union back in the centre of health policy-making. After a decade of adjustment, the CSMF's national strategy had succeeded in restoring union leverage. The profession had clearly adapted to the Fifth Republic and acquired once again the ability to frustrate national policy.

When the 1978 deficit was forecast and it appeared that the growth of health care expenses was continuing unabated, the context of policy-making had evolved once again. A wide-ranging attack on the outstanding problems was made both feasible and desirable by recent political and economic developments. The threat from the Left had disappeared: in the government's view, the Socialist-Communist alliance would not recover from the loss of the 1978 legislative elections. Moreover, President Giscard d'Estaing had adopted a neo-liberal strategy to deal with the deepening recession. In order to encourage the business community to become more aggressively competitive, and to protect the purchasing power of the lower-salaried workers, the government wished to avoid raising parafiscal taxes. It was resolved, therefore, to bring the entire health care system under unified control and remove the major obstacles to cost containment. Identifying the doctors as the principal generators of health care expenses, in both hospital and ambulatory care, the government in effect decided to declare war on the medical profession.

Its policies emerged in separate stages, focusing at first on the hospitals, then on the physicians' unions. In 1979, the Health Ministry acquired discretionary authority to phase out excess bed capacity in the public hospitals, targeting 7,000 beds. The concept of prospective global budgets for hospitals was also introduced, implying the necessity for administrators to live within fixed means. Neither of these measures was actually implemented until the Socialists came to power, but the battle was joined. The Minister also got the CNPF and the labour unions to agree to increase the payroll tax wage base by 5 per cent in order to balance the 1978 Social Security deficit. The CNAMTS was consequently instructed to hold 1979 fee schedule increases below the inflation rate.

The next phase set in motion the government's vigorous and co-ordinated strategy to break the dynamics of spiralling health costs and destroy the doctors' corporate power.[10] To meet expected Social Security deficits in 1979, a special surtax of 1 per cent would be imposed on all salaries for eighteen months; the doctors' fee increases scheduled for 1979 and 1980 were suspended. Henceforth, the growth of overall health expenses would be linked to the rate of increase of GDP, a rough indicator of the CNAMTS' ability to pay; in practical terms this meant that doctors would be under pressure to reduce diagnostic and therapeutic prescriptions in order to see their real income progress.

Then, on explicit instructions from the government, the sickness fund exploited medical union divisions to impose a new national contract (whose main outlines had been drawn up in the ministries), under which physicians were invited to choose individually between two 'sectors' or forms of participation. In the first sector, local sickness funds continued to pay the social insurance premiums for those doctors who applied the negotiated fee schedule. In the second sector, doctors were free to charge higher fees ('with tact and moderation') but had to pay their own premiums. Since the patient was reimbursed the same amount in either case, the costs of higher fees were thus to be shifted from the sickness funds to the consumer.

The government's strategy was to keep a tight lid on the fee schedule while creating an exit option; market forces in the second sector (i.e. a rapidly growing supply of doctors) were expected to keep fees down, the equivalent of price deregulation in the industrial sector.[11] The CSMF denounced an economic rationale in health care as an intolerable constraint on professional autonomy; the union accurately assessed the two-sector policy as one likely to counter their pressures for fee increases. Even worse, the possibility of exercising individual options deprived the union of its position as negotiator for the profession. Nevertheless, the signature of a smaller rival union was enough to bring the new contract into effect, and shortly thereafter, 99 per cent of the office-based doctors joined individually.

The Giscardian policies in the health field were significant because they meant that both the employers' association (through the CNAMTS) and a conservative government were intent on challenging the privileged position of the medical profession, making doctors carry a larger share of the burden of the recession. Curiously, the political implications of the concerted attack on the doctors were simply ignored; Giscard d'Estaing was convinced he could win the 1981 presidential elections without the doctors' union. The new agreement strengthened the mechanism for tightly controlling physicians' fees, but the government had hardly begun to consider other factors involved in the still unchecked high growth rate of health expenses.

Socialist rigour and *médecine libérale*

When the Left came to power in 1981, the health system was not the priority issue that restoring economic growth and reducing unemployment were. But these are not unrelated policy goals: the health care delivery system is labour-intensive, and employs more than 700,000 people directly. It is also highly inflationary, and the Socialists were not insensitive to the financial consequences of Social Security deficits.

Social policy as a whole had, of course, significant ideological implications. The Social Security system itself was viewed as a victory for the working class, and the Socialists and Communists were committed to extending benefits as a means of reducing social inequalities. Their thinking on the organization of the health care delivery system was expressed in the 1972 Common Programme, in Mitterrand's campaign platforms of 1974 and 1981, and in the 1980 Socialist Project. They were clearly aware of the inherent complexities of the system, and they intended only to refurbish it, not to redesign it.

The basic features of the Socialist health reforms focused on the financing and administration of both the Social Security system and the public hospital network, seen as the centrepiece of a vast public health service. The Socialists planned no broad-scale attack on the private office practitioners, but neither did they commit themselves to perpetuating the fee-for-service payment. They sought to promote pluralism in health care. Although many doctors, especially among the younger ones, were optimistic about new directions, most of the profession feared for the survival of médecine liberale, particularly with the appointment of a Communist as Health Minister and a left-wing Socialist as Minister of National Solidarity, in charge of Social Security.

The early measures adopted by the government during its expansionary period differed little from those of its predecessors. The 1 per cent payroll surtax which the Barre government had recently withdrawn was reinstated, and the employers' contribution was increased considerably. The Health Minister suspended the *numerus clausus* on entering medical students initiated two years earlier, but reinstated it in 1982. Mitterrand's pre-election promise to renegotiate the doctors' national contract discussions was quietly forgotten. Instead, the fee schedules were again frozen in July 1981 for six months. Shortly after the CNAMTS and the physicians' unions had negotiated new fee increases, in June 1982, the government imposed a four-month general freeze on wages and prices, affecting all doctors (except those in the deregulated second sector).

The main thrust of the government's policy aimed at the public hospitals, and here it faced stiff opposition from vested interests. The national negotiating process had succeeded in bringing office practitioners under control, but had not touched the entrenched power of the *grands patrons* in the public hospitals. Presiding over sizeable specialized service units and enjoying immense prestige and incomes and life appointments, the public hospitals' service directors were immune to pressures to contain costs. The Barre government had engineered some schemes to reduce their powers, but had faltered in implementing them.

One measure struck at the corner-stone of the 1958 Hospital Reform, phasing out the specialists' lucrative privilege of consulting and hospitalizing their private patients in the public hospitals. Fewer than 4,000 of the more than 15,000 full-time physicians benefited from this privilege, but they were in effect using the highly sophisticated public facilities for private gain. The reform was accompanied by substantial fringe benefits to compensate in part for the loss of income.

The government's second measure attacked the hospital physicians' power at its roots by breaking up the specialized service units over which the *grands patrons* ruled like feudal lords. A blue-ribbon panel, commissioned by the Prime Minister in 1983 to examine the public hospitals, had suggested creating discipline-defined clinical departments as instruments of more rational functioning and management of the public hospitals.[12] Despite the support of the younger physicians and the non-medical staff, the virulent opposition of the *grands patrons* delayed implementation until 1985, and even then, very few departments were set up.

The combination of these measures, the growing number of doctors, and the decline of their purchasing power, produced major demonstrations, primarily in Paris, during 1982. United in opposition to what they considered Socialist-Communist threats to basic liberties, the doctors joined forces with other health professionals, lawyers, and architects, to protest. The general themes of the movement obscured the fundamentally divergent interests among the doctors, but the demonstrations contributed to the emerging public sentiment that the government was losing popular support, as local elections would soon prove.

The government's policy shift to 'Socialist rigour' in July 1982 saw the Health Ministry placed under a broad Social Affairs Ministry, led by Pierre Bérégovoy. Observing that hospital expenses were still growing at more than 20 per cent a year, Bérégovoy instituted two hospital finance reforms to curb costs. The global budget process, introduced into the public hospital network progressively as of January 1984, required regional health funds and hospital administrators to negotiate annual hospital expenditure ceilings. As a result, the annual increase of hospital expenditures declined to 8.5 per cent in 1985.[13] Second, a minimum daily payment was instituted, as an incentive for patients to resist prolonged hospital stays.

Although the CNAMTS had been involved with the government strategy since 1980 to control health care expenditures, its resistance to several of the Socialists' measures — viewed as potential threats to *médecine libérale* — led the government to try to break up the CNPF-FO alliance which prevailed on the fund's administrative board. The Left had been committed since the Common Programme to abrogate the 1967 Jeanneney Ordinances and return the management of the Social Security boards to the elected representatives of the workers. They were hoping in fact to place the CFDT and the CGT delegates, who had been excluded from policy matters, back in control. Although the distribution of board seats favoured the labour unions, the Social Security elections of October 1983 were heavily politicized and became one more test of the government's (un)popularity. The opposition parties, the CNPF, and the physicians' unions campaigned for the moderate labour unions (FO, CFTC and CGC), who won most of the seats, upsetting the government's plans, and the CNPF–FO coalition remained intact.

By keeping fee schedule increases below the rate of inflation and imposing constraints on the hospitals, Bérégovoy's cost containment policies succeeded in balancing the Social Security accounts. In fact, a substantial surplus in 1983 was enough to wipe out the 1982 deficit. Another surplus in 1984 allowed the government to abolish the 1 per cent income surtax and help keep Mitterrand's promise to reduce fiscal pressures. In attempting after 1982 to demonstrate that social justice and prudent financial management were not incompatible, the Socialists by and large maintained the health policies of their predecessors. Their five years in power — with its successes and disappointments — did much to persuade them that state-directed strategies must still obey economic realities;[14] their term in office also served to clear the air, to free both the non-Communist Left and the moderate Right of the ideological heritage which had shaped and constrained their policies for so long.

The return of neo-liberalism

When the conservative coalition (the Gaullist RPR and the centrist UDF alliance) returned to power in 1986, France seemed finally to be catching up with the conservative mood prevailing in Britain, the USA and West Germany. Prime Minister Jacques Chirac had quietly broken with the traditional Gaullist emphasis on the state as symbol of the national interest and adopted the Thatcher–Reagan model, discovering the virtues of the free market and the vices of bureaucratic *dirigisme,* and espousing the themes of deregulation and individual initiative.

The fundamental thrust of the RPR–UDF alliance's domestic programme was thus anti-statist: it promised to privatize the major nationalized industrial and banking groups, reduce public debt and budget deficits, eliminate subsidies to private industry, remove price controls and deregulate the credit sector and currency exchange, eliminate administrative control of private-sector layoffs, and so on. Their neo-liberal, market-orientated programme contained no broad-scale attack, however, on the welfare state. On the contrary, French public opinion was still wedded to egalitarian principles,— and the broad consensus on the Social Security system required safeguarding it from perennial financial difficulties. The supply-side approach dictated restoring economic growth, in order to reduce unemployment and Social Security deficits.

The conservative agenda in health care promised greater responsibility to health professionals, hospital managers, and financing institutions, and greater managerial and budget autonomy to hospitals and clinics. It also hinted vaguely about greater competition among private complementary insurers. On the whole, however, because their predecessors had fallen in line with the cost-containment strategies adopted since 1979, the conservatives found little room to manoeuvre and few areas in which to innovate.

By 1986, the public had heard too often the dire warnings of Social Security's imminent collapse to accept any radical systemic changes. An IFOP poll showed 85 per cent of the French deeply attached to their '*Sécu* ' as they knew it; more than half of those polled wanted additional revenues raised from the employer contributions, not their own.[16] The government, however, was committed to reducing the share of taxes in the GDP.

Given these constraints, the government had to navigate carefully. Its strategy was therefore to maintain the cost-containment priority, which would reassure the public, demonstrate its responsible and effective governance, and keep its critics quiet; at the same time, it needed to regain the support of the medical community, not only for electoral reasons, but also to secure its acquiescence and co-operation in the efforts to control health expenditures. Consequently, the government promised fee increases in ambulatory care, but only if the volume of medical procedures and prescriptions were kept in line. Gaining the hospital physicians' good will required reversing the Socialist measures with the most symbolic value.

The first objective was to finance the immediate Social Security deficit for 1986 (estimated between 6 billion and 25 billion francs). The only solutions available, until more extensive consultations and consensus-building could take place, were fiscal. Over the Finance Minister's objections, the government increased payroll deductions and re-established the 1 per cent income surtax the Socialists had applied between 1983 and 1985. To meet the even larger 1987 deficit (15–40 billion francs), Social Affairs Minister Séguin introduced a politically courageous, but highly unpopular reform of insured benefits, involving increased patient co-payments, which saved the sickness fund nearly 12 billion francs.

Concerning the public hospitals, the RPR–UDF platform of 1986 was committed to restoring the private sector which the Socialists had phased out. The stated goals of Health Minister Barzach, a physician herself, were to improve the articulation between ambulatory and hospital care and to reverse the flight of competent physicians from the public service.[17] She did recognize the widespread criticism on ethical grounds of abuses of the private sector, and promised a 'moralization' of the practice. The 1987 Hospital Law made the right to private practice dependent on a contract negotiated between physician and hospital management, subject to prefectoral (i.e. state) approval. Furthermore, the privilege was no longer transferable between hospitals. Private activity would be limited to two half-days a week; and the hospital would collect the fees, deducting its share. The Law also re-established the hospital services which the Socialists has abolished, but under new conditions which provided for the appointment by the Health Minister of service directors to renewable five-year terms, subject to consultation and peer evaluation, in place of the life appointments.

The French health care system in the 1980s

The 1980s have thus witnessed much more than continuity with the fiscal imperative which emerged in the late 1970s. Although there has not been any sharp break with the past, the subtle, pragmatic and qualitative changes which have taken place combine to make the health care system today substantially *different* from what it was at the beginning of the Fifth Republic. A public enterprise mentality has replaced the public service concept, with consequences in authority patterns, management techniques, reimbursement mechanisms, and the configuration of the delivery system.

There has been a sifting out of roles and powers between the managers of the system, the state and the sickness funds. In its domain, the state has applied a firm grip on supply: cutting in half the number of students admitted into the second year of medical school, reducing hospital capacity, and capping both hospital expenditures and physicians' fees in ambulatory care.

The public hospital system has been redesigned to focus on the highly technical medical procedures, while ambulatory care is being made more flexible and adaptable to the cultural and demographic changes taking place in French society. Alternatives are being developed to hospitalization for non-medical social cases (the elderly and the mentally disturbed, for example), placing them when feasible in appropriate centres, or in home care with paramedical assistance.[18] The medical community has been exploring French versions of Health Maintenance Organizations (HMOs),[19] multi-disciplinary public care clinics, day hospitals, and so on.

Modern managerial and accounting techniques are being introduced into the hospitals. In financing, the prospective budgeting procedure has already created incentives to improve efficiency. Reliable, sophisticated means of determining hospital costs are being developed; analytical accounting was introduced in 1985 to give hospital administrators a means of examining their expenditures by cost centres (administrative, hotel charges, clinical, medico-technical). To make the hospital budgets real tools for forecasting needs, the Ministry's Hospital Division has worked out a French version of the Diagnostic Related Groups,[20] and is currently collecting standardized exit data on patients.

This strategy of flexibility in health care delivery requires a more sophisticated gatekeeper role for the family doctor, directing his patients to the appropriate diagnostic and therapeutic centres when necessary. To enhance the pivotal role of the general practitioner, the government began revamping the medical school curriculum, in order to make general medicine a different kind of specialization; it has also begun closing the gap between the fees of GPs and specialists.[21]

In the course of this reshaping of the health care delivery system, the sickness funds have also diversified and extended the scope of their role, in the public hospitals and in ambulatory care.[22] As the intermediaries between the state and the medical profession, it was the CNAMTS which redesigned the national agreement in 1980 to defuse conflict over the fee schedule by opening up the second sector. Since then, the focus of negotiations has shifted to finding acceptable ways to get physicians to re-examine how they practice their art: to identify not only the best remedy for a given affliction, but the best remedy at the lowest cost, a perspective foreign to most doctors' training. Tripartite discussions were undertaken to set up professional review procedures which, while respecting professional confidentiality, should provide qualitative, not just quantitative, analyses of medical behaviour and its financial consequences to help in this pursuit.[23]

Conclusion

The French health care system has for two centuries been characterized by a shifting public and private balance; in the nineteenth century, the state was called upon to help the profession regulate the medical market, by controlling supply (to eliminate quacks), and to create demand (public health campaigns, medical care for the poor). The public–private mix today seems, none the less, to satisfy most French - patients and physicians alike — who find that their system is an excellent compromise between the egalitarian but financially strapped British National Health Service and the technologically advanced but profligate American way. Consumers receive high-quality care, accessible to all, at not too great a cost, while preserving a certain measure of individual choice. This consensus has served over the past three decades as a formidable constraint in policy-making, precluding radical change and guiding both Left and Right towards consensual policies.

Given the direction of change during the 1980s, it seems likely that the next decade will focus on increasing the efficiency and reducing the scope of the public sector, assigning greater roles to the private sector, whether private insurance, private clinics, or consumer responsibility. Although the sickness funds are not likely to be affected directly, the completion of the European single market in 1992 will surely bring in competition from private British and German insurers. One possible scenario would be to limit mandatory coverage to 'major risks', leaving complementary insurance to the consumer, providing income supplements to protect the less well-off.

After thirty years of the Fifth Republic, there appear to be profound changes under way in French political culture, as the 1988 presidential and legislative campaigns suggested. The intense ideological debates opposing a free-market economy and a state-regulated economy, so characteristic of France in the 1950s and 1960s, now seem outdated; a new consensus on the relative role of state and market is taking shape, indicating recognition of the new and highly competitive international environment which emerged in the 1970s. The evolution of French health care policy illustrates a modern industrial democracy's capacity to preserve its particular national values while adjusting to changing circumstances.

Notes

1. Douglas E. Ashford, 'The British and French Social Security Systems: Welfare State by Intent and by Default' in Ashford (ed.), *Nationalizing Social Security* (Greenwich, JAI Press, 1985); Robert Launois, 'L'Economie et la politique de la santé', unpublished paper presented at the Université de Rennes, 1984.
2. Simone Sandier, 'Les dépenses de soins médicaux en France depuis 1950', *Revue Française de Finances Publiques*, 2 (1983).
3. Victor Rodwin, *The Health Planning Predicament: France, Québec, England, and the United States* (Berkeley: University of California Press, 1984); Jean-Claude Stéphan, *Economie et pouvoir médical* (Paris: Economica, 1978).
4. Gérard de Pouvourville, 'Faut-il centraliser le système de santé?', *Projet* nos 179–80 (1983).
5. Rodwin, *Health Planning*.
6. A.T. Lachand, 'Sur la maîtrise de dépenses', *Le Monde*, 29 September 1979.
7. Launois, 'L'Economie'.
8. Jean-François Lacronique, 'The French Health Care System' in Gordon McLachlan and Alan Maynard (eds), *The Public/Private Mix for Health* (London: The Nuffield Provincial Hospitals Trust, 1982).
9. Robert Launois and Daniel Le Touzé, 'L'Analyse économique des mesures prises en France afin de maîtriser la croissance des dépenses sanitaires' in Didier Truchet (ed.), *Etudes de droit et d'économie de santé* (Paris: Economica, 1980).
10. The Elysée and Matignon staffs never forgave the CSMF leader, Jacques Monier, for having criticized the government during the 1978 legislative elections campaign.
11. The assumption that the health sector was a market like any other, and that patients would be — could be — discerning consumers, went largely unchallenged in government circles. (Personal interview with Dominique Coudreau, Director of the CNAMTS, 1984.)
12. *Le Système de Santé Français: Réflexions et propositions* (Paris: La Documentation Française, 1983). See also André Demichel, 'La Réforme hospitalière: éléments pour une problématique' in *Revue Française de Finances Publiques*, 2 (1983); and Jean-Marie Clément, *Les Réformes Hospitalières, 1981-1984* (Paris: Berger–Levrault, 1985). Health Minister Ralite's original proposals, which had medical and non-medical personnel electing department directors, were modified in May 1983 when Edmond Hervé took over the portfolio, to have them appointed by the Ministry, on recommendation of medical committee, for four years.
13. Jean-Paul Séguéla, Report (no. 689) of the Cultural, Family, and Social Affairs Committee of the National Assembly, on the Hospital Reform Bill, April 1987.
14. See, for example, Bela Belassa, 'Five Years of Socialist Economic Policy in France: A Balance Sheet', *The Tocqueville Review*, vol. 7 (1986); and Peter A.

Hall, 'Socialism in One Country: Mitterrand and the Struggle to Define a New Economic Policy for France' in Philip G. Cerny and Martin A. Schain (eds), *Socialism, the State and Public Policy in France* (London: Frances Pinter, 1985).

15. See Olivier Duhamel *et al.* (eds), *SOFRES: Opinion Publique 1986* (Paris: Gallimard, 1986).

16. Published in *L'Humanité Dimanche* , 25 May 1986.

17. On TV in January 1987, Minister Barzach complained that two-thirds of the 1,800 vacant hospital posts remained unfilled.

18. Jean de Kervasdoué, former Director of Hospitals in the Ministry of Health, estimated that at least 30 per cent of a given day's hospital admissions should not be there at all. See 'Prescrire l'hôpital', *Prospective et Santé* , no. 43 (Fall 1987).

19. Several experts have devised a system called *Réseaux de Soins Coordonnés* (RSC) — Coordinated Health Care Networks — in which, for example, the sickness funds provide a uniform annual payment, and patients choose among competitive pre-paid programmes, depending on the coverage they seek; they could opt for more extensive coverage, if they are willing to pay extra. See Robert Launois, Béatrice Majnoni d'Intignano, Victor Rodwin and Jean-Claude Stéphan, 'Les Réseaux de Soins Coordonnés: Proposition pour une réforme profonde du système de santé', in *Revue Française des Affaires Sociales* , 1 (1985).

20. The Groupes Homogènes de Malades, or GHM. See Armand Hatchuel, Jean-Claude Moisdon, and Hugues Molet, 'Budget Global Hospitalier et Groupes Homogènes de Malades', *Politiques et Management Public* , vol.3, no. 4 (December 1985).

21. The steady growth in the number of doctors over the 1980s brought about an oversaturation in the most desirable locations for setting up practices. Combined with the slow evolution of the fee schedules since 1980, this high density resulted in stagnating incomes for most doctors, declining incomes for GPs. See CREDES, 'Géographie économique de la santé', *Revue de socio-économie de la santé* (November 1986). The market for specialists, however, is not so Malthusian. Overall, doctors' purchasing power showed modest (1-2 per cent) real increases since 1984, according to a Centre d'Etudes des Revenus et des Coûts study (13 July 1988).

22. See Antoinette Catrice-Lorey, 'L'Assurance Maladie et le Système de Santé', *Revue Française des Affaires Sociales*, no. 43 (July-September 1987).

23. See, for example, *Le Monde*, 24 February 1988. Evaluation techniques were initially sponsored by Prof. Emile Papiernik, a Socialist consultant; Health Minister Barzach chose to set up her own committee, but the objectives have not been modified.

Part V: Foreign Policy

14. Franco-Soviet relations and French foreign policy: between adjustment and ambition

Dominique Moïsi

Introduction

France's dilemma between the need for security and the desire for independence is the product of a complex, triangular set of relations, between France and the United States, France and West Germany, and France and the Soviet Union. In so far as the latter is partly conditioned by the two former, understanding fully France's relations with the Soviet Union requires taking into account France's relations with its main ally and guarantor, the United States, and with its main European partner and former rival, West Germany. France is the Western European country whose position since the 1960s has been the least anti-Soviet and the most anti-American, a position which clearly evolved in the late 1970s and early 1980s, as France's allies tended to become more sceptical of the United States and to mellow toward the Soviet Union.

France's relations with the Soviet Union are dominated by five factors. The first is her vision of her world role and her claim to mini-superpower status has created a particular context, which gives the Soviet Union a double role: first as the country to be resisted, within the framework of an Atlantic solidarity, but also as the country with which to promote dialogue and co-operation so as to bolster France's claim to an ambitious international existence.

The second is that, given the centralization of the French foreign policy process, especially since the Fifth Republic, the definition of France's policy towards the Soviet Union is essentially the privilege of the executive, and in particular of the President alone, with the help of his advisers and the Foreign Ministry. The absence of divisive debates between the executive and the legislature, or among the various agencies of the executive, has probably led to a greater continuity in French Soviet policy. Even the 'cohabitation' of a President and a Prime Minister representing opposing political forces between March 1986 and May

1988 did not alter the essential unity of France's policy towards the Soviet Union.

The third is that the existence of a French Communist Party (PCF), long representing, despite its recent decline, a sizeable sector of the electorate, has been important in the definition of France's policy towards the Soviet Union, all the more so since the PCF seemed to align itself faithfully with Moscow. The presence of the PCF has alternately given French governments a greater awareness of the risks of destabilization promoted by Moscow, as in the late 1940s, or the conviction that conservative governments could acquire the tacit allegiance of the Communists, through a policy of *détente* with the Soviet Union and resistance to and differentiation from the United States.

The fourth factor is the role of the intelligentsia: French intellectuals have helped shape Franco-Soviet relations, as a positive force in the postwar years with often active support for the Soviet regime, or by their benign neglect of Soviet repression in Czechoslovakia in 1968. On the other hand, intellectuals played a negative role for the Soviet Union in the 1970s, when their belated discovery of the Gulag, combined with immediate criticism of Soviet expansionism in Afghanistan, led to a major deterioration of the Soviet image in France.

The final factor is the economic dimension, although initially it proved to be of secondary, if not marginal, importance in a country where *raison d'état* and ideological debates prevail. By the 1970s, though, starting with President Pompidou, economic deals with the Soviet Union became both a symbol and a concrete element of the privileged relationship between the two countries. Greatly influenced by Samuel Pisar's vision of economic exchanges as the 'weapon of peace', Giscard d'Estaing's France could combine two myths: obeying the law of the market and pursuing an independent policy. Economic rationality became an alibi and a justification for political choices and a card which the Soviet Union used as best it could.

The substance of policy

History and ideology are the two main components of a relationship that took on a different nature after the Second World War, when France, no longer a great power, found itself confronted with the emerging threat of a new superpower, the Soviet Union. In this context, there were two sides to France's policy: it sought to adjust while at the same time refusing the new givens of this situation. A double orientation thus arose, based on the need to resist the new Soviet challenge through the Atlantic Alliance and the need to exist independently, through a policy of differentiation within the Alliance which in turn implied a different policy toward the Soviet Union. Whenever the global East–West crisis assumed a character of urgency, the French rallied behind the United States (as in the Berlin, Cuban or Euromissile crises). Whenever East–West tensions receded, the French played their own cards toward Moscow in a dual effort of differentiation from the United States and of competition with respect to West Germany. This was a somewhat dangerous trend, since relations with the Soviet Union, in effect, became one of the main criteria by which to judge France's international clout and standing, with the Soviets as potential arbiters of a Franco-German competitive partnership. The competition was bound to be unequal, since the Soviet Union could play on France's vanity and fears of Germany. France could become a partner in a game in which the Germans were the real and only stake.

The long history of Franco-Russian ties is played and sometimes overplayed by both the French and the Soviet governments to fulfil different but complementary objectives. The recent Paris exhibition on 'France and Russia in the century of Enlightenment' was a perfectly illuminating example of that dual trend. The French were proud of this reminder of their once great power, of a time when France was clearly a model for Russia and a source of political, intellectual and artistic inspiration. The Soviet leadership was pleased to stress the continuity with Russia's great rulers of the past, thereby de-emphasizing ideological differences. This unifying function of history can be played efficiently because geography, having had the good grace of giving France and Russia no common borders, made them most of the time allies against the country in between, Germany, their common threat. The Soviet Union and its Eastern European clients consistently use common cultural values and history to drive a wedge between France and the United States, and between the United States and West Germany. For a country like France which relishes all evocations of its own glorious past, this long history of relations and very often alliances with Russia is an important ingredient in the relationship with the Soviet Union.

In December 1944, the Franco-Soviet Alliance, purportedly against Germany, corresponded to de Gaulle's attempt to reinsert France diplomatically into the international system by having her play the arbiter between the Anglo-Saxons and the Soviets whose alliance was already beginning to appear in difficulty. This French ambition was thwarted since Moscow did not support France's international claim to be a major partner in the concert of victorious powers. After the Second World War it was only reluctantly that France accepted the new framework of an international order which reduced her status and imposed on her the strict rules of solidarity with allies. The irresistible rise of the Cold War in Europe, the need to resist Soviet destabilizing tactics with the economic, political and ultimately military help of the United States, could only condemn the illusory dream of Foreign Minister Georges Bidault of having France play an intermediary role between East and West.

However, the passions underlying the European Defence Community debates in the 1950s illustrated France's psychological difficulty in switching from the German to the Soviet threat. By 1954, the negative alliance between the Gaullists and the Communists, on top of the divisions among the Socialists themselves, defeated French ratification of the EDC Treaty. The purported denationalization of the French army, coupled with the rearmament of Germany, seemed a far greater threat than the real presence of Soviet divisions, whose danger seemed removed and abstract compared with the impending prospect of German soldiers within a European army. In the Suez crisis in 1956, the dual veto of the superpowers condemned to failure the last anachronistic attempt by European colonial powers to play at gunboat diplomacy in the new international system. France's humiliation reinforced its resolution to possess the necessary means to enhance its status and bolster its independence against the diktat of the two superpowers. France's independent nuclear force in effect introduced a new element in her relationship with the Soviet Union, but one that corresponded well to France's traditional attempt to combine security with regard to the Soviet Union and independence within the alliance from the United States.

In 1958, de Gaulle's return to power in the midst of the Algerian drama coincided first with the successive crises of Berlin and Cuba, then with the onset of *détente*. This proved to be the ideal context for fixing de Gaulle's principles: firmness towards the Soviet Union and solidarity with the United States in time of acute East–West crises; dialogue with the Soviet Union and enlargement of France's diplomatic margin of manoeuvre with the United States, through a policy of calculated differentiation in periods of relaxed tensions. These were the two pillars of a policy whose validity and limitations were both demonstrated between 1962 and 1969. De Gaulle's trip to Moscow in June 1966, coming so shortly after France's departure from the integrated military apparatus of NATO, was wrongly denounced by many as a reversal of alliances. The two actions were perfectly complementary in the context of a policy of '*détente*, entente and co-operation' which de Gaulle wanted to establish.

De Gaulle's famous and ambiguous appeal for a Europe from the Atlantic to the Urals could be accepted, within limits, by the Soviet Union as long as the latter was integrated into the geographical scope of this European scheme, and as long as her control of Eastern Europe was not threatened. For de Gaulle an approach so different from the traditional 'geography of values', made possible by the American nuclear umbrella, could alter the nature of the international system in Europe. Less integration in Western Europe would encourage less control of the Soviet Union in Eastern Europe. Could not France's distance from NATO be presented as an indirect appeal to the people of Eastern Europe to try the same with Moscow? De Gaulle's trip to Moscow in June 1966 was followed by a series of visits to Poland in 1967 and to Rumania in 1967.

Unfortunately for de Gaulle, his vision did not fully correspond either to the reality of the international system, as was proven by the Soviet invasion of Czechoslovakia (the second *coup de Prague*) in August 1968, or to France's capacity for independent action, as demonstrated by the Events of May 1968. The *coup de Prague*, a mere traffic incident on the road to *détente* according to Michel Debré, had, however, a stabilizing impact on détente, which was fully pursued in a parallel if not competitive manner by the French, the Germans and the Americans. France's approach to détente was mainly political; for the Americans, the strategic arms control component constituted the clear priority, whereas for the Germans the emphasis was on the human and economic dimensions of *Ostpolitik*. France's political approach stemmed directly from her desire for a central international role, one that would transcend her regional limitations. Successive French governments, therefore, have always been systematically worried either by phases of excessive direct *rapprochement* between the two superpowers, potentially leading to what is characterized as a condominium, or by phases of excessive tensions and confrontation, which would leave France with no diplomatic margin of manoeuvre within its own camp. For the French therefore, the ideal dialogue between the two superpowers must be slow and difficult — but there must be dialogue.

This specific French approach to the Soviet Union, which combines independence and therefore differentiation within the Western Alliance and the search for a maximum security, has led to the adoption of original positions on three major questions pertaining to the relationship with the Soviet Union. First, what is the geographic scope of the Soviet threat, and where should Western solidarity stop, given the geographic limitations of the Atlantic Alliance? Second, what is the specific contribution that France should make to the arms control process, given its need to protect the credibility of its independent nuclear deterrent? Third, to what an extent should the French or the Europeans join the Americans in their policy of sanctions or embargo towards the Soviet Union?

A fourth question, though less divisive, is worth mentioning, and is linked to the treatment of Eastern Europe. In its policy of *rapprochement* with the Soviet Union, should France use the traditional East European channels and recreate links existing between the two world wars, or should France conversely punish the Soviet Union for the repression she imposes on her unhappy and rebelling satellites?

The question of the geographic extension of the Atlantic solidarity to non-NATO areas has undergone cyclical evolution. It reflects as much respective French and American interests as it measures reactions to the Soviet Union's Third World ambitions. During the Fourth Republic, while the French were engaged in a desperate battle to keep parts of their Empire against the irresistible process of decolonization, Paris tried to convince Washington of the altruistic nature of its colonial stands. How could the United States not support France, when it was ultimately against Moscow's revolutionary and world-wide ambitions that she was acting in Indochina and Algeria!

During the 1960s, once decolonization was completed, the positions were reversed. The Americans, engaged in the Vietnam war, unsuccessfully tried to convince the French to give them at least political support in their global defence of Western interests in Asia. Since that time, with the notable exception of the Carter period prior to the 1979 Soviet invasion of Afghanistan, the French have tried to give a regional and not a global interpretation to Third World conflicts. The French refusal to join the Americans in a concerted action in Third World areas of unrest expresses a different interpretation of the nature of these conflicts, and therefore a different appreciation of the best ways to confront them. It also corresponds to a willingness to protect the process of *rapprochement* with the Soviet Union, an attitude that led to the American–European debate on the divisibility of *détente*. For the French, to interpret Third World conflicts through East–West military lenses was to miss their essentially regional, local, even 'tribal', socio-economic and cultural origins. A joint Western approach could only reinforce anti-Western feelings in areas such as the Persian Gulf, where the Western presence, through resistance to the modernization process, is one of the main sources of destabilization.

It was only during the Carter presidency, and within the very specific African contest of the Kolwesi affair, that the French gave the Americans lessons in responsible behaviour against the indirect Soviet threat. Most of the time the reverse was true, and the French emphasized the legitimacy of the Soviet presence in the Middle East, for both historical and geographic reasons, denouncing the illusion of any effort to promote peace in the Arab–Israeli conflict which excluded the Soviet Union. A certain willingness to preserve a process of *détente* with the Soviet Union in Europe pushed the French government to react initially in a very muted manner to the Soviet invasion of Afghanistan in December 1979, an attitude that was reversed when President Mitterrand came to power.

In the field of arms control, France's approach once again revealed its global attitude to the United States and the Soviet Union, and the French need to combine independence and security, to the extent possible. For France, especially since the Fifth Republic, disarmament must obey four principles: it must be real, implying therefore a reduction of, and not simply a limit to, arms growth; and it must be global, non-discriminatory, and subject to control. France's nuclear efforts in the 1960s ran directly counter to the logic prevailing in the American–Soviet approach to arms control, which in its bipolarity symbolized the very division of Europe. France therefore opted for the policy of the 'empty chair' between 1962 and 1978, refusing to occupy its seat on the Disarmament Committee in Geneva. When France shifted position in 1978, under the impulse of

Giscard d'Estaing, it proposed among various measures the convening of a Conference on Disarmament in Europe to deal with the problem of the conventional disequilibrium in Europe in favour of the Warsaw Pact. This proposal corresponded to another French priority: the need for a third great power to make an independent and original contribution to the problems of disarmament.

The issue of Eastern Europe has been traditionally absent from French preoccupations, or was perceived in a purely derivative manner. 'The other Europe' was seen either as a way to open or foster channels of communication with Moscow (de Gaulle's early strategy in the mid-1960s), or as a means to reinforce *détente* on an economic basis as in the 1970s, or as a potential obstacle to *détente* (as shown by the events in Prague in 1968). Eastern Europe's always secondary or accompanying role in French concerns did not preclude the old strategy of 'reverse alliances', a traditional French pattern used by the Eastern European regimes themselves, either independently or on behalf of Moscow. Public emotions played a modest role in the Polish crisis of December 1981, but did not seriously affect French resolution to react in a discrete manner.

A traditional attempt to promote *raison d'état* above all other concerns was in keeping with French willingness to approach the Soviet Union on a state-to-state, non-ideological basis. The question of sanctions against the Soviet Union following the invasion of Afghanistan, and the 1980 'military coup' in Poland provided another source of West–West tensions and exemplified France's emphasis on the need to dissociate economic exchanges with the East from their political and even military implications. But it also embodied France's and Europe's irritation with an America that seemed at the same time too ideological and too economically orientated, overemphasizing the capacity of the West to influence developments in the Soviet Union through a policy of economic pressures. In France, most analysts felt that the Soviet Union could always transcend what would be considered in the West as basic economic demands, by a strict control over its society and a recourse to autarchy. On the other hand, one may wonder to what extent the Europeans were not refusing to see the real help they were giving to the Soviet military effort or aggressive political strategy by refusing to consider the possibility of linkages between Soviet behaviour and Western attitudes.

The role of images

There exists a direct relation between the way France sees herself and the way she views the world, and the Soviet Union in particular. France's fascination with her own past pushes her to give a high priority to the historical dimension of political phenomena. Inheritor of a prestigious past, of a long tradition as a nation-state, France naturally seeks in others what she looks for in herself: a sense of continuity and tradition, eternal goals beyond the floating nature of different regimes. De Gaulle's view of history, his personification of nations, has had a long-standing impact on the way France perceives the Soviet Union. Tempted to see eternal Russia under the Marxist mantle, France voluntarily neglected for cultural but also for immediate political reasons the ideological nature of the Soviet regime. Ideology was not supposed to interfere with historical links or immediate, détente-orientated political concerns.

In a famous and ambiguous statement about a Europe that would stretch from the Atlantic to the Urals, de Gaulle constituted a perfect negation of the enduring ideological nature of the East–West divide. Pompidou's pragmatism or Giscard d'Estaing's inexperienced idealism only confirmed this difficulty for French governments to integrate the ideological dimension of the Soviet regime. Animated by an optimistic, positivist vision of the world, convinced of his own superiority, Giscard d'Estaing was the least able to understand the Soviet Union. When he first went to Moscow in 1975, he dreamed of attenuating the ideological competition with the Soviet Union. Such a non-ideological approach to the Soviet regime risked putting France, and more globally the West, in a structurally weak position. Negotiating processes, by their very nature, tend to create the illusion of an ideologically and culturally homogeneous world, when in fact it is divided. Henry Kissinger, a great admirer of de Gaulle in his search to restore a world order, dreamed of recreating the conditions of the nineteenth-century balance of power. He could only fail: the Soviet Union is not the Hapsburg or Roman empire. In an atomic age the Soviet Union does not and cannot want war, but it cannot want stability, either, without losing its legitimacy.

Mitterrand's coming to power in 1981, in the context of deteriorated East–West relations, introduced a break in this tradition of concern for détente and preservation of co-operation. Interrupting the pattern of bilateral Franco-Soviet summit meetings, formally established during Pompidou's presidency, Mitterrand intended to fulfil a moral (given Afghanistan) and political role, while reassuring the United States about the reliability of Socialist France, despite the presence of Communist ministers in the government. Mitterrand was also seeking to be more in tune with the policies of de Gaulle, whose influence over time seemed to overtake the more traditional Socialist role-models, such as Jean Jaurès, Aristide Briand and Léon Blum, who had been Mitterrand's previous references. This change could only confirm André Malraux's dictum that 'everybody is, has been, or will be a Gaullist'.

Mitterrand's change of attitude towards the Soviet Union in 1984–5 illustrated perfectly France's hopes and fears with regard to East–West relations. It also incarnated France's perception of its obligations and responsibilities toward its main allies, foremost among them the United States and West Germany. In 1984, when the Reagan administration was trying, largely for domestic political reasons, to re-establish contact with the Soviet leadership, why should France refrain from doing the same? Mitterrand's France had given ample proof of its faithfulness to the Atlantic Alliance with its steadfastness in the Euromissile quarrel. Having reassured the Americans, and been reassured by the evolution of West Germany away from the 'sirens of pacifism', Mitterrand could return to the traditional French aim of helping bridge the growing gap of misunderstanding between East and West. Such a goal is always appreciated in Moscow, since it allows the Soviet Union to play on French pride by singling them out from the European pack, as Gorbachev's trip of October 1985 showed. In this particular case, the Soviets demonstrated respect for French firmness on the Euromissile issue while approving France's critical stance towards President Reagan's Strategic Defense Initiative (SDI).

French intellectuals have played an important role in developing the Soviet Union's image in France. In the early 1950s, at the peak of the Cold War, the intelligentsia was fascinated with the revolutionary essence of the Soviet experiment, and full of understanding for the excesses taking place in 'the Motherland of socialism'. But in the early 1970s they belatedly discovered the totalitarian nature of the Soviet system from Alexander Solzhenitsyn's *Gulag* trilogy. Concurrently, Soviet expansionism from Africa to Afghanistan brought French intellectuals to see the world in starkly different terms. This shift coincided with and was a reason for the spectacular fall of the French Communist Party, victim of its own Stalinism, whose popular support dwindled by more than half to less than 10 per cent. The combination of the intellectuals' reversal and the French Communist Party's continued Stalinism helped produce an image of the Soviet Union which was noticeably worse in France than in the rest of Western Europe in the late 1970s and early 1980s, and which, to add insult to injury from the Soviet standpoint, coincided with a visible decline of anti-Americanism in France. It is probable that the weakening of America's military supremacy has made her cultural dynamism more acceptable in France. While France was discovering the values of the alliance during the Euromissile crisis, its citizens, in their quest for a more open and modern society, began looking to the United States as the incarnation of the values of openness, dynamism and inventiveness.

In 1984–5, France returned to the traditional dialogue with the Soviet Union, and witnessed an evolution of the Soviet image that could be characterized as the 'banalization of evil'. The Soviet Union was not going to improve its record on human rights, moderate its world ambitions or reform its economy or society. Since little could be done to influence Soviet domestic policies, it was better to be resigned, and to resume a dialogue and normalization, already begun by the United States, that could not be left to France's main European partners either, West

Germany or Great Britain. Significantly, however, the French intelligentsia pursued its anti-totalitarian denunciations even as *raison d'état*
prevailed once more.

The process

Compared to the American process, French foreign policy-making is
quite simple. The intricate checks and balances between the executive
branch and Congress, and the sophisticated, suicidal games within the
executive, that seem to fit only a truly isolationist America rather than the
foreign policy needs of the world's leading power, simply do not exist in
France. Following monarchical tradition, France's centralized foreign
policy decision-making has been strengthened by the Fifth Republic's
presidentialism and by France's choice of a strategy based on an
independent nuclear force. The legislature thus has neither the means
nor the desire to challenge foreign policy choices of the nuclear
monarchy.

The press, which has never become a fourth power in France, does not
play a divisive role either. External expertise plays only a marginal role.
Experts who were not even considered during de Gaulle's period have
been introduced into the system with the creation in 1973 of the Planning
Staff at the Foreign Ministry. This channel produced much consultation
in the late 1970s, during the divisive debates provoked by the Soviet
invasion of Afghanistan, but nothing serious came out of them: the
'experts' were not prepared to give responsible and practical advice, and
the 'professionals' were not open to listening to them. France's lack of
effective channels of communication between the administration and the
universities precludes the existence of fruitful cross-fertilization among
the administration, its in-house experts, and the 'outsiders'.

The cohabitation experience of 1986–8 modified the rules of the game
somewhat, without diminishing executive prerogative. When the executive is divided, foreign policy is no longer the clear domain of a single
leader. The French Prime Minister reinforced his role in diplomacy, but
the President remains the highest authority in constitutional terms, a pre-
eminence symbolized by his ultimate control over the nuclear trigger.
Concerning the Soviet Union, continuity largely prevailed and France's
language remained firm and without illusion. America's uncertainties
and Gorbachev's reserved diplomatic dynamism in arms control could
only stimulate French unity against the spectre of disarmament by
obsolescence. In so far as Mitterrand is ultimately faithful to a certain
Gaullist vision, and the French have been vaccinated against excessive
illusions by the impending diplomatic threat against their nuclear
deterrent, the Soviet government could do little to benefit from a relative
'Americanization', that is, confusion of the French foreign policy process
brought about by 'cohabitation'.

In defining the interaction between France's policy towards the Soviet Union and the domestic process, it is necessary to assess the complex and ambiguous role of the French Communist Party, and Moscow's constant support for French conservative governments and Gaullist continuity. Soviet regimes seem always to have considered that Gaullist principles were the best they could hope for. A conservative government was appreciated not only because of the 'soundness' of its foreign policy principles, but also because it did not represent an ideological threat in a clearly Manichean vision of the world. Moscow gave clear sign of its support for Chaban-Delmas's candidacy in 1974 and for Giscard d'Estaing in 1981, consistent but unsuccessful choices. Today, Moscow seems to be giving particular consideration to the heir of Gaullist tradition, Raymond Barre. Could one assume that there is a link between the long-time suicidal impact — for the Left's chances of coming to power — of the French Communist Party's negative tactics, and Moscow's diplomatic and strategic calculus? It is fair to say that the French Communist Party's counter-productive strategies may be the result, not so much of sophisti-cated diktats from Moscow, but of its own blunders in interpreting its historical decline. Whatever the right interpretation, conservative gov-ernments in France have always behaved as if there were a tacit understanding, if not a clear alliance, between Paris and Moscow on the role of the French Communist Party.

Foreign policy considerations *per se* played only an indirect role in the presidential elections of 1981. At the time, Giscard d'Estaing's modera-tion toward the Soviet Union, in spite of the invasion of Afghanistan, was not popular among a majority of Frenchmen. But this element was only part of the President's isolation from the people, which led to his defeat.

Future policy direction

Recent public opinion surveys suggest that the French are not impervious to the new image offered by Mikhail Gorbachev. At a time when Irangate has revealed the underside of democracy, it is tempting to focus on Soviet reforms. The existence of this new and more positive image of the Soviet Union should not be overemphasized, however: public opinion is by nature volatile, and images are easily influenced. It is therefore essential to distinguish between the trendy and the trend.

'Normalization' and the return to a more traditional (some would say Gaullist) position on East–West matters — distinct from the American position, yet not to be confused with the seeming equidistance of the mid-1960s — came progressively as a result of many mutually reinforcing factors. First of all, the Western diplomatic victory itself led to a transition from a scene dominated by the Euromissile quarrel to one dominated first by the United States' infatuation with SDI and then by the arms control dialogue between the superpowers.

No longer worried by the regional balance of forces in Europe, and reassured by the conservatives' victory in West Germany, the French basically saw in the American desire to transcend a nuclear world a threat to their own security and to their mini-superpower nuclear-based status. SDI reawakened in them the spectre of a neo-isolationist 'Fortress America' willing to unlink its security from that of Europe. The French also viewed the idea that weapons could successfully fight a war in space as a reflection of the inherent optimism of the American character, in contrast to the more cynical and tragic view of the world that Europeans have learned. Conservative by necessity, in spite of their attachment to arms control, the French could only see America's new revisionist stance, based on an increased aloofness towards the nuclear sword, with growing discomfort.

After March 1986, the period of cohabitation added an element of confusion in France's attitude towards SDI, although Mitterrand and Chirac's differences over SDI were largely exaggerated for domestic purposes. In their respective comments both men had in fact largely concentrated on different aspects of SDI: the President's reservations stemmed from the strategic implication of SDI, whereas Chirac's more favourable comments were aimed at the individual and technological spin-offs of the United States' programme, and translated a desire not to miss the boat's departure on its profitable technological/economic journey. In fact, French firms like Matra had not waited for the official green light to join in the bidding for SDI-derived contracts.

The negative impact on Franco-American relations of these first frictions over SDI was reinforced by a gradually shifting image of the United States and the Soviet Union in the French psyche. The Reykjavik non-summit — an 'earthquake' for many Europeans in spite of its failure — followed by the revelations of Irangate, revived in France an old and rather negative image of the Americans, a mixture of condescension and irritation: they appeared unpredictable and adventurous, with unreliable and probably incompetent diplomacy. At the same time, under the energetic leadership of Gorbachev, the Soviet Union was benefiting from a less unfavourable image, even if French reservations about the Soviet Union and scepticism towards *glasnost*, were still more pronounced than in any other Western European country. For the French, not unlike their European partners, Reykjavik constituted a daring, unprepared diplomatic venture, confirming the impression that, as a result of a mixture of amateurism, moralism and the search for immediate domestic political gains, the Reagan administration was trying to define a new world beyond nuclear deterrence, thus destabilizing a world order based on the balance of terror. Beyond the fear that the superpowers would once again jointly manage the world, there was the apprehension that the benefits of the Euromissile victory would be lost, resulting in a growing military imbalance in Europe. This fear, which other Europeans shared, was reinforced among the French by the feeling that sooner or later their own nuclear forces would be counted in any future negotiations, and that Europe would eventually be left to face Soviet conventional superiority alone.

In fact, in the arms control debate on the double zero option, the very reasons that spared France from the pacifist waves of the early 1980s and made her firmer than any other European country in her resistance to Soviet ambitions in the Euromissile crisis, account for why she was initially the most reserved country in the climate of blossoming arms control. In the Euromissile debate, France had the least to fear and the most to gain from a firm stance. Because of her special status within NATO, Euromissiles were not going to be deployed on her territory. Because of the existing consensus on nuclear deterrence and the quasi-monopoly of the Communist Party on the pacifist movement, popular opposition was the least significant. Because of her somewhat inflated international ego, France was not threatened by any kind of cultural identity crisis, unlike most of her European neighbours. The Intermediate-range Nuclear Forces (INF) negotiations had reversed this proposition, and France rightly or wrongly felt she had the least to gain, and the most to lose, from the agreement and its 'dangerous logic'.

Yet France's public comments have not reflected the depth of French worries, because of a mixture of diplomatic realism towards the United States, concern for European cohesion, and domestic calculation. Even President Mitterrand became with time increasingly positive towards the INF process. As French presidential elections were nearing, Mitterrand had been growingly espousing arms control and disarmament in Europe, as if returning to his late-1970 Socialist stance. This evolution suggests that it was unrealistic for a medium-size power to express, to no avail, its reservations or apprehensions concerning the irresistible coming together of the two superpowers on arms control. Out of concern for European unity and given the state of West German public opinion, Mitterrand also deemed it necessary not to appear too distant in emotions and positions from the Federal Republic. How also could a country that had been so active in the 1970s in favour of disarmament appear so negative about the first agreement ever on arms reductions? According to some of the President's conservative critics, such an attitude was reinforced by electoral considerations: a candidate in need of the votes of the Left — Socialists and Communists alike — could not divorce himself from an electorate in favour of arms control and East–West dialogue.

In the largely Franco-French debate on the value or the risks — a window of vulnerability or a window of opportunity — of an INF agreement for France and Europe, one dimension has been omnipresent: the European one. It all looks as if the negotiations had hastened an awareness of and greater openness to the issue of a Common European Defence; but this pedagogic value has not — yet — translated itself into dramatic breakthroughs. In spite of symbolic gestures such as the recent joint Franco-German manoeuvres, or the creation of a joint Defence Council between the two countries, there is a gap between the modesty of the measures undertaken, and the sense of urgency and novelty resulting from the new international configuration linked to the present East–West dialogue and arms control process. It would be unfair to single out France's responsibilities. Yet the process of cohabitation itself, between 1986 and 1988, slowed down France's European initiatives, whereas the crisis of the French economy and its decreasing competitiveness within Europe limited her international and European clout.

Franco-German relations in their complex intensity are a perfect illustration of this state of affairs. Never has the dialogue been more frequent between the French and the Germans, but this frequency has not fostered qualitatively deeper relations. In fact, as the very bases of European post-war stability — American protection over Europe, and reliance on nuclear deterrence — are being questioned, France and West Germany's visions of the world appear increasingly divergent. De Gaulle's France in the mid-1960s was a revisionist power intent on modifying the existing European security system. Today's France is at heart a status-quo power, whereas West Germany's deepest hope would be to transcend 'Yalta'. The long-term prospect of a denuclearized world cannot be seen in the same light in Paris and Bonn. As long as West Germany's hope remains France's fear, as long as the French want to preserve above all a policy of independence, as long as France's defence posture remains purposefully ambiguous towards a Federal Republic whose demands are equally unclear, as long as a mixture of structural differences — France is a nuclear power outside of NATO, the Federal Republic just the reverse — and emotions prevails, the Franco-German nucleus of Europe will be bound to remain central but insufficient.

The joint effort of these two countries stands as a major post-war achievement, living proof that Europeans can transcend their divisive past. But such bilateralism is no longer enough. A multilateral approach is needed to transcend the Franco-German structural deadlock and to accommodate British sensitivity to what London tends to see as an excessive flirtation between Bonn and Paris.

There are two prerequisites for a new European multilateral policy: the good will of the United States and a redefinition of the alliance that would give the European pillar more weight. The United States must be convinced of its duty to encourage European security efforts by deeds, not just by words. She should, for example, persuade Prime Minister Margaret Thatcher that there is no contradiction between Britain's duties to NATO and its responsibilities to Europe. Equally crucially, Washington should make sure that the flow in NATO arms procurement goes both ways across the Atlantic. Europeans and Americans alike must understand that the best way to have more Europe tomorrow is to have more alliance today — and an alliance that is more balanced toward Europe. France must show greater pragmatism and flexibility if this is to work. France could, for example, return to the NATO planning group — a symbolic gesture that would prove a new French concern for the sensitivities of the other Europeans, who have never fully accepted France's self-proclaimed 'specificity'.

15. France and Europe*

Philippe Moreau Defarges

At the end of the Second World War, France found herself caught up in a radically new European situation. The Old Continent was gradually separated into two blocs, and France took part in setting up the Atlantic Alliance. In addition, Germany, her hereditary enemy, was divided, and with the onset of the Cold War, the United States became determined to consolidate and rearm the western half. At the end of the 1940s, therefore, the unification of Europe represented for France at once a necessity and a choice: it was a question of defining a new relationship with Germany (or, at least, West Germany). In a broader sense, this European perspective obliged France to seek other means to balance her diplomacy.

Elements of permanence, elements of ambiguity

Especially since the beginning of the Fifth Republic (but also under the Fourth), France has sought to assert a foreign policy which was her own — 'independent', in the Gaullist terminology. Several permanent features of French foreign policy result from this aspiration: the claim to great power status, the nuclear strike force, the ties with Africa and the Third World among them. From this point of view, the European dimension appears as an advantage, giving to French diplomacy a broader framework. For example, it was a French initiative that led the European Community to develop an innovative mechanism for trade and co-operation between Europe and Africa (the Yaoundé and Lomé Conventions).

But a unified Europe is also a set of constraints, at once stiffening the requirements of economic and monetary discipline, and obliging each of

*Translated and adapted by the editor. Portions of this chapter were adapted from Philippe Moreau Defarges, 'La France et l'Europe: le rêve ambigu ou la mesure du rang', *Politique Etrangère* , no. 1 (1986).

the member states[1] to live together. Whether it is the customs union, agricultural policy, monetary policy, or perhaps, in the future, defence policy, by its very existence, Europe limits its member states' capacity to act. Faced with a European entity, France needed to find a flexible compromise between independence and solidarity, sovereignty and integration.

Two different sources — contradictory, yet complementary — marked French policy. For Jean Monnet, the 'Father of Europe' in the early 1950s, the object was to create multiple opportunities for concrete interdependence (in such areas as coal and steel production and trade), to accustom once hostile nations to mutual interpenetration, and thus to circumvent national resistance. Monnet dreamed of a United States of Europe; as a businessman, Monnet was above all a pragmatist concerned with practical organization.[2]

For de Gaulle, on the other hand, European unification could not melt away the nation-states; it could at best associate them in joint economic or political tasks. Whereas for Monnet, Europe would prove its existence in the process of coming to life, de Gaulle placed greater emphasis on the given political and national realities.

This dual inspiration is a reminder that France made a historic choice in the early 1950s, despite some procrastination because of the perennial German problem. This option for Europe, which originated in the Fourth Republic, took on an increasingly irreversible character under the Fifth. In retrospect, two moments appear capital. First, upon returning to power in 1958, General de Gaulle was won over to the creation of the European Community, scheduled to begin on 1 January 1959. He understood how vital it was for France and her economy to undergo the shock of the opening up of borders, of competition. Second, in 1983, faced with a seriously deteriorated financial situation, President François Mitterrand chose to keep the French franc in the European Monetary System. Experience taught the Socialists that in managing the French economy, they were doomed to respect Community rules and work in co-ordination with France's partners, and above all with West Germany.

Monnet or de Gaulle? Since 1958, official discourse has remained rather faithful to the Gaullist vision, centred on nations; in reality, each President has accepted a certain logic of integration: for de Gaulle, the customs union and the Common Agricultural Policy; for Georges Pompidou, Community finances; for Valéry Giscard d'Estaing, the European Monetary System; for François Mitterrand, the completion of the single market by 1993.

From de Gaulle to Mitterrand, another constant feature has been the will to construct a European Europe, founded in its own values, and thus distinct from both the United States and the Soviet Union. On numerous occasions, France has repeatedly portrayed herself as the promoter of a Europe with its own will and voice: from the Fouchet Plan (for a union of

states) to the veto of British membership in the 1960s; from the theme of
European Union to the joint industrial projects (e.g., Ariane or Airbus) in
the 1970s; and in the 1980s, the insistence on the necessity — in light of
the single market — to develop a joint economic strategy *vis-à-vis* the
United States and especially Japan.

This European Europe, however, raises two series of questions. First,
how can it fit into the existing linkages within the broader Western
framework (in particular, trade, currency, defence)? Each member state
has its own conception of the fit: for example, the United Kingdom's
'special' ties with the USA; West Germany's conviction — which France
shares— that Western European defence is inseparable from the Atlantic
Alliance. In short, must a European Europe assert its independent
existence? Or can it only be viewed as part of the group USA–Europe–
Japan?

Second, what balance does France strike between her independence
and her membership in the European entity? In certain fields, such as her
autonomous nuclear strike force, her ties with the Maghreb and with sub-
Saharan Africa, France insists on retaining her freedom of manoeuvre in
questions which she considers essential; so, of course, does West Germany
in its relations with the Soviet bloc, or the UK in its friendship with the
USA.

The evolution of France's European policy since 1958

The de Gaulle years (1958–69) were marked by three spectacular and
precarious elements: the loosening (not without difficulties) of the blocs
and especially the vague rebirth of a Pan-European space; the confirmation of Europe's economic strength; and the deepening of the Franco-
German relationship, at least between 1958 and 1963. De Gaulle's 'Grand
Design', to use Alfred Grosser's expression,[3] was built around the pre-
eminence of the political, the quest for a Concert of Europe system,
adapted to the twentieth century. This idea of concert illustrates the
theme of de Gaulle's European diplomacy: it inspired the 1961 Fouchet
Plan, and when that failed, it dominated the 1963 Franco-German
Treaty. The European goal, however, was but one of the elements of
Gaullist policy, which aimed at preserving France's great power status:
only a European concert could prevent the consolidation of the
American-Soviet monopoly over the affairs of the world.

A hierarchical confederation of states which, by its political nature,
would have overall responsibility for European unification, however, was
not acceptable to France's partners or to partisans of 'supranationality'.
Here we note one of the paradoxes, or one of the misunderstandings of
Gaullist diplomacy: de Gaulle had France— and the other member states
— assume fully the obligations of European integration, when he aborted

British efforts to set up a broad free trade zone (1958), when he respected the deadline of 1 January 1959, when he linked the achievement of a customs union with the adoption of a common agricultural policy (1962), and finally, when he refused to postpone, in the aftermath of the Events of May 1968, the abolition of customs barriers within the Community, on 1 July 1968. And yet, de Gaulle's rhetoric contained all that was distasteful to those who believed in Europe. And at the end, the Gaullist policy entered an impasse precisely because of the conflicting interests of the nation-states who were to form its foundation. The Franco-German axis, reinforced by de Gaulle and Adenauer's heightened awareness of the need to create 'something durable', remained equivocal: for the 'old Frenchman', Germany was no longer and must never again be a great power; for the 'old German', the security and equilibrium of his country required being anchored to the West. And while de Gaulle seemed to propose an anti-American Europe, halfway between East and West, West Germany in particular considered there was no security without the American nuclear shield.

But de Gaulle was above all the heir of Joan of Arc. And his European policy came up against the British question. On two occasions (January 1963 and November 1967) de Gaulle vetoed British entry into the Common Market, and yet his vision of a Europe of states was also shared by London. In fact, the problem was simpler than that. France's five partners in the European Community seemed haunted by the hegemonic temptation of the country of Louis XIV and Napoleon; only England could provide the indispensable counterweight. For de Gaulle, it was not possible to admit Great Britain 'without tearing, without breaking, what already exists'.[4] That country — whether in its purchase of agricultural products, in the status of the pound sterling, or especially in its special ties with the United States — would have to convert to Europe and show proof of the metamorphosis.

In retrospect, the Gaullist years established France's European commitment, already well developed during the Fourth Republic, as irreversible: the Common Market and the Common Agricultural Policy were set up. Of course, de Gaulle asserted his firm opposition to any process which would escape the control of the nation-states; as the 1966 Luxembourg 'compromise' demonstrated, Europe had to be built on the unanimous agreement of all member states. From the Schumann declaration of May 1950, proposing the European Coal and Steel Community, to the December 1969 summit at The Hague, proposing the completion and the deepening of the European Community, France had defined the issues. But by 1969, the era of a French Europe was closing.

Succeeding de Gaulle as President, Pompidou drew the lessons of the preceding period: France put an end to the European impasse and lifted French opposition to British entry into the European Community. Still, he remained fundamentally faithful to the Gaullist vision: independence, a Europe of states, the dialogue with the Soviet bloc, and so on. During his presidency, the first steps towards monetary union were taken, as well as towards common industrial and regional policies. Pompidou insisted on asserting a European point of view *vis-à-vis* the United States following the first oil shock in 1973–4. Thus, under Pompidou, France could still be persuaded that her European dream was intact.

None the less, in the dialogue with the Soviet bloc, there was the German thorn: with the blossoming of *Ostpolitik* in 1970–2, West Germany renewed her traditional vocation as a privileged partner of Eastern Europe. *Détente* was no longer to be France's private preserve. And France appeared torn between her ambition to be the leading force for integration and the weight of her interests. As of 1970, Pompidou foresaw the inclusion of 'Latin' Europe (Spain and Portugal) into the Community. Yet France was concerned about her own agricultural sector and dragged her feet throughout the long negotiations on the membership of these two young democracies; eventually bilateral Franco-Spanish discussions were needed to work out the difficulties.

Under the presidency of Valéry Giscard d'Estaing (1974-81), despite his less classical, more world-orientated rhetoric, French policy remained largely dominated by the same confrontation between the ambitions inherited from de Gaulle and the political and economic realities, which imposed compromises and ambiguities. It is important to stress the intensity of the Franco-German dialogue, established on a very personal level between Giscard d'Estaing and Helmut Schmidt. None the less, the closeness of the Franco-German couple could not eliminate the imbalance between the two economies, nor the weight of the United States.

From the perspective of European integration, the Franco-German relationship helped to launch the European Monetary System in 1979. Economic interdependence and monetary turbulence incited the prudent emergence of a European monetary sphere, protected from the fluctuations of the dollar. In defence, Giscard sought to reshape the balance between the options of independence and European solidarity by adopting the hypothesis of a forward defence, that is, based in West Germany.

And finally, Giscard d'Estaing adopted in his own way the theme of a European Europe, through the institutionalization of a dialogue at the summit: he developed a series of regular bilateral meetings (not only Franco-German, but also Franco-British, Franco-Italian and Franco-Spanish); and, most importantly, he initiated in 1974 the European Council, a forum for periodic meetings of the Community's heads of government or state. While it is true that the Council has often been taken up with secondary issues, it none the less gave Europe an institutional framework for conceiving and initiating policy, and gradually accustomed Europe to developing its own point of view at the highest levels. Giscard also helped set up, beginning in 1975, the annual economic and political summit meetings of the seven major industrial democracies. In 1979, there was even a brief attempt to establish a Euro-American political dialogue through the gathering of the leaders of just France, the United States, the United Kingdom and West Germany.

As Europe became less French (could it be otherwise?), France's intermediary role between the two Europes — East and West — also seemed to run into difficulty. The Brezhnev–Giscard summit of October 1975 was interrupted by the Soviet leader's diplomatic 'cold'. And following the Red Army's occupation of Afghanistan in December 1979, the meeting between the two men in Warsaw, in May 1980, created embarrassment and ambiguity.

During his presidency, François Mitterrand curiously maintained the same pattern in France's relationship with Europe as his predecessor. Naturally, he substituted a Lamartinian lyricism, with a touch of Marxism, for Giscard's management-orientated modernism. And Socialist France dreamed of a European-level social policy. But the Europe of Helmut Schmidt (and later Helmut Kohl) and of Margaret Thatcher was incorrigibly free-market and prosaic. The stubborn dream had to be pursued through other paths, such as joint projects for space exploration (the 'Eureka' project, 1984), and advancing European integration with the European Single Act.

And France had to protect her rank. This objective led Mitterrand to assert the specificity of France's policy outside Europe: a joint European approach to the Middle East conflict was shelved; France's Third World vocation was revived; and a renewed dialogue with the Soviet bloc was pursued. On balance, however, it was by preserving France's participation in the European Monetary System in 1983 and by committing his government to a long-term policy of rigour that François Mitterrand confirmed that France's natural milieu, her framework, was the Europe of the European Community.

Still, the 1980s introduced at least three new features. First, the Europe of the Twelve has become a heterogeneous, complex area, encompassing fully developed countries and those less so (Ireland, Greece, Spain, Portugal). Other countries are seeking membership, whether Mediterranean (Turkey and even Morocco) or from 'neutral' Europe (Austria and Sweden). On the one hand, France enjoys a median position, at the crossroads of Latin, Germanic and Anglo-Saxon cultures; on the other hand, this Europe is no longer bipolar (France/West Germany), but multipolar (France, West Germany, Great Britain, and also Italy and Spain).

Second, new realities — international economic competition, the weight of the United States, the breakthroughs of Japan and industrial Asia — are obliging the European Community to adjust its goals. As a result, a different cleavage has made its appearance. Mrs Thatcher's Great Britain emphasizes the dismantling of trade barriers, deregulation and competition: Europe must adapt to the world marketplace. France, however, is once again worried about European specificity in the face of advanced technologies or of Japanese competition: the single market of 1993 must not dilute the European identity, but, on the contrary, reinforce it.

Third, while the European Community has continued to increase interdependence among the member states (from trade to agriculture, from industry to currency), these states, as political entities with their own concerns, have varied in their evolution. In this regard, West Germany remains the pivotal country.

The Franco-German axis is still as fundamental for the two states. For Bonn, the dialogue with Paris reinforces and replenishes its ties with the West; German leaders know that this reconciliation with the hereditary enemy certifies that West Germany is a country like others, democratic and reasonable. For Paris, the linkage with Bonn is vital as much for the pursuit of European unification as for security against the Soviet threat. In short, neither state can advance without the other. But West Germany is no longer the timid and constrained country, under watch by Washington and Moscow, that it was during Adenauer's time in the 1950s and 1960s. West Germany today is the the third industrial power, behind the United States and Japan; its *Ostpolitik* makes Bonn Western Europe's principal spokesman with the Soviet bloc.

Throughout the 1980s, French policy has been based on the European foundation and has helped to consolidate it: resolving the issue of the British contribution in 1984, accelerating the negotiations on Spanish membership in 1985, promoting the single market and monetary union in 1986. French behaviour towards Europe seems guided by two sentiments: the certainty that the choice of Europe remains the right choice (especially given the closeness of the Franco-German axis); the acceptance of a European Community certainly less coherent than that of the Six, during the 1960s, but incorporating the key components of Western Europe. In this environment, France has endeavoured to prepare and shape the discussion of European issues through the expansion of her bilateral dialogues.

The future and its uncertainties

From the economic perspective, France's European option has always been and remains governed by two motives: to bring the French economy out of its traditional protectionism (characteristic of the end of the nineteenth century and the first half of the twentieth century); and to integrate that economy in a Common Market which, while competitive, softens the shock of international competition. In sum, economic Europe implies both an opening — towards the other member states — and a common defence against third states.

France has thus always linked two dimensions, the dismantling of internal Community barriers, and the setting up of a common trade policy. The 1993 deadline for the single market gives new life to the ongoing debate: if Europe becomes totally free and transparent, can it and must it remain without protection against the Americans, the Japanese and the South Koreans, who fear a fortress Europe? This question concerns such key sectors as automobiles, electronics and aeronautics. The British approach favours free trade and openness towards the world market. France remains faithful to the themes of organized markets and disciplined trade. For France's European policy, this is one of the major stakes.

From the point of view of Europe's institutions, France has insisted, especially since de Gaulle, that the process of European integration remain under the control of the member states. This has meant that any transfer of authority from states to the Community must be decided with clarity, by unanimous agreement.

Nearly forty years after its beginnings, European integration has reached an extraordinary complexity, in industry, agriculture, services and currency for example. Still, political matters (i.e. defence and diplomacy) continue to be basically the responsibility of each member state, even if means of co-operation have been expanded. What kind of political Europe? France believes it to be a necessary achievement, but the consensus among the 'major' states (West Germany and Great Britain, in particular) remains vague, as each has its own concerns: German reunification, for Bonn, and the special relationship with the United States, for London.

From an external perspective, the European Community with its twelve member states is henceforth an essential international actor, one of the three pillars of the Western economic system, at the crossroads between the free world and the Soviet bloc. Moreover, by 1993, it will become the leading marketplace in the world. But what does this Europe seek? What roles can it play between East and West, North and South? As was the case during the *détente* of the 1970s, Europe at the end of the 1980s seems united on questions of principle (such as human rights), but fragmented in everyday action: West Germany is gambling on the success of the Gorbachev experience, while France and the United Kingdom are more circumspect.

France has always promoted the idea of a European Europe, with its own voice, particularly in East–West relations. Has the moment finally come, at the end of the twentieth century, with doubts about continued American military presence in Europe and the promises of openness held out by Gorbachev? Will the dream finally catch up with reality? Such is the difficult challenge of the second Mitterrand presidency.

Notes

1. Since 1951, these have included France, West Germany, Italy, Belgium, the Netherlands and Luxembourg; in addition, the United Kingdom, Ireland and Denmark joined in 1973, Greece in 1981, and Spain and Portugal in 1986.
2. See his *Mémoires* (Paris: Fayard, 1976).
3. See Alfred Grosser, *Affaires Extérieures: La Politique de la France, 1944–1984* (Paris: Flammarion, 1984); and *The Western Alliance: European–American Relations since 1945* (New York: Continuum, 1980).
4. De Gaulle's press conference, 27 November 1967.

16. The Fifth Republic and the Third World*

Marie-Claude Smouts

Analysing French policy toward the Third World from the perspective of public policy-making is an interesting exercise. France is indeed the only major power to have not *one* policy but several, not *one* instrument, but several agencies of economic development assistance. She is the only power with separate ministries for handling relations with countries said to be of the inner circle — more or less, the former colonies of sub-Saharan Africa — and countries of the rest of the world. France displays the greatest gap between an ambitious, candid, and generous rhetoric, and a conservative practice weighed down by history.

She is probably the least successful in integrating the psychological consequences of decolonization. Her ambitions of grandeur still feed on the dreams of distant horizons. She cannot imagine herself powerful without a presence beyond her borders and an influence overseas. In what other country could a minister write, without being accused of neo-colonialism: 'France has a decisive role in preserving peace in the world, for which she has three major pieces on the international chessboard: a permanent seat on the UN Security Council, an independent nuclear strike force, and an African dimension'?[1] Coming after nearly thirty years of African independence, such a remark does not seem incongruous in France, but expresses a widely shared sentiment. There is no apparent contradiction in presenting La Coopération (economic development assistance) as 'the heir of colonization, which was in its time praised as the great undertaking capable of making France a powerful and respected nation',[2] and asserting in equally good faith: 'Regardless of the views of the professional cynics, La Coopération is the expression of fraternity and of friendship between populations'.[3]

The theme of a generous France with a 'good image' in the Third World is part of a national heritage that every government of the Fifth

*Translated by the editor.

Republic has nourished with great care. Paradoxically, it is neither entirely accurate nor completely false. Consequently, the French position remains a mystery for many foreign observers, and the question posed by a journalist about France's African policy could apply as well to her overall North–South policy: 'How can France do everything she does and get away with it?'[4]

The weight of history

The African Priority

The decolonization of the African countries south of the Sahara was, as we know, France's only politically successful decolonization.[5] In the middle of the Algerian war, at a time when France was thrown in the dock by all the non-aligned countries, the system of economic development assistance created for French-speaking Africa succeeded in transforming a lost sovereignty into a durable influence. Most of the colonial bureaucracy was converted into agencies of assistance. A elaborate network of administrative structures and political accords has allowed the former colonizer to take charge of the organization of the national administration in most of these new states, as well as their problems of development, public investment, and at times even security.[6] Moreover, the importance of cultural assistance and the creation of a French franc zone have given the Franco-African association the exceptional nature of an integrated zone on both linguistic and monetary levels.

For the French political class, this double integration constitutes such an indisputable advantage that no government has sought to alter it. Several characteristics of French policy towards the Third World result from decisions taken when Africa represented a major economic invest-ment, according to the specialists. The system of economic development assistance was conceived for a specific geographic zone, French-speaking black Africa. A separate ministry was set up, with important means and specialized agencies: the Development Assistance Fund (Fonds d'Aide et de Coopération) and the Central Economic Aid Office (La Caisse Centrale de Coopération Economique). Everything that a policy of economic development assistance implies in the way of 'expertise', determination, and continuity, has been focused on the countries of the 'inner circle', to which 75 per cent of French bilateral aid is directed.[7] Such a degree of 'Africanization' of Third World assistance delayed the formulation of a global and coherent policy for the other countries. Those outside the 'inner circle' are generally dealt with without method or foresight. Even the countries of North Africa, with which France has 'privileged' relations and which receive some 16 per cent of her bilateral aid, are outside the 'circle' and suffer from the administrative incoherence created by this situation: is Algeria, for example, eligible for loans from the Central Economic Aid Office?

Yet, the question of regrouping the agencies responsible for economic development assistance in the developing countries was raised very early on. In 1964, the Jeanneney Report proposed giving to a single agency, attached to the Foreign Ministry, responsibility for defining and implementing the whole of France's economic development assistance policy without geographic distinctions. But the reform undertaken in this direction by the Pompidou government in 1966, like that of the Socialist government in 1982, ran into the same type of resistance. They were both similarly swept away by succeeding governments.

A compartmentalized system

This administrative partitioning initially had a certain relevance in emphasizing both French priorities and the specificity of Franco-African relations. Over the years, its rigidity engendered a number of distortions. By excessively specializing, France cut herself off from other development experiences — in Latin America and Asia — and acquired the reputation of perceiving Third World problems only through the African prism. A Mexican diplomat summed it up bluntly: 'It would appear that for France, the Third World consists only of Burkinabe peasants'. And this 'Africanization' is incomplete, in so far as the large English-speaking countries are not within the competence of the Ministry for *Coopération,* which leads to absurd situations: Nigeria, for example, whose economic weight is greater than that of all the countries covered by the Development Assistance Fund, is excluded from the Ministry's competence, while all its neighbours are in the 'inner circle'. In the absence of any real co-ordination among the administrative services, this split between French-speaking and English-speaking countries is consequently accentuated, and the conditions for regional co-operation, unavoidable in the long term, are all the more complicated.

The Ministry for *Coopération* manages only roughly one-fifth of all French public aid. The rest is divided among thirteen ministerial bureaux, each endowed with its own funds and specific agencies. As a whole, the system is extremely complicated. For just industrial development assistance, for example, there are no less than some twenty different bureaux in different ministries, each with its own field of competence and its own techniques: *Coopération,* Economics and Finance, Research and Industry, Foreign Trade, National Education, as well as the various technical ministries.

There is blatant scattering of means, and the dispersal of decision-making centres hampers the definition of a coherent, long-term policy line. Without the co-ordination of a central agency, the instruments of development assistance are diluted in a bureaucratic logic in which inter-agency competition for influence and concerns of the moment prevail. Admittedly, the Foreign Affairs Ministry occupies a central position in the system. It manages relations with some ninety Third World countries outside the circle. It is in charge of cultural assistance, and its important Bureau for Cultural, Scientific and Technical Relations aims two-thirds of its funds towards the developing countries. It also ensures a French presence in North–South negotiations taking place within the United Nations: UNCTAD and the specialized agencies. Yet one may wonder whether, over the years, the Ministry of Economics and Finance has not become the real authority for French policy towards the South. On the one hand, the nature of aid has changed; on the other, the centres of interest have changed.

France's multilateral aid, infinitesimal in the early years (2 per cent of all development aid in 1964, 10 per cent in 1969), has settled at around 27 per cent in recent years. Half of this multilateral aid goes to the European Community; some 8 to 10 per cent goes to UN agencies; the rest goes to the International Monetary Fund, the World Bank, and to regional banks by means of the Ministry of Finance. The Ministry also controls Treasury loans and the mechanics of the French franc zone; it shares tutelary authority over the Central Economic Aid Office with the Ministries of *Coopération* and of Foreign Affairs, and over food aid with these latter ministries and that of Agriculture as well. The volume of public expenditure on the Third World thus controlled directly by the Ministry of Economics and Finance is now much greater than that administered by the Foreign Ministry's Bureau of Cultural, Scientific and Technical Relations. Moreover, the last few years have seen an increasingly marked geographic specialization of the instruments of financial aid, which tends to reinforce the weight of the Finance Ministry and to marginalize that of the Ministries of *Coopération* and of Foreign Affairs.

In the 1960s tension appeared between the desire to preserve a sphere of influence focused on French-speaking Africa and the wish to redeploy aid towards the high growth countries, sources of vibrant markets. It intensified during the 1970s, when it became evident that adapting the French economy to the new patterns of world demand required, among other things, a restructuring of exports. The concern to reconcile maintaining traditional co-operation for political reasons and restructuring of aid for commercial reasons led to diversifying the instruments of assistance according to region. Traditional aid — grants from the Development Assistance Fund and long-term, low-interest loans from the Central Economic Aid Office — went to black Africa. Aid to restructure exports towards the more buoyant markets of the Third World (e.g., Indonesia, Brazil, Egypt) was carried out thanks to the spectacular development, after the first oil shock, of Treasury loans and their incorporation into governmental financial protocols.[8] The debt problem, predominant since 1982, gave the Finance Ministry additional influence in defining the policy towards Latin America, but also towards the better-off (and thus more indebted) countries of Africa, by means of the Club of Paris and its machinery for rescheduling debts. Asia, on the other hand, is seen essentially from a commercial point of view, at once for the competition that these newly industrialized countries represent and for the expansion that their dynamism foreshadows.

A specific discourse

For nearly twenty years, lofty political discourse provided a sense of unity to French diplomacy towards the Third World. The circumstances lent themselves to it; France had things to say to a South emerging on the world scene. The public dialogue between the industrial and the developing countries offered a framework.

Master in one's own house

By the time of the first UNCTAD meeting in 1964, when for the first time the Third World found a form of diplomatic expression with the Group of 77, France was no longer burdened by the Algerian problem, was strengthened by a peaceful decolonization in black Africa and endowed with stable institutions. She was a nuclear power; she was enjoying an exceptional rate of growth. She could finally take her place in the universe beside the 'two giants'. The efforts of the developing countries to organize themselves into a non-aligned political force coincided with the Gaullist ambition of a multi-polar world in which middle-range powers would have a margin of manoeuvre next to the two superpowers. The expression 'Third World', rarely used by the founder of the Fifth Republic, appeared in his speeches of this period, with a clearly geopolitical meaning: 'There are great realities in the world, in the middle of which France lives. There are two currently colossal countries, the United States and Soviet Russia..., China..., Western Europe..., and finally the Third World of Africa, Asia, and Latin America'. France would show the peoples who aspire to better lives and seek their autonomy how to approach the world when one is not a superpower.

   With the diplomatic recognition of China (27 January 1964), the state visits to Latin America (1964–5), and the Phnom Penh speech (1 September 1966), de Gaulle sought to extend to broader horizons the policy of independence and restructuring of power that gave him difficulty in the Western sphere (the failure of his NATO directory scheme and of the Fouchet Plan). He offered to the states of the Third World the model of an independent country which dares to defy the

American hegemony and rejected the logic of blocs. This effort brought him a prestige all the greater because the image of the United States at this time was deteriorating world-wide.

By contrast, France was fashioning herself an image as a power concerned for law and justice. She disapproved of the 'unjust' and 'detestable' war carried out in Vietnam. She condemned 'the opening of hostilities by Israel' in 1967 and declared that 'conquest by arms does not establish a right to occupy a territory'. And when the coalition of Southern states sought to challenge the liberal economic order, France was not worried. Was she not the first to denounce the hegemony of the dollar on the international monetary system? To criticize the egotism of a super-power which exports its inflation at the expense of the rest of the world?

This convergence between France and the Third World runs into evident limits. France encourages peoples to be 'masters in their own houses', but does not have the material means to help them increase their autonomy. The opening towards Latin America and Asia in the mid-1960s led to no concrete results. Quite a few years later, François Mitterrand would discover for himself the limits of his possibilities in Central America and southern Africa. Despite his desire to prevent the East–West rivalry from poisoning the situation in Nicaragua and El Salvador, to ensure that South Africa and the superpowers did not remain the only interlocutors of the front-line countries, he had to be satisfied with symbolic gestures and verbal encouragement. France does not have the means to rival with the grip of the two great powers, nor even that of a major regional power.

This refusal to allow the conflicts of the South to become necessarily encompassed in the East–West problematic has none the less remained part of the legacy. It has marked French diplomacy and indicated that France does not intend to support the United States in all its initiatives in the Third World. More recently, this logic has been visible in the support give to the Contadora group, the condemnation of the American bombing of Grenada (1982), and the refusal to allow American planes to fly over French territory for their Libyan raid (April 1986). And when French interests coincide with those of the United States in the defence of Western interests, France means to choose freely the moment and the means of action (troop commitments in Zaïre, Chad and Lebanon). An assertion of such independence allows France to portray herself as a neutral third party, with her own analysis of the Third World's crises, and capable of understanding the South's aspirations.

The North–South stakes

France's perception of North–South relations has been marked by the permanence of her interests outside Europe and by the features of her economy. Her overseas territories and departments make her the world's third largest maritime power. Her ability to continue nuclear testing is dependent upon her presence in the South Pacific, where she remains the only foreign power with full political sovereignty over inhabited islands. She is the only European state whose strategic thinking links national security to the maintenance of peace in the Third World, on a par with the conventional defence of Europe; the only one who has created the means — with a single instrument, the Rapid Deployment Force — to help her allies in Europe, in Africa, and in the Middle East.

By her presence in strategically importance regions (Djibouti, for example), France seeks to play a role of dissuasion and stabilization. This ambition has given her a special place among the Western countries. This position is fragile, however, and France knows it; it assumes the relative stability of the international environment and the existence of governments with which a minimum of dialogue is possible. France alone could not guarantee the stability of black Africa and of North Africa if too many governments were simultaneously threatened. More than other powers, France is conscious of the existing linkage between political stability, external security and the economic situation in the countries of the Third World. Therein lie the main stakes of North–South relations.

When Jacques Chirac said, 'Poverty is the fertilizer of Marxism',[9] and François Mitterrand stated: 'When a superficial economic liberalism — the enemy of true freedom — prevails, the dominator forgets that the exploitation of the dominated will bring about his own downfall',[10] they were both expressing, each in his own style, the same idea and the same fear: the collapse of their interlocutors and the multiplication of uncontrolled situations. France has become particularly sensitive to the need for a dialogue between the industrialized and the developing countries, thanks to the precariousness of her sphere of influence, the increasing tensions in the Middle East and along the shores of the Mediterranean, the vulnerability of her overseas territories to the convulsions around them, and the co-existence at home between French and North Africans, epitomizing many of the aspects of North–South relations.

From 1973 to 1982, France worked unceasingly to open up this dialogue, in every form. During 1973–4, President Georges Pompidou and his Foreign Minister, Michel Jobert, refused to join the oil consumers' alliance (the International Energy Agency) organized by the United States against OPEC; instead they proposed an international conference on energy, sponsored by the UN. After his election as President in 1974, Valéry Giscard d'Estaing floated the idea of a limited conference 'on energy and the related international economic problems' (Conference on International Economic Co-operation, 1975–7). In the early 1980s, France supported the idea of worldwide negotiations in which all North–South questions would be handled simultaneously. At the Cancún

(Mexico) meeting of the leaders of the seven major industrialized countries, François Mitterrand committed himself personally to reviving the theme. At France's insistence, reference to this project was wrested from President Reagan during the Versailles summit in June 1982.

More fragile than others, the French economy is more vulnerable to international disorder. Thus, contrary to the United States or West Germany, France did not hesitate to use the terminology of the New Order in fashion during the 1970s. She espoused certain demands of the Third World in denouncing monetary anarchy, the 'erratic' floating of exchange rates, the excessive level of interest rates in the United States. With a solid national tradition of defending farmers, and the experience of the stabilization funds which provided price support during the French Empire for agricultural goods from overseas, France was naturally open to the idea of organizing the markets for basic commodities. Ever since 1964, she favoured commodity agreements, making them her principal theme and the symbol of her openness to the problems of the South. If the fourth UNCTAD meeting in 1976 adopted the 'integrated programme' and the 'common fund', it is because of the efforts of France's representatives (especially Stéphane Hessel). If the STABEX mechanisms were inserted — and maintained — in the Lomé Conventions, it is due in large part to France's obstinacy.

France's foreign aid policy, which places her among the biggest spenders among the OECD countries, allows France to present herself in international organizations as the spokesman for the poor countries within the European Community. She can play the role of intermediary in the EC, the Group of 77, and the United States. Her rhetoric and her diplomacy guarantee she will be heard among these authorities.

Forced multilateralization

In the 1980s, the North–South dialogue was interrupted, the South came apart, and the institutions in which a semblance of dialogue remained (i.e. the UN, UNCTAD) were gradually deprived of their substance. 'Serious' things take place elsewhere — at the IMF, the GATT — inauspicious places for lyrical oratory. No doubt, the discourse remains unchanged (see, for example, Mitterrand's speech to the seventh UNCTAD meeting in 1987, very political and 'very well received'), but it leads nowhere. The commodity agreements are not working; the foreign aid theme is less successful. The hot topics of the day are structural adjustment, foreign debt, protectionism. On these points, however, France has nothing original to say, and is even at times more intransigent than her Western partners.

With the end of the North–South dialogue, an important part of France's diplomacy is in suspension, precisely that which gave her prominence and gave her a flattering image of herself. What she could offer — a conceptual framework, a set of procedures — no longer had the same usefulness, since the dialogue had shattered into multiple, separate, case-by-case negotiations on the debt, on food aid, on trade, and so on, while the South was coming apart. The situation was all the more delicate for France, as she had adjusted less well than others to the evolution of the world economy. Long accustomed to trade surpluses obtained in the protected markets of the French franc zone, then thrown into a short-sighted 'major contract' policy, she fitted poorly into the new international division of labour and began running up a foreign trade deficit.

Her jittery and protectionist behaviour hurt her reputation — particularly in Asia — and her presence outside the African continent is inadequate to her world-wide ambitions. Even in Africa, her action probably preserved a certain political status quo, but could not prevent economic, social and cultural difficulties from accumulating. The economic crisis is there, and will not go away. A major part of French policy towards the South is now devoted to drawing the international community's attention to the less developed countries (LDCs), most of which are in Africa. The tripling of the IMF's structural adjustment facility, demanded — and obtained — by Economics and Finance Minister Edouard Balladur, the building up of the resources of the International Development Agency, the preparation of a new conference on the LDCs, all demonstrate this concern. In the same vein, France is slightly vexed, but not displeased, that the IMF and the World Bank are intervening more and more in the countries in her sphere of influence to impose conditions that she approves of and was unable to impose unilaterally.

This forced multilateralization can, of course, be seen in the European framework. The relations between the Community and the ACP (African, Caribbean and Pacific) countries are considered the most successful example of what a contractualized relationship between industrial and developing countries can be, and France has worked hard for the adoption and renewal of the Lomé Conventions (after those of Yaoundé). The recent enlargement of the Community will probably open up the game even more and make Euro-African relations less and less exclusive.

Thus France's ability to speak with a different voice has been progressively reduced, all the more so since, with the conversion of not only the Gaullists, but also the Socialists, to free market ideals, France's position is no longer distinguishable from that of her German, British or even American partners. The only political space still open is that of the French-speaking countries, revived in the last few years with the goal of creating a counterweight to North American cultural hegemony. Otherwise, 'the grand policy' towards the Third World has given way to a day-by-day and technocratic management quite distant from the ambition that the Fifth Republic's heads of state — from de Gaulle to Mitterrand — sought to give it.

Notes

1. Michel Aurillac, Minister for *Coopération* in the Chirac Cabinet (1986–8), in *L'Afrique à coeur* (Paris: Berger-Levrault, 1987), p. 59.
2. Ibid., p. 37.
3. Ibid., p. 250.
4. Tamar Golan, 'A certain mystery: how can France do everything it does in Africa and get away with it', *African Affairs* (January 1981).
5. Much later, Djibouti's accession to independence was also considered as a success. On the other hand, that of Vanuatu, formerly the New Hebrides, led to a nearly complete break in relations.
6. See Patrick Cadenat, 'La France et le Tiers Monde: Vingt ans de coopération bilatérale', *Notes et Etudes documentaires*, 14 January 1983 (Paris: La Documentation Française), for a description of the co-operative structures and agreements.
7. In early 1988, thirty-four states were covered by the Ministry of Economic Aid and Development Assistance, all from Africa and the Indian Ocean, except for Haiti and four tiny islands in the Antilles. In addition to the seventeen former French colonies, these included Zaïre, Burundi, Rwanda, Mauritius, the Seychelles, Cape Verde, Gambia, São Tomé and Príncipe, Guinea-Bissau and Guinea. One should note that Vanuatu was not in the 'inner circle', but Mozambique and Angola, after having been excluded by the Chirac government, were once again authorized to receive funds from the Development Assistance Fund.
8. For a fuller treatment of these issues, see Jacques Adda and Marie-Claude Smouts, *La France dans le nouveau désordre Nord-Sud* (Paris: Editions Karthala, 1989).
9. In the preface to Michel Guillou, *Pour un dialogue Nord–Sud* (Paris: Albatros [Collection Club 89], 1984).
10. Speech before the Council of Governors of the International Fund for Agricultural Development (FIDA), 22 October 1984.

Conclusion

Paul Godt and Vincent Wright

The ambitions of the Fifth Republic

Fundamental reform had been on the French political agenda since the Liberation. The institutions of 1946, adopted for lack of consensus on more radical change, were faithful to traditional parliamentary practice, and came to be dominated by undisciplined parties and fluctuating coalitions representing at times barely half the electorate; as a consequence, important policies would lack coherence or continuity or both. In addition, its considerable successes notwithstanding, the Fourth Republic was overwhelmed by the number of pressing domestic and international problems and hampered by *immobilisme* . Efforts to eliminate the most harassing of the parliamentary delaying tactics, and thus to enhance state capacity to handle major issues, were not enough and came too late.

Brought back to power by the military uprising in Algiers in May 1958, de Gaulle was aware of the fate of other 'crisis-liquidators' who, like Mendès France in 1955, were cast aside when no longer needed. Invited to extricate France from her Algerian dilemma, he therefore chose to 'seize the opportunity offered...' to obtain authority to draft a new constitution, founded on the pre-eminence and stability of the executive, as he had urged in his famous Bayeux speech of June 1946. This new republic would enable de Gaulle to pursue an interconnected set of lofty ambitions.

The overarching, unifying goal was to restore to France her traditional prestige and national independence, lost in the demise of the Third Republic, the humiliation of the Occupation, and the economic and military realities of the post-war world. France's earlier status as a major power had been largely conditioned on possessing a world-wide empire, and de Gaulle had been among its staunchest defenders; yet, by 1958, he recognized that France's colonial possessions stood in the way of national *grandeur*. In a world dominated by the Soviet and American 'hegemonies',

France could have neither influence nor independence whilst weighed down by colonial conflict. To restore France's freedom, de Gaulle thus had to grant Algeria hers. Decolonization required asserting civilian authority over the army and control by Paris over the colonial administration, both pre-conditions of another Gaullist ambition, erecting a strong state.

In the Gaullist view, the state had become the forum for servicing or accommodating private interests, a product of France's traditional political and social cleavages. The Gaullist state would become the activist, interventionist — in a word, *dirigiste* — promoter of the national interest, blending its traditional *Colbertiste* role with a 'social Keynesianism', as Christian Stoffaës has called it. This ambition will be the driving force behind efforts to gain control over the financial circuits; to defend the value of the franc; to develop an internationally competitive industrial network; to mobilize key public- and private-sector actors through the planning process in a state-directed strategy to overcome the hazards of the marketplace and the traditional resistance to change.

Creating a strong state meant setting up institutions adapted to the national temperament ('the Gallic propensity for quarrels and divisions'), and capable of providing order, efficiency, stability and cohesion in governmental processes. Given France's 'perpetual political effervescence', executive power could no longer depend on political parties, those archaic intermediaries that distorted the general will, but had to derive from a head of state capable of articulating the national interest above the *intérêts particuliers* and guaranteeing continuity. Not a simple figure-head, the President that de Gaulle anticipated would be the keystone in the institutional arch, endowed with potent and potential powers, especially in times of emergency. His government, needing coherence and discipline, would need to be more than a 'mere collection of party delegations' (quotations are from de Gaulle's speech at Bayeux, 16 June 1946.).

The strong state required bringing a nearly autonomous civil bureaucracy under the control of the government, whilst freeing both from harassment by a legislature dominated by parties and colonized by special interests. The Fifth Republic's Constitution consequently imposed numerous constraints upon Parliament: its sovereignty was inherently limited by the creation of a Constitutional Council with judicial review authority and by the definition of its law-making capacity; parliamentary control of the executive was diminished by having the President, not the Assembly, create the cabinet, by making cabinet membership incompatible with a legislative mandate, and by making it very difficult for parliament to amend legislation or the budget and to force the government to resign.

De Gaulle's objectives for France's place in the world, for the colonial empire, for civil society, were indeed ambitious; while it is not evident that the French understood their complexity, it is clear their sense of national pride was stirred. The nearly 80 per cent of the voters who approved the new Constitution in the 1958 referendum demonstrated both the popular rejection of the Fourth Republic and the depth of de Gaulle's personal legitimacy.

By the time of de Gaulle's resignation in 1969, many of these ambitions had been achieved. France's prestige in the world was high: as a nuclear power, independent of the United States (NATO forces had been invited to leave French soil), France had become a useful partner in dialogue for the Soviet Union. The Paris–Bonn axis within the European Community added to that prestige and reinforced French leverage in European matters: for a decade, France had been able to exercise an effective veto on British membership. Having settled the Algerian problem and decolonized whilst preserving considerable political and economic influence among her former possessions, France spoke with a respected voice in Third World affairs. The civil and military bureaucracies, still vigorous, had been brought under government control. The state had perfected powerful instruments of intervention to achieve its will in the economic and social fields, as its growing proportion of GNP attested.

In addition, many policy communities had undergone substantial restructuring, because of state voluntarism. In agriculture, the resistance to modernization embodied in the FNSEA was circumvented by developing a privileged relationship with the reformers of the organization's youth movement. In health care, the medical profession's corporate influence was countered, and policy-making was shifted to public or para-public agencies. The leftist unions' control of the Social Security system was broken by redesigning its management structure. Not all changes were to the advantage of the state: whilst the *bouilleurs de cru* lost their sway, Breton — and later Corsican — autonomists gained some.

The Gaullist regime was consolidated, executive authority strengthened, acquiring both popularity and legitimacy, as Mitterrand's candidacy — and defeat — demonstrated in the 1965 presidential elections; even the profound challenge of the May 1968 events could only shake the regime temporarily, not dislocate it. The anti-regime parties of the extreme Right had disappeared, whilst those of the Left were effectively marginalized. Meanwhile, the majority coalition supporting de Gaulle was solidified (the Gaullist party was the first ever to win a majority of Assembly seats alone, in June 1968), and provided stable and broad support for government's policy initiatives. Parliamentary power was subdued, almost to the point of extinction.

These politico-institutional developments were underpinned by a vibrant, dynamic economy, growing (although unequally distributed) prosperity, increasingly universal welfare-state provisions, and a dominant statist and social-democratic ideology. In sum, after a decade of the Fifth Republic, France had achieved the highly enviable status of a strong, assertive, prestigious, and powerful country, with solid, legitimate, and respected institutions.

The limits of the strong state

Twenty years later, a different picture of the Fifth Republic emerges, as the political class has discovered the limits of state action in a volatile and interdependent world. The demise of the Bretton Woods system, following the abandonment of fixed parities in March 1973, has diminished state capacity to use exchange rates as an occasional instrument of macroeconomic policy. The prevailing trend in the capitalist democracies toward liberalism and deregulation has simply made France's traditional forms of *dirigisme* outmoded. As Philip Cerny has shown, France can no longer insulate itself from the world in which it lives: the 'strategic state' is on the decline.

The European integration process, seen earlier as a means of increasing France's political manoeuvrability by giving her a wider stage and enhancing her economic strength by exposing French firms to the rigours of international competition, has proved instead to be the source of numerous externally-imposed constraints. Several key sectors and policy instruments are effectively under the aegis of Brussels (agriculture, steel, state subsidies and mergers, for example), reducing the state's capacity for independent adjustment in the service of national interests. The challenge of 1992 will further accentuate this tendency, by withdrawing additional sectors of economic control from the unilateral decisions of member states. France clearly made the commitment to forgo sovereign use of national instruments, as Philippe Moreau Defarges points out, when President Mitterrand decided to remain in the European Monetary System in 1983, despite the enormous pressures on the franc.

Similarly, the increasing multinationalization and transnationalization of 'French' firms has meant that major investment and strategic decisions affecting trade balances, inflation rates, the value of the franc, national income, and employment are made elsewhere and on criteria other than national interest; even public enterprises cannot escape this evolution.

The prolonged adjustment crisis into which the world's industrial economies have been plunged since 1974 has also had its impact upon the state. First, of course, the *trente glorieuses* came to an end, closing thirty years of fabulous post-war growth whose steady flow of benefits allowed governments to postpone difficult distributional decisions. In addition, the crisis disrupted the economic planning process, as currency fluctuations or market shifts invalidated the most careful calculations. Likewise, *l'aménagement du territoire* , the land-use rationalization schemes initiated during the growth period of the 1960s, has become a luxury.

The ineffectiveness of counter-cyclical policies to deal with the crisis independently was proved in 1981–3, when the Mauroy government was obliged to devalue three times and eventually adopt politically costly deflationary measures. Apart from the relatively brief reflationary policy in 1981–2, the crisis produced a decade and a half of slow (or negative) growth, declining investment, extensive deindustrialization (massive in steel and textiles), regional problems, incipient inflation, persistent trade imbalances, seemingly incorrigible budgetary deficits, as well as pervasively high unemployment. These nagging problems were not peculiar to France, of course, but in a political system known for its high capacity for state intervention, they demonstrated more clearly than elsewhere the finite limits of state action. The Socialist strategy to develop central instruments to direct economic adjustment, by nationalizing key industrial sectors, spending more on technology and research, and managing private-sector credit, simply failed before the enormity of the task.

Consequently, as Christian Stoffaës makes clear, a new political-economic culture has emerged, emphasizing the need for developing competitive advantages, increasing mobility of capital and labour, gaining access to international capital markets, raising profit margins, and granting greater managerial autonomy: in a word, the French state has rediscovered the virtues of the firm. Today's rhetoric stresses not statism, but modernization and the market.

The changes in the international and European environment coincided with and were related to the emergence of domestic constraints. The perennial tensions between fierce French individualism and Jacobin bureaucratic impulses had always resulted in strengthening the paternalist state, which the French habitually feared or denounced, but to which they inevitably turned for protection, status or material benefits. The very diverse social developments of the 1960s and 1970s — the rekindling of regional identities, student protest, urbanization, worker discontent, nascent consumerism and environmentalism, for example — focused on the state as the source of either the problem or the solution, highlighting the disadvantages of the extended state.

Ironically, it was during the Socialists' term in office that the bell began to toll for *étatisme* in France. Mitterrand's first government, under the impulse of Prime Minister Mauroy and Interior Minister Defferre, both big-city mayors, pushed forward with territorial decentralization, transferring significant powers to local elected officials. Initially inspired by administrative functionalism in the 1950s and 1960s, decentralization reached its heights in the 1980s in part because of the need to relieve the saturated state of the pressures of responding to local demands. As new problems appeared on the agenda — for example, the telecommunications revolution which necessitated regulation, the immigrant problems which called for a new consensus on nationality, the seemingly uncontrollable growth of social expenditures — one state response was to seek a horizontal diffusion of authority, creating new agencies such as the Audiovisual Authority (now in its third version), blue-ribbon panels such as the *Comités des Sages* to propose reform of the Social Security system and the nationality laws, and the various policy tsars (for drugs and highway safety, for example) to symbolize and help legitimize the reform effort.

The difficulties the Socialists encountered in trying to impose new sets of voluntaristic policies on the vast, compartmentalized state administration suggested there were limits to state interventionism and provided sobering lessons for both the Socialists and the Gaullists, who had shared the statist approach. The Socialists adopted more pragmatic and innovative approaches, praising the entrepreneurial spirit and focusing on the adaptive capacities of medium-size firms. Mitterrand's public commitment to reduce the very high share of GDP taken up by state taxes, a consequence of declining revenues to finance incompressible social programmes, was another step away from statism. Jacques Chirac, benefiting from the failures of both the Socialists and their predecessors, and fearing a challenge from the liberal Centre, began leading his party away from traditional Gaullism and formulating a supply-side critique of the 'Socialist state'.

Nationalization was no longer viewed by any except the Communist Party as an effective means of asserting public will in the economy. The Fabius government first considered selling off assets of some state-run firms as a way of forcing adaptation to the market and developing competitiveness; the conservative coalition that succeeded him made privatization the centre-piece of both their political and economic strategies.

The last twenty years have also produced a sharper definition of the constitutional state in France. The relationship between President and Prime Minister has become more balanced and the division of labour between them more clearly understood: in 1976, Jacques Chirac became the first Prime Minister to resign because he lacked the means to govern as he saw fit; ten years later, the same Chirac was able to lead a conservative government without much interference from a Socialist President. And relations between government and Parliament have also taken a new turn, as both government supporters and opposition have perfected techniques of scrutiny and control. To some degree, and ironically, Parliament's more constructive role is related to the emergence of the Constitutional Council, whose judicial review function has become a critical factor in the legislative process; the opposition's access to the Council has served not only to revive Parliament, but also to create an additional external constraint upon the government.

Policy-making in the Fifth Republic became more technical and complex than ever before, and increased executive discretion only widened the gap between the political process and the mass public. The early years of the regime were marked by major outbursts, until key interest groups learned new channels of access to shape policies. When the politics of economic adjustment undermined the growth consensus carefully nurtured during the *trente glorieuses* — May 1968 notwithstanding — it became at once more imperative and difficult for government to mobilize popular legitimacy behind its policies. The 1980s have seen a growing number of demonstrations, by *lycée* students, health and other professionals, public sector employees, and so on; *la rue* has acquired an impact precisely because of the need for — and failure to marshal — acquiescence for zero-sum policies. There are, of course, broad areas of political consensus: the institutions, the mixed economy, the welfare state. Yet, consequent to the presidentialization of the regime, the traditional parties have diluted their ideological content, key groups have been frustrated by or excluded from the policy-making process, and France appears to be suffering from what Stanley Hoffmann has called a problem of *encadrement social*, the failure to develop effective means of interest intermediation.

A final assessment

Entering the last decade of the twentieth century, France remains among the world's leading nations, both economically and militarily. The experiences of the past twenty years, however, have restricted the Fifth Republic's ambitions; today they are more modest, less assertive and voluntaristic, on the European and world stages, and in domestic affairs.

There is a new balance between state, market and civil society. France remains firmly a mixed economy, but the public role is more circumscribed, especially after various *affaires* — Pechiney and the Société Générale, to take recent examples — which discredited state fiddling in the marketplace.

The institutional architecture of the Fifth Republic is demonstrably stable, yet it is also fluid and adaptable, as cohabitation and Prime Minister Rocard's relative parliamentary majority have both amply demonstrated. The regime has survived its many challenges intact and legitimate, though not without significant problems. The still vast public sector shows many areas of *malaise* : in education, the penal system, transportation, the public hospitals. The rapidly expanding world of communications seems to leave France vulnerable to forces beyond her control. The more than four million immigrants and the assorted native minority communities raise difficult questions about French cultural identity and the implications of a pluralist society. Concomitantly, deindustrialization and the disappearance of the traditional working class have challenged both the divided labour movement and the parties of the Left to redefine their values and political strategies, whilst the National Front's assumption of the PCF's role as spokesman for the alienated, with its growing sociological and structural roots, similarly challenges the centrist drift of the conservative parties.

The Fifth Republic has also had its share of paradoxes. It took a general to restore the army to its place, a liberal (Giscard d'Estaing) to expand the welfare state, and a Socialist to embrace the market. The Gaullist ambition to strengthen the state unquestionably succeeded, and yet sovereignty has never been less sure (European Community rules, multinational corporations, the global stock market, and so on). It was also de Gaulle's ambition to assert 'the general interest', but the increasing degree of interpenetration between public and private obfuscates the distinction. Likewise, de Gaulle sought to create a regime to defeat the political parties, yet today's principal parties are powerful electoral machines without which — as Raymond Barre has learned — it is impossible to capture the presidency.

It is not enough to assert that the Fifth Republic has largely succeeded in realising its ambitions. One senses today that France is entering a new era. The successful alternation of Left and Right in power has removed much of the drama of political life; elections are no longer *choix de société*, and participation rates have declined (marginally) in consequence. The approach of the single European market, with all its uncertainties, challenges and opportunities — and no doubt its disappointments — fascinates some and worries others, but most recognize that tomorrow's French society will be considerably different.

There are still important problems to be faced. Among the social problems is the growing number of marginals, the *exclus* : the long-term unemployed, workers in dying industries with non-transferable skills, the young unequipped for today's job-market, the hold-overs from the traditional economy (the small merchants and the subsistence farmers), the dependent elderly, for example. In the political sphere, the social and intellectual cleavage between the political class and the mass public persists: the former are still recruited mainly from the upper-middle class, have been trained in the *grandes écoles* , and share a sense of the national interest; they are also still engaged in what the more pragmatically orientated public continues to perceive as a sterile Left–Right debate. Until this gap has been narrowed, and until a new socio-political coalition has been forged to support the new policy directions, policy-making in the Fifth Republic is likely to continue to suffer from problems of legitimacy.

In the final analysis, despite significant discontinuities with the Fourth Republic in many areas, the chapters in this volume have demonstrated that, in other areas, the Fifth Republic has continued the trajectory. The Fourth Republic began modernizing the French economy, transforming a tradition-bound, dissensual agrarian society into a major industrial democracy. Where it faltered, in decolonization and institutional reform, the Fifth Republic carried on. In doing so, it created the necessary conditions to pursue economic and social modernization, on firmer ground.

Index